Think BIG With THINK ALOUDS

Grades K-5

To Mike, the BHE.

Think BIG With THINK ALOUDS

Grades K-5

A **Three-Step Planning Process** That Develops Strategic Readers

Molly Ness

Foreword by Douglas Fisher

resources.corwin.com/ness-thinkalouds

FOR INFORMATION:

Corwin
A SAGE Company
2455 Teller Road
Thousand Oaks, California 91320
(800) 233-9936
www.corwin.com

SAGE Publications Ltd.
1 Oliver's Yard
55 City Road
London EC1Y 1SP
United Kingdom

SAGE Publications India Pvt. Ltd.
B 1/I 1 Mohan Cooperative Industrial Area
Mathura Road, New Delhi 110 044
India

SAGE Publications Asia-Pacific Pte. Ltd.
3 Church Street
#10-04 Samsung Hub
Singapore 049483

Publisher and Senior Program Director: Lisa Luedeke
Senior Acquisitions Editor: Wendy Murray
Editorial Development Manager: Julie Nemer
Editorial Assistant: Nicole Shade
Production Editor: Melanie Birdsall
Copy Editor: Melinda Masson
Typesetter: C&M Digitals (P) Ltd.
Proofreader: Sally Jaskold
Indexer: Kathleen Paparchontis
Cover and Interior Designer: Gail Buschman
Marketing Manager: Rebecca Eaton

Printed in the United States of America

Library of Congress Cataloging-in-Publication Data

Names: Ness, Molly.

Title: Think big with think alouds, grades K–5 : a three-step planning process that develops strategic readers / Molly Ness.

Description: Thousand Oaks, California : Corwin, [2018] | Includes bibliographical references and index.

Identifiers: LCCN 2017007100 | ISBN 9781506364964 (pbk. : alk. paper)

Subjects: LCSH: Oral reading. | Reading (Elementary)

Classification: LCC LB1573.5 .N47 2017 | DDC 372.45/2—dc23
LC record available at https://lccn.loc.gov/2017007100

This book is printed on acid-free paper.

SFI label applies to text stock

19 20 21 10 9 8 7 6 5 4 3 2

Contents

Foreword xi
Douglas Fisher

Acknowledgments xv

CHAPTER 1 The Genius of Think Alouds: To Think Big, Readers Need to Hear What "Big" Sounds Like 1

What Think Alouds Are 4
What Think Alouds Are Not 10
Why Think Alouds Are Relevant Today 13
The Educational Theories Behind Think Alouds 14
Practice Makes Perfect: The Three-Step Process to Planning Think Alouds 15
Read Once: Identifying Juicy Stopping Points 16
Read Twice: Determining Where and When to Think Aloud 16
Read Three Times: Writing the Scripts on Sticky Notes 16
A Final Note About the Three-Step Process 17
How to Use This Book 17
Final Thoughts 18
Ready for a Trial Run? 19

CHAPTER 2 Think Aloud With Focus: Five Comprehension Strategies That Go the Distance 23

How Think Alouds Benefit Our Readers 24
Arming Yourself With the Five Essential Think Aloud Strategies 25
Standing on the Shoulders of Giants 26
A Note About the Strategy Symbols 27
A Note About the Sentence Starters 28
The Five Essential Think Aloud Strategies 28
Asking Questions 28
Making Inferences 31
Synthesizing 34
Understanding the Author's Purpose 35
Monitoring and Clarifying 37

Final Thoughts 39
Ready for a Trial Run? 39

CHAPTER 3 Read Once: Identifying Juicy Stopping Points 41

An Overview 41
Using Poetry in Kindergarten 43
Using Narrative Text in Third Grade 45
Using Informational Text in Fifth Grade 45
Final Thoughts 50
Ready for a Trial Run? 56

CHAPTER 4 Read Twice: Determining Where and When to Think Aloud 59

Examining the Original Stopping Points in "Sick" by Shel Silverstein 61
Examining the Original Stopping Points in *Enemy Pie* by Derek Munson 63
Examining the Original Stopping Points in *Eyes and Ears* by Seymour Simon 68
Final Thoughts 75
Ready for a Trial Run? 76

CHAPTER 5 Read Three Times: Writing the Scripts on Sticky Notes 77

Signaling for Think Alouds 79
Think Aloud Sentence Starters 81
DIE TEMPLATE FOR USING SENTENCE STARTERS 82
SPINNER TEMPLATE FOR USING SENTENCE STARTERS 83
THINK ALOUD SENTENCE STARTERS 84
Introducing the Three-Column Chart 86
The Think Aloud Scripts for Our Model Texts 86
THE THINK ALOUD CHART 87
Final Thoughts 100
Ready for a Trial Run? 100

CHAPTER 6 How Did They Go? Teachers Share Successes and Challenges 101

Inside K–5 Classrooms: A Yearlong Study 102
Lessons Learned From the Yearlong Study 103
Lesson 1: Planning a think aloud requires a clear structure and process. 104
Lesson 2: Teachers' abilities to think aloud and confidence in the strategy grow tremendously over time. 105

Lesson 3: Teachers are eager for additional and ongoing support in thinking aloud. 107
Ideas to Hone Your Thinking Aloud **107**
Evaluating Your Own Thinking Aloud **108**
Final Thoughts **120**
FEEDBACK FORM FOR THINK ALOUD REFLECTIONS 121
Ready for a Trial Run? **123**

CHAPTER 7 Students Do: Tips and Tools for Helping Your Readers Think Aloud on Their Own 125

Using Gradual Release of Responsibility to Scaffold Think Alouds **125**
The "I Do" Phase 126
THINK ALOUD CATCHER 128
The "We Do" Phase: Introducing the Think Along 129
"WE DO" CHART 130
The "You Do" Phase 142
Encouraging Self-Evaluation With Think Alouds **144**
Applying Think Alouds Across Content Areas **144**
SELF-EVALUATION CHART FOR READERS 145
Thinking Aloud With Visuals **147**
Final Thoughts **150**
Ready for a Trial Run? **151**

Appendices

Appendix A: Sample Think Aloud **153**
Appendix B: Sample Texts **156**
Appendix C: Think Alouds for Sample Texts **162**
Appendix D: Think Aloud Sentence Starters **168**
Appendix E: Three-Column Think Aloud Chart **171**
Appendix F: Think Aloud Script for *The Circus Ship* by Chris Van Dusen **172**
Appendix G: Think Aloud Script for *A Bad Case of Stripes* by David Shannon **181**
Appendix H: Think Aloud Self-Evaluation **185**
Appendix I: Think Aloud Scripts **186**
Appendix J: Putting It Together: Think Aloud Scripts **221**
References **249**
Index **255**

Visit the companion website at
resources.corwin.com/ness-thinkalouds
for downloadable resources.

Companion Website Resources

Visit the companion website at
resources.corwin.com/ness-thinkalouds
for downloadable resources.

REPRODUCIBLES

Die Template for Using Sentence Starters

Spinner Template for Using Sentence Starters

The Think Aloud Chart

Feedback Form for Think Aloud Reflections

Think Aloud Catcher

"We Do" Chart

Self-Evaluation Chart for Readers

APPENDICES

Appendix A: Sample Think Aloud

Appendix B: Sample Texts

"The Owl and the Pussy-Cat" by Edward Lear
The Sandwich Swap by Her Majesty Queen Rania Al-Abdullah and Kelly DiPucchio
The William Hoy Story: How a Deaf Baseball Player Changed the Game by Nancy Churnin

Appendix C: Think Alouds for Sample Texts

Think Aloud for "The Owl and the Pussy-Cat" by Edward Lear
Think Aloud for *The Sandwich Swap* by Her Majesty Queen Rania Al-Abdullah and Kelly DiPucchio
Think Aloud for *The William Hoy Story: How a Deaf Baseball Player Changed the Game* by Nancy Churnin

Appendix D: Think Aloud Sentence Starters

Appendix E: Three-Column Think Aloud Chart

Appendix F: Think Aloud Script for *The Circus Ship* by Chris Van Dusen

Appendix G: Think Aloud Script for A *Bad Case of Stripes* by David Shannon

Appendix H: Think Aloud Self-Evaluation

Appendix I: Think Aloud Scripts

Teaching Asking Questions in Grades K–2: *Smoky Night* by Eve Bunting
Teaching Asking Questions in Grades 3–5: *Who Was Anne Frank?* by Ann Abramson
Teaching Making Inferences in Grades K–2: *Miss Nelson Is Missing!* by Harry Allard
Teaching Making Inferences in Grades 3–5: *The Stranger* by Chris Van Allsburg
Teaching Synthesizing in Grades K–2: *My Lucky Day* by Keiko Kasza
Teaching Synthesizing in Grades 3–5: *The Story of Ruby Bridges* by Robert Coles
Teaching Understanding the Author's Purpose in Grades K–2: Inform: *Lizards* by Laura Marsh
Teaching Understanding the Author's Purpose in Grades K–2: Entertain: *Private I. Guana: The Case of the Missing Chameleon* by Nina Laden
Teaching Understanding the Author's Purpose in Grades K–2: Persuade: *I Wanna Iguana* by Karen Orloff
Teaching Understanding the Author's Purpose in Grades 3–5: *Balloons Over Broadway: The True Story of the Puppeteer of Macy's Parade* by Melissa Sweet
Teaching Monitoring and Clarifying in Grades K–2: *My Name Is Sangoel* by Karen Lynn Williams and Khadra Mohammed
Teaching Monitoring and Clarifying in Grades 3–5: *Simple Machines: Wheels, Levers, and Pulleys* by David Adler

Appendix J: Putting It Together: Think Aloud Scripts

Thinking Aloud With Nonfiction in Grades K–2: *Apples* by Gail Gibbons
Thinking Aloud With Poetry in Grades K–2: "The Dentist and the Crocodile" by Roald Dahl
Thinking Aloud With a Narrative Picture Book in Grades K–2: *Last Stop on Market Street* by Matt de la Peña
Thinking Aloud With Historical Fiction in Grades K–2: *The Watcher: Jane Goodall's Life With the Chimps* by Jeanette Winter
Thinking Aloud With a Narrative Picture Book in Grades 3–5: *Doctor De Soto* by William Steig
Thinking Aloud With a Chapter Book in Grades 3–5: *The Year of Billy Miller* by Kevin Henkes
Thinking Aloud With Poetry in Grades 3–5: "Casey at the Bat" by Ernest Thayer
Thinking Aloud With a Narrative Picture Book in Grades 3–5: *An Angel for Solomon Singer* by Cynthia Rylant

Foreword

I have spent years working out ways for students to access more complex texts than they can read on their own. The solution is not a simple one, but rather requires a complex set of experiences that students must have if they are ever going to be able to understand texts that stretch their understanding. One popular way for providing students access to complex texts is close reading instruction. During close reading, students read and re-read a short piece of text, engaging in collaborative conversations with their peers in response to the questions they have or that their teachers ask, marking on the text as they go, successively getting to deeper and deeper understanding. It's a slow and laborious process, and yet one that allows students to collaboratively read a text that is complex. What is missing from many conversations about close reading are the other types of instruction students need to become skilled.

In addition to close reading, students need to read a lot of texts. Focusing on close reading, while I believe is important, has the potential to crowd out the very necessary wide reading that students need to do each day. Simply said, wide reading builds background knowledge and vocabulary, both of which are critical to understanding complex texts. Students who read a lot are more likely to activate their background knowledge when they are reading something that is complex. Thus, wide reading can assist students in understanding complex texts during close reading lessons. In addition, wide reading builds students' habits. I worry about students who are provided excellent reading instruction but do not engage in sufficient practice for that instruction to stick. I'm not suggesting that wide reading is the solution for students' reading needs, but rather that students have to engage in sufficient practice so that the instruction approaches recommended by the teacher have a chance of becoming students' habits.

And that's where this book by Molly Ness comes in. Another way to provide students with access to complex text is to model through think alouds. It's an effective approach for providing students with ideas and recommendations that they can use when they read. While modeling, teachers can provide students a glimpse inside the mind of a reader who is actively engaged in meaning making. Over time, and with practice, students begin to engage in the same types of thinking that their teachers model.

I think of this as an apprenticeship model for developing readers. My father tells the story of his time as a journeyman apprentice in sheet metal working. He has installed heating and air conditioning systems for over 40 years. He learned to do this by spending time with an expert, listening to this person—Bud was his name—describe the decisions made each day as they faced different situations. As Bud used to say, "No two buildings are alike, but everyone wants them to be comfortable." He described the adaptations he had to make to ensure that the air would flow correctly and taught my father to think like this when he was installing a new system or repairing one that did not work correctly.

I want the same thing for students as they learn to read. They deserve to have opportunities to experience the thinking of someone who has more experience and different ideas. They need to hear examples of the thinking that unlocks the ideas inside of a text so that they can try those processes on as they read. And they need to be guided in the cognitive processes that an expert uses. Simply said, thinking is invisible. All we have, and all Bud had, is talking about our thinking. And that's the key to effective think alouds, which Molly Ness so skillfully demonstrates in this book. Molly understands that modeling with think alouds is more than providing the example of the cognitive work that readers need to do. Providing students with an example of an appropriate prediction or an apt summary can unlock a specific text, but it will not ensure that students are apprenticed to the type of thinking that they need to do on their own. Instead, modeling with think alouds needs to include metacognition: thinking about thinking. When teachers provide students with an example of a prediction, they need to show students how they arrived at the prediction. When teachers demonstrate the types of questions they have as they read, they need to explain where those questions came from. That's what makes the difference. And that's what Bud did for my dad. There is a building in San Diego that reminds my dad fondly of his time as an apprentice. He tells me, "The columns that the architect wanted were blocking a lot of the air flow. And the columns made it hard to run enough lines. Bud thought about this for several days before he figured it out. He walked me through that building, room after room, telling me how and why we were going to add returns and angle the vents. And it worked. I've used that same technique so many times."

I understand that you're not likely worried about the installation of heating and air conditioning systems, but you are probably concerned about the most effective ways for ensuring that students develop a set of skills that serve them well as they read. An important part of the instruction necessary for students to read well, and at higher levels than they do on their own, is fully explained in this book. Without modeling through think alouds, students are likely to guess at texts and struggle to understand them. And they are unlikely to develop strategies that they can try, much less habits that they can use, when they are reading on their own. As Molly notes, it's time to "think big" so that students have a chance at becoming increasingly literate.

—Douglas Fisher
Professor, San Diego State University
Author, *Rigorous Reading* and *Visible Learning for Literacy*

Acknowledgments

My sincere gratitude goes to the following:

To Wendy Murray, for her enthusiastic support of my work and her keen editing.

To the Corwin team, for your work on my behalf.

To Doug Fisher, for inspiring this work so many years ago and for following its path.

To Rye Free Reading Room, for the sanctuary and the resources.

To Doug Distefano and Deb Rosado, for opening their classroom doors to me.

To my parents, who begrudgingly learned to whisper when I shut myself in the parlor to write.

To Callie, for reminding me about the joys of reading and for understanding how much my work means to me.

And to Mike, for everything.

Publisher's Acknowledgments

Corwin gratefully acknowledges the contributions of the following reviewers:

Melissa Black
Co-Principal at Harlem Village Academies Elementary School
New York, NY

Helen Comba
Literacy Consultant
Westfield, NJ

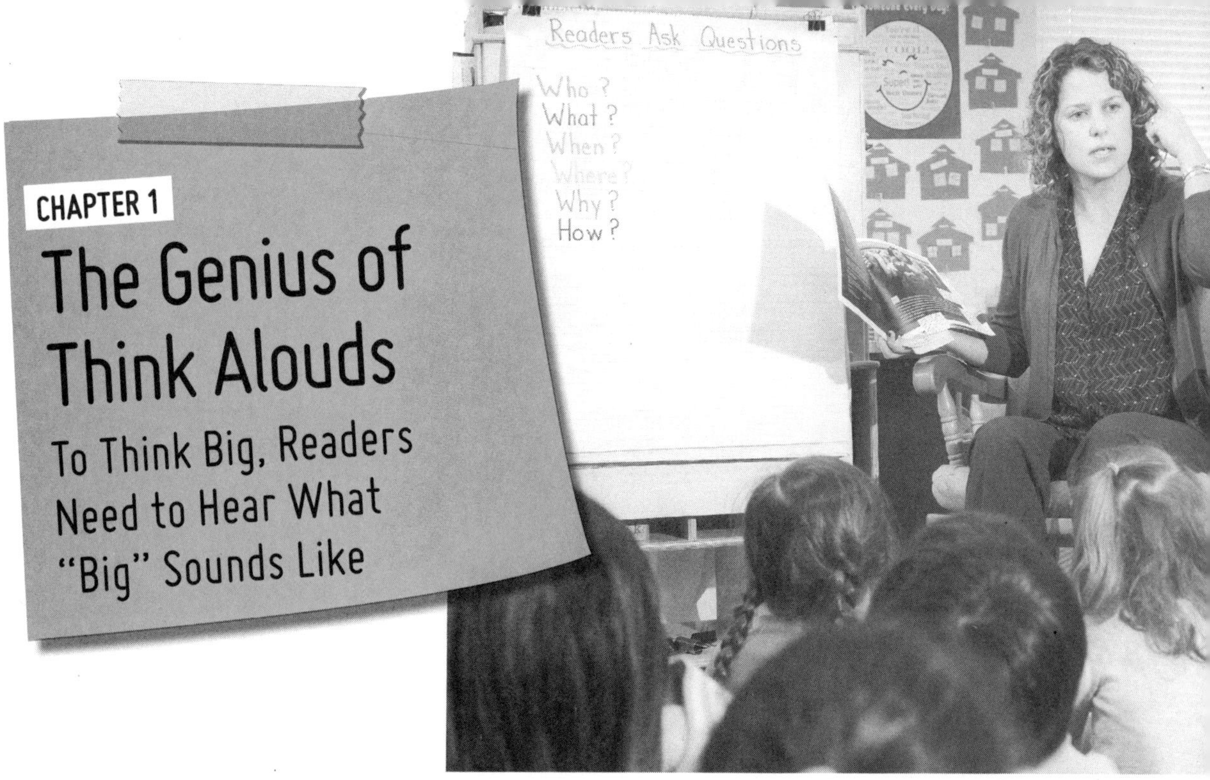

CHAPTER 1

The Genius of Think Alouds

To Think Big, Readers Need to Hear What "Big" Sounds Like

© Rick Harrington Photography

Several years ago, I attended a professional conference. Teachers crammed into a hotel ballroom to see literacy gurus Nancy Frey and Doug Fisher give a keynote on reading comprehension. In the session, Doug made an offhand comment, stating, "We all know that think alouds are highly effective, yet teachers don't do them or can't do them."

I left that conference feeling unsettled, because I knew there was truth in what he said; he had his finger on the pulse of what was going on in classrooms. I had always put great stock in think alouds and as a professor had presumed my graduate students would go out into classrooms and use the strategy seamlessly. When it came to think alouds, I was a lifelong card-carrying member! As a classroom teacher, I had used them during my routine read alouds so that my students were privy to the thinking I did while engaged with a text. As a clinician at a university reading clinic, I consistently saw the multiple ways think alouds benefited readers who struggled to comprehend. As a coach and mentor for novice teachers, I modeled think alouds to showcase their effectiveness.

Upon my return to New York and to my life as a teacher educator, Doug's statement still nagged at me. Maybe think alouds were the equivalent of the recommendation to eat six servings of fruits and vegetables a day—it's something we know we *should* do, but don't always get to. If it was indeed the case that teachers don't think aloud, why not? I did what I call "geeking out"—I dove into research, and set up my own yearlong investigation exploring these questions. (Perhaps this bookish tendency explains why celebrity sightings for me include reading researchers, rather than Hollywood stars or famous athletes.) My project, outlined below and described in further detail in subsequent chapters, aimed to address these questions that Doug's observation had raised:

- Were there data about the frequency with which teachers think aloud? How likely are teachers to include this strategy in routine classroom instruction?
- In teacher training and professional development, how well do we prepare teachers to think aloud? Where do teachers struggle to think aloud? Where do teachers succeed?
- Are there factors that hold teachers back from thinking aloud? Are there other obstacles, besides the lack of instructional time? Do teachers feel too exposed or self-conscious in doing them?
- Might think alouds be hard to master because they involve making use of complex skills simultaneously? Why have they not caught on?

My research goal was to discover actual implementation of think alouds, with an eye to naming the challenges so as to improve teachers' ability to think aloud. With current and former students, I formed a research team of early-career teachers. We spent a year focusing entirely on thinking aloud in K–5 classrooms. We read about think alouds in professional books and journals. I modeled think alouds—both effective and intentionally ineffective ones—in my university courses. We watched and critiqued videos of teachers thinking aloud. My participants wrote and implemented multiple think aloud lesson plans. Across the year, teachers grew in their confidence in creating think aloud lessons with logical stopping points, a variety of relevant comprehension strategies, and rich monologues designed to help young readers understand the metacognitive processes of reading.

The spoiler alert here regarding the research findings is that when teachers received meaningful instruction on why, how, and when to think aloud from me, they increased their own self-efficacy in creating well-prepared think alouds. In short, I discovered that it was the careful *planning* of think alouds that mattered most. This research study is further described in Chapter 6, but summarized in the following table.

A Yearlong Investigation Into K–5 Teachers' Think Alouds

Who were my participants?	Almost 70 early-career teachers in K–5 classrooms
What did I study?	I examined the ways in which teachers approached think alouds, the reading comprehension strategies teachers incorporated during think alouds, and the ways in which teachers might improve their confidence in and ability to think aloud.
Where did this investigation take place?	My participants conducted their think alouds in their K–5 classrooms. As the head of their research team, I directed them in online and face-to-face reflective sessions. Some of the participants were enrolled in my literacy courses at a graduate school of education in a major metropolitan area.
When did this occur?	This research team met over one academic year.
Why did I undertake this project?	My objective was to explore how to better prepare teachers to conduct think alouds. I wanted to understand the successes and challenges that teachers encountered while thinking aloud.
How did I conduct the study? What were my methods?	From each teacher, I collected and analyzed three think aloud lesson plans. Teachers also video recorded their think alouds and analyzed their own instruction. All participants also completed a written questionnaire.
So what did I find?	Teachers made significant growth in both the number and the variety of reading comprehension strategies they incorporated. Teachers realized that effective think alouds require advance preparation and deep knowledge of both an appropriate text and relevant strategies.

The lessons learned from the elementary teachers who planned, implemented, transcribed, and reflected on think aloud lessons are the basis for this book. A year after conducting that project, this book is the result of what I discovered about teachers' usage. Based on my research—and the lessons I learned from teachers' think alouds—I developed a step-by-step process for implementing think alouds in K–5. This process is the heart of the book, because it really makes the think aloud strategy far easier to pull off successfully. Most important of all? Think alouds become classroom instruction students like—a lot. Over the years, I have seen the bewildered looks from students suffering from their teachers' poorly executed think alouds. I've observed teachers—with the best of intentions—transform their think alouds into endless monologues more suitable for an off-off-off-Broadway play. But with the strategies outlined in this book, the think aloud becomes an energized, brief instructional burst that involves young readers to the point that they can more easily take on the strategies modeled. With this book, I aim to

- Explore what a think aloud is and what a think aloud is not
- Demonstrate the power of thinking aloud in building students' engagement and reading comprehension

- Dispel the myths that think alouds are too labor-intensive or time-consuming to occur in routine classroom instruction
- Delineate my three-step planning process so that think alouds can be easily implemented across grade level and text genre

The title of a 2008 article in the *Journal of Adolescent and Adult Literacy* by Diane Lapp, Douglas Fisher, and Maria Grant about interactive comprehension instruction reads, "You can read this text—I'll show you how." In the same vein, the subtitle of this book that was in my head as I wrote it was "You can think aloud—I'll show you how." My aim in this book is to make think alouds, a widely recommended instructional strategy, commonplace in today's classrooms.

What Think Alouds Are

Before I dive headfirst into defining think alouds, I'll give you a glimpse into the thinking aloud I did with a newspaper article I encountered in *USA Today*. Just to exemplify the multitude of comprehension strategies that I used with a common, everyday sort of text, I've written out the exact thoughts that went through my head as I read. If I were thinking aloud in front of young readers, I'd say these things aloud—hence the name *think aloud*. A second think aloud from an additional news article can be found in Appendix A.

This think aloud showcases the richness of all of the reading strategies and maneuvers that we—as proficient readers—do every day. In this short article, I stopped eleven times—to visualize, to predict, to make inferences, to clarify, to set a purpose for reading, and to deduce the author's purpose. My guess is that if you had read this article, and I had flagged particular stopping points, your thought process and internal conversations would be quite similar, because these stopping points are in a sense prompts from the author. Getting good at selecting these stopping points is the crux of what I want to teach you in this book. This experience was not cumbersome for me to plan—it happened in my bathrobe over my morning cup of coffee. With practice, think alouds are low-stress to plan and enjoyable to share with your students, and even have that great combination of high entertainment and high impact on students' progress as readers.

Before too long, your students will be ready to apply the active meaning-making process you model to their own reading. You'll read about the dice activity shown here in Chapter 7.

A Sample Think Aloud With *USA Today*	
What the Text Says	**What I Think**
"A 'Whopper' of a Burger Bill"	*This title gives me some clues as to what this article is about. I know that whopper means "a lot" or "big." Maybe it's about an expensive hamburger. But I also know that a Whopper is a kind of hamburger that one particular fast-food chain sells. So maybe this article is about Burger King selling a really expensive hamburger. In any case, I'm intrigued enough by this title to keep reading so that I can find out if either of my predictions is accurate.*
A quick meal at George Beane's neighborhood Burger King ended up costing a lot more than he expected when he got the $4,334.33 bill.	*How is it possible that a meal at a fast-food restaurant cost more than $4,000?*
Beane ordered two Whopper Jrs. and two Rodeo cheeseburgers when he pulled up to the drive-through window last week.	*I don't often eat at Burger King, so I'm unfamiliar with what a Rodeo cheeseburger is. But still, two of them can't cost enough to lead to such an expensive bill. And it seems like the author is giving me an important clue that this happened at a drive-through window. I wonder what role the drive-through window holds in this story.*
The cashier, however,	*Uh-oh. This word, however, seems to be an important signal word. I predict the next thing I will read is an explanation of this crazy bill.*
forgot that she'd entered the $4.33 charge on his debit card and punched in the numbers again without erasing the original ones—thus creating a four-figure bill.	*Wait, I'm unclear on exactly how the cashier made this error, so let me reread for clarification. I really need to understand how we got to this big number. It might help me to visualize exactly what the cashier did. As I reread, I can see that she punched in $4.33 on the register. But then she double entered that same amount. So on top of 4.33, she punched in another 4.33. She must have hit enter or return on the cash register before she realized her mistake—so the final sum was $4,334.33.*
The electronic charge went through to George and Pat Beane's checking account Tuesday and left the couple penniless.	*The author told me that it was a debit card, so before anyone realized the mistake, the bank took out over $4,000 from their account. There must not have been enough in their account, and so the balance went to zero.*
Their mortgage payment was due and they worried checks they had written would bounce, Pat Beane said.	*Did they have overdraft protection from their bank? What might the consequences be if their mortgage check did bounce? Would the bank charge them additional fees for bouncing a check?*

continued...

...from previous

What the Text Says	What I Think
"We were thinking, 'No, not now!'" she said of the overcharge.	*I find this "not now!" statement curious. It sort of makes me think that the timing of this episode was problematic—that maybe it wouldn't have been such trouble if this charge had happened another time—like not when their mortgage payment was due. But I know that there would never be a good time for this mistake to happen to me!*
Terri Woody, the restaurant manager, said Burger King officials tried to get the charge refunded.	*Who are Burger King officials? How high up the corporate ladder did they go to try to fix this error? What did they try? Calling the bank and debit card company?*
But the bank said the funds were on a three-day hold and could not be released, Pat Beane said.	*I don't understand what "the funds could not be released" means. I think it means that the bank took the funds out and put them on hold for three days.*
Burger King did not charge the Beanes for their meal, and the couple got their $4,334.33 back on Friday.	*So it sounds like Burger King just erased their meal entirely. They got a free meal for the inconvenience of the mistake!*
"For those three days, those were the most expensive value burgers in history," Pat Beane said.	*This article leaves me with lots of questions. What is the most expensive burger ever? I'd assume it would be something made of Kobe beef. Did the Beanes ever eat at that particular Burger King again? Is it more likely to have this kind of mistake in drive-through than in walk-in? Maybe people are less likely to check their receipts as they drive off than when they are standing waiting for their food to be prepared. Did the bank penalize the Beanes in any way? And I'm really interested in the author's underlying message here. Is the author trying to place blame for this error? Whose fault was it? We could blame the cashier for her mistake, but isn't it the customer's responsibility to check his receipt? To me, the takeaway of this article is to double-check receipts for everything!*

The passage above demonstrates how applicable think alouds are to the texts that adult readers encounter. But what about the poetry, storybooks, and expository text that we use to teach and that fill our classroom libraries? To give you a quick overview of the ease with which think alouds can be applied to some of the most recognizable children's texts, I've provided very brief think alouds on the next pages.

A think aloud is a teaching strategy in which a proficient reader (in this case, the teacher) verbally reports or models his or her thinking as he or she approaches the text. Think alouds require a reader to stop periodically, to reflect on how a text is being processed and understood, and to relate orally what reading strategies are being employed (Baumann, Jones, & Seifert-Kessell, 1993; Block & Israel, 2004). My favorite definition of a think aloud comes from Baumann, Seifert-Kessell, and Jones (1992), who described it as

Synthesizing With *My Name Is Yoon* by Helen Recorvits	
What the Text Says	**What I Think**
My name is Yoon. I came here from Korea, a country far away. It was not long after we settled in that my father called me to his side. "Soon you will go to your new school. You must learn to print your name in English," he said. "Here. This is how it looks." I wrinkled my nose. I did not like YOON. Lines. Circles. Each standing alone. "My name looks happy in Korean," I said. "The symbols dance together. And in Korean my name means Shining Wisdom. I like the Korean way better." . . . I did not want to learn the new way. I wanted to go back home to Korea. I did not like America. Everything was different here.	*The most important idea here is that Yoon is homesick. She is in a new country with a new language. She misses her home and what is familiar.*

Making Inferences With *The House on Mango Street* by Sandra Cisneros	
What the Text Says	**What I Think**
The boys and the girls live in separate worlds. The boys in their universe and we in ours . . . They've got plenty to say to me and Nenny inside the house. But outside they can't be seen talking to girls . . . Nenny is too young to be my friend. She's just my sister and that was not my fault. You don't pick your sisters, you just get them and sometimes they come like Nenny.	*The author doesn't come right out and say it, but I can infer that the narrator is a girl. I know this because of the clue "we in ours"—the narrator is saying that she's in a different world than the boys, so she must be a girl.* *I'm also getting the sense that the narrator doesn't really like her younger sister. The language "just my sister" and "not my fault" makes it sound like she finds her younger sister annoying.*

Asking Questions With *Sarah, Plain and Tall* by Patricia MacLachlan	
What the Text Says	**What I Think**
The sheep made Sarah smile. She sank her fingers into their thick, coarse wool. She talked to them, running with the lambs, letting them suck on her fingers. She named them after her favorite aunts, Harriet and Mattie and Lou.	*Why would someone smile about sheep? Does she like the feel of their wool? Is wool itchy when it grows on sheep, or is it only itchy in sweaters? Do people think it's odd that she talks to animals? Does this mean there are only three lambs on this farm?*

Monitoring and Clarifying With *Owls* by Gail Gibbons	
What the Text Says	**What I Think**
Most owls have the same basic characteristics. The male is usually a little smaller than the female. There are two different types of owls. Owls with round facial disks are *Strigidae* owls. Owls with heart-shaped facial disks are *Tytonidae* owls.	*I don't understand what a facial disk is. I'm wondering if a facial disk is the same thing as a skull, or if it is just a fancy way to say face. Maybe if I keep reading I can clear up this confusion.*

Understanding the Author's Purpose With *Henry's Freedom Box: A True Story From the Underground Railroad* by Ellen Levine	
What the Text Says	**What I Think**
Henry needed an excuse to say home, or the boss would think he had run off. James pointed to Henry's sore finger. But Henry knew it wasn't bad enough. He opened a bottle of oil of vitriol. "No!" cried James. Henry poured it on his hand. It burned his skin to the bone. Now the boss would have to let him stay home.	*Here I get the sense that the author is trying to tell me about her feelings toward both slave owners and the protagonist Henry. Henry already has an injured finger, but it's not bad enough for the boss to excuse him from work. That makes me think the author sees the boss as cruel. Then Henry pours this poisonous liquid onto his own skin—so harmful that it burns him to the bone! Here the author is giving me clues that Henry is so determined to stay home that he will hurt himself for an excuse. He's brave to hurt himself for something he really wants. This passage tells me an important characteristic of Henry and of the boss.*

"the overt, verbal expression of the normally covert mental processes readers engage in when constructing meaning from a text" (p. 144). When I examine this definition, I tease out the following essential subcomponents:

- Think alouds are transparent efforts to show the deliberate reading actions by the teacher.
- Think alouds are a language-based activity, where the teacher talks through the thought processes he or she employs while reading.
- Think alouds guide the sophisticated process of reading comprehension, making and extracting meaning from a text (Snow, 2002).
- Think alouds are meant to be quick explanations—not lengthy or convoluted extrapolations—of what is going through the mind of a proficient reader.

To further define think alouds, let's examine some of their important characteristics.

What Think Alouds Are

- Think alouds are purposeful.
- Think alouds are a powerful metacognitive tool.
- Think alouds build students' independent abilities to comprehend text.
- Think alouds are an essential step in learning.
- Think alouds apply to all classroom contexts and content.

Think alouds are purposeful. An effective think aloud has clear connections between the text and the strategies you're modeling. A well-planned think aloud begins with a careful perusal of the text, focusing on the opportunities inherent in that text. An effective think aloud logically connects those text elements to comprehension strategies. Mysteries, for example, are logical texts to use for think alouds about generating predictions. High-quality narrative texts for children, like *A Bad Case of Stripes* (Shannon, 1998), *Charlie and the Chocolate Factory* (Dahl, 1964), and *Tuck Everlasting* (Babbitt, 1975), offer ample opportunities to make inferences and to think through the author's purpose. Expository texts, like the works of Gail Gibbons and Seymour Simon, are prudent choices to encourage students to generate questions. As explained by Lapp and colleagues in 2008, teachers who provided effective think alouds "allowed the text to guide their selection of the comprehension strategy to be modeled" (p. 380). This is a crucial point; whenever we model a strategy or reading behavior with a think aloud, it has to be wholly natural—that is, completely a strategy that would bubble up authentically in the mind of a reader approaching that particular text.

By the end of this book, you'll be ready to examine a text and connect its features to the most relevant comprehension strategies and to subsequently generate the think alouds to model those comprehension strategies. When we don't carefully consider the alignment between our lesson's objective, a particular text, and the logically related comprehension strategies, we diminish the power of our think alouds.

Think alouds are a powerful metacognitive tool. An essential component of think alouds is metacognition, or awareness of one's own thinking and learning processes. Readers with metacognitive knowledge have a clear understanding of themselves, the tasks in which they engage, and the thinking strategies to apply to these tasks (Thomas & Barksdale-Ladd, 2000). To conduct think alouds, teachers must be aware of their own reading strategies (Duffy, 2003; Maria & Hathaway, 1993). To facilitate this process, I provide an exercise to encourage you to become metacognitive in Chapter 2.

Think alouds build students' independent abilities to comprehend text. Think alouds help readers to monitor their comprehension. Through a think aloud, students can see that getting through a text requires stamina and struggle. In order to comprehend a text, purposeful readers interact with text by questioning it, wondering about it, slowing down, and rereading it. Through think alouds, teachers facilitate students' independent abilities to follow similar cognitive processes (Davey, 1983). Our aim is to model, guide, and coach students on our thought processes with comprehension being the ultimate goal. As developing readers watch the think aloud, they internalize the skill until they are ready to emulate the work of a proficient reader. This process occurs through gradual release of responsibility (Pearson & Gallagher, 1983a), an important theory described later in this chapter and in Chapter 7. Reading rock stars Doug Fisher, Nancy Frey, and Diane Lapp (2011) wrote that when teachers think aloud "in a conversational manner of a text, in a way that illustrates and scaffolds for students how to build the new knowledge and language about a topic and about the features and the structure of the text, our students are one step closer to being proficient and independent comprehenders" (p. 232).

Think alouds are an essential step in learning. As teachers, we see the term *think aloud* most frequently appear in journals and books about reading comprehension. But if we were to pause and think about the skills that we showcase, model, and teach on a daily basis—outside of the realm of reading—we'd likely realize that thinking aloud is a natural way to showcase our internal thought process. In his seminal text, *Improving Comprehension With Think-Aloud Strategies*, Jeffrey Wilhelm (2001) compares his process of learning to whitewater canoe to think alouds. I made a text connection here when reading Wilhelm's book, when I used a think aloud to model my (not-so-effective!) approach to skiing to my five-year-old. We stood at the top of a slope, visually surveying what lay ahead. I thought aloud with comments like "I see an icy patch right there, so I'll be careful to avoid it" and "If I feel like I'm picking up speed too quickly, I'll remember to snowplow to slow myself down." It would not have been enough for her just to watch my motions down the hill or to direct her from the sidelines on exactly what to do. And though I am certainly not a proficient skier, my thought process and coaching gave her enough guidance to ease her down the mountain. I'm not sure if I was prouder of her for getting down her first real slope on her own, or of myself for not breaking a bone in the process! For the skills that we teach both inside and outside the classroom—be it cooking with a grandchild, teaching a friend how to play mah-jongg, or working on a chip shot with a golf partner—we rely on think alouds as a teaching strategy.

Think alouds apply to all classroom contexts and content. In other words, think alouds are widely applicable. Not every think aloud occurs as a teacher is perched in her rocking chair, with the whole class of students sitting in rapt attention on the rug. With my planning approach, teachers can—and should—think aloud in their guided reading groups, in one-on-one conferences, and in their content-area instruction. Think alouds are powerful across grade levels and genres. They have the same power for a first grader in a narrative text as they do with a fifth grader navigating through expository text. To demonstrate this point, I provide think alouds spanning the K–5 continuum of poetry, narrative, and expository text. I've even included think alouds on text features such as the Author's Note and important visuals and graphics.

What Think Alouds Are Not

After exploring the qualities of think alouds, I aim to rule out any misconceptions about think alouds with some myth busting.

What Think Alouds Are Not

- Think alouds are not extemporaneous.
- Think alouds are not an all-you-can-eat buffet approach to modeling strategies.
- Think alouds are not a check for understanding.
- A think aloud is not a turn and talk.
- Most importantly to this text, think alouds are not impossible!

Think alouds are not extemporaneous. Too often as a novice teacher, I believed that I would be able to think aloud on the spot. I believed that because I was a proficient reader who comprehended nearly any text I tackled, I would be able to generate meaningful think aloud statements off the cuff. I was wrong! Instead, I stumbled to explain how I made an inference. I relied on a small number of relatively simple and familiar strategies—I made predictions over and over again, but pushed aside using text structure and using context clues. I asked questions that were merely checks of comprehension, rather than opportunities to build comprehension. From this experience, and as showcased in a later chapter about my yearlong research study with teachers, I realized that think alouds require thoughtful planning and significant knowledge of a text. In their examination of the read aloud practices of highly effective teachers, Fisher, Flood, Lapp, and Frey (2004) found that expert teachers preview and practice their text selections prior to conducting classroom read alouds. The same practice is true for teachers who approach think alouds as another instructional technique that requires diligent planning and preparation.

Think alouds are not an all-you-can-eat buffet approach to modeling strategies. A think aloud is not a time to sample from every reading comprehension strategy in the history of reading research. Let me illustrate the point with a story from my twenties, when I tagged along with my parents on a business trip to Asia. We stayed—all expenses paid—at a particularly swanky hotel and woke up in the morning to an expansive breakfast buffet at its premiere restaurant. Throwing caution to the wind, I gorged. I piled my plate with lox and pancakes and dim sum and eggs Benedict. Despite my parents' warnings (and disgust!), I ate plate after plate. There was no connection to the purpose of breakfast: fueling my body with nutrients and proteins to supply energy for the day ahead of me. There was no connection between the foods on my plates: I ate meringues before fruits, waffles next to steak. And much to my parents' chagrin, I spent the rest of the day horribly ill. The problem with a buffet is that you eat so many foods that you don't remember the taste of anything specific. Just as I filled my plates with a smattering of unrelated and excess food, too often teachers employ think alouds that are not strategic. Think alouds are not intended to be random samples of multiple strategies; with a think aloud, it is more effective to focus on a few focal strategies that relate coherently both to the text and to the lesson's objective. Too many strategies in a think aloud leave the student not remembering anything specific.

Think alouds are not a check for understanding. As teachers, we ask lots and lots of questions of our students. We might even say that asking questions is second nature to the seasoned teacher. Teachers spend approximately 80 percent of instructional time asking questions; teachers ask between three and four hundred questions each day (Leven & Long, 1981). That figure translates into up to two questions every minute, around seventy thousand a year, or two to three million in the course of a career. A think aloud, however, is the time for teachers to model, demonstrate, and showcase their thinking—not a time for us to check in with students to see what *they* are thinking. We know from Dolores Durkin's (1978) milestone investigation of elementary classrooms that many teachers believed that they were teaching comprehension, when instead they were assessing their students' comprehension. While thinking aloud, I encourage you to squash your natural instincts to assess your students' understanding. Our time is better spent using think alouds as the teacher's time to shine and to dominate discourse.

A think aloud is not a turn and talk. In a think aloud, the teacher generates the thinking. In a turn and talk, all students participate in the discussion. This distinction in who holds the primary responsibility for generating language is an important feature in understanding think alouds. While turn and talks provide valuable experiences for children to generate academic language and to practice the social norms of conversation, they are not best used during teacher-generated think alouds.

I once observed a second-grade teacher attempt to think aloud with the 1986 William Steig narrative *Brave Irene. Brave Irene* tells the story of a young girl whose mother is a seamstress. Her mother—despite being very ill—has sewn a gown for a duchess to wear to a ball. When Irene offers to take the dress to the duchess, Irene's mother refuses. After some persuasion, Irene convinces her mother to get in bed. Irene travels through a harsh blizzard to deliver the dress to the duchess. I watched as the teacher read the following line: "She coaxed her mother into bed, covered her with two quilts, and added a blanket for her feet." The teacher directed students to turn and talk with their neighbors about what they thought the word *coax* meant. She then allotted five minutes of precious instructional time to have students share out their thoughts; every student incorrectly reported that *coax* means to lead someone into bed. Students lost out on the chance to see how their teacher tackled the challenge of unfamiliar vocabulary. And they may have been more likely to remember the fifteen incorrect definitions of the target word than the single correct one from the teacher! Rather than modeling how to use text clues to deduce the meaning of unfamiliar vocabulary, this think aloud became a turn and talk gone wrong.

Most importantly to this text, think alouds are not impossible! Many of the teachers I have worked with expressed initial uncertainty or apprehension about how to think aloud. They were intimidated by what they believed to be a complex process. Research—though increasingly outdated—suggests that teachers may struggle with modeling the complex process of thinking aloud (Dowhower, 1999; Duffy & Roehler, 1989; El-Dinary, Pressley, & Schuder, 1992; Jongsma, 2000; Pressley, 2002). However, since the publication of that research, our field has advanced in practitioner-friendly manuals and articles on how to think aloud. Teachers today are savvy enough to understand where and why students struggle with a text. I take comfort in the words of a participant in my yearlong study, who explained the following:

> There are many steps between knowing what an effective teaching strategy is, and knowing how to do it. The more I prepared and tried out think alouds, the more confident I became in my knowledge that this was something I both *should* do and *could* do.

What strikes me most from the comment above is this teacher's conviction about the instructional value of think alouds, as well as her self-efficacy about how to approach them. Just as our K–5 students need to increase their self-efficacy about their reading abilities, teachers need to build their procedural, adaptive, and reflective knowledge on applying think alouds with confidence (Snow, Griffin, & Burns, 2005).

Why Think Alouds Are Relevant Today

The high academic standards in classrooms today hold students accountable to sophisticated levels of reading comprehension; students are asked to compare and contrast, to evaluate and analyze, to explain their thinking with text evidence, and to judge and interpret. It is no longer enough for a student to recall basic facts and events while answering the lightweight questions that teachers pose (Williams, 2010). Gone are the days when a crafty student could substitute his or her background knowledge for subtle nuances in text-to-self connections; now we demand concrete text evidence. Instead, we expect a kindergartner to compare and contrast the adventure of the owl in Arnold Lobel's *Owl at Home* (1975) to that of the owl in the Edward Lear poem "The Owl and the Pussy-Cat" (Lear, 1871) (Common Core State Standards Initiative, 2010, RL.K.9). While reading *Charlotte's Web* (White, 1952), third graders must differentiate their point of view about Wilbur the Pig from that of Fern Arable, as well as from that of the narrator (CCSS Initiative, 2010, RL.3.6). We demand that fourth graders make inferences between the protagonist's actions and a cholera outbreak in *The Secret Garden* (Burnett, 1911). Students don't naturally learn these skills on their own; they build these skills through the carefully planned think alouds delivered by proficient teachers.

Think alouds also tie into today's instructional push for close reading. Close reading is the instructional practice of having students critically examine a text, especially through multiple readings. To engage in close reading—or critical reading—students must be ready to interrogate a text and dig deep into the author's purpose in writing it. As explained by Fisher and Frey (2012), close reading is usually teacher centered, with the teacher modeling through a shared reading. Inherent in teacher modeling are think alouds, where the teacher can showcase the text-dependent questions and the repeated readings of short passages of complex text.

The Educational Theories Behind Think Alouds

Underpinning the notion of teaching students to think aloud is Pearson and Gallagher's (1983a) work on the *gradual release of responsibility.* Originally developed for reading instruction, this instructional framework shifts the cognitive load from the teacher to the student. The goal of this framework is for students to take on the responsibility for the focal task so that students work independently. This model consists of several purposeful steps, moving from the teacher as model, to joint responsibility of the teacher and learner, to independent practice and application by the learner:

1. **Teacher-provided explicit description of the strategy.** Here the teacher defines the strategy in student-friendly language. The teacher explains the benefits of the strategy, as well as how and when to use it.
2. **Teacher modeling.** The teacher models, explains, thinks aloud, and shows students how to do a particular skill. Students observe as the teacher holds the primary responsibility.
3. **Guided instruction.** Here, teachers prompt, question, facilitate, or lead students through tasks that increase understanding of a particular text. The student and teacher work together to apply the metacognitive strategy.
4. **Collaboration.** In a group setting, students work collaboratively to practice the strategy. Here the teacher observes, coaches, provides feedback, encourages, and clarifies.
5. **Independent practice.** Students are now ready to try the strategy independently. Here the teacher assists, evaluates, and responds.

The overall notion of the gradual release of responsibility is to progress in a cyclical and fluid fashion from teachers holding the primarily instructional role to students holding the primary responsibility for their learning. As students hold More responsibility, they can competently and independently apply a new learning strategy. This process is explained in further detail in Chapter 7.

Practice Makes Perfect: The Three-Step Process to Planning Think Alouds

Jeffrey Wilhelm literally wrote the book on thinking aloud, first in 2001 and later with a 2013 revision. In his text, Wilhelm cites research that identifies the six recursive steps to explicit instruction:

1. The teacher explains what is meant by the focal reading comprehension strategy.
2. The teacher explains the rationale for the reading comprehension strategy.
3. The teacher explains when to use the strategy in authentic reading experiences.
4. The teacher models how to perform the strategy.
5. The teacher guides learner practice.
6. Students independently use the strategy.

© Rick Harrington Photography

Here, second-grade teacher Doug Distefano and I plan a think aloud. If you are getting started with think alouds, it's helpful to work with a colleague.

As I work in classrooms and with teachers, I have witnessed far too much of Steps 1 and 2. Teachers are quick to explain what an inference is and why it helps us become purposeful readers. They provide a definition of author's purpose, and convince their students of its importance in reading. Yet we fall short on Step 4; there is not nearly enough modeling. The overarching objective of my book is to expand on Step 4—or the "teacher does/student watches" step (Wilhelm, 2013). I delineate this process into three easy steps so that teachers can readily think aloud, from start to finish. This three-step process, explored in detail with multiple examples, is unique to this text.

Read Once: Identifying Juicy Stopping Points

The first step in thinking aloud is a close examination of the text. We peruse the text searching for the comprehension opportunities in its pictures, words, and layout. We begin planning our think alouds with a stack of sticky notes in hand. The purpose of this first reading is to mark the pages or paragraphs where we identified "juicy stopping points." A juicy stopping point offers a range of possibilities, either comprehension opportunities or stumbling blocks. Chapter 3 provides guidelines to help you recognize these stopping points. In my first reading, I may identify upwards of fifteen juicy stopping spots in a standard children's picture book!

Read Twice: Determining Where and When to Think Aloud

In our second reading, we examine each stopping point and critically reflect on the need for that particular point. The goal here is to truly focus on what stopping points are appropriate and related to the overarching objective of the think aloud. Chapter 4 provides reflective questions to determine the usefulness of each juicy stopping point. The aim is to narrow down our original stopping points to a more manageable number. These reflective questions help to identify the stopping points that are critical versus those that can be eliminated. Because the overarching goal of the think aloud is to model metacognitive processes, we do not want to overwhelm our students with stopping unnecessarily and detract from the comprehension process. The process of condensing and eliminating stopping points also must be purposeful. We must keep several factors in mind as we make our decisions, including our overall purpose for selecting this particular text, our learning objectives in this lesson, and which comprehension strategies are familiar or unfamiliar to our students prior to reading this text. After our second reading, we typically end up with about five to seven stopping points; these are the bare bones of the think aloud that we will model in front of our students.

Read Three Times: Writing the Scripts on Sticky Notes

The goal of our third reading is to identify the script of exactly what we will say in front of students. We literally write out, in first-person narrative, what we will say in response to a text, so as to give students the chance to eavesdrop on our reading processes. Fisher, Frey, and Hattie (2017) write that think alouds should use "I" statements, explaining that the first-person pronoun "activates the ability—some call it an instinct—of humans to learn by imitation" (p. 58). Chapter 5 provides a wide variety of sentence starters or prompts to jump-start the script writing.

A Final Note About the Three-Step Process

I've adapted the three-step process from Lapp and colleagues' (2008) work with struggling adolescent readers. In their observations of a high school science teacher's interactive read aloud, they conclude that think alouds "were neither unplanned nor inconsequential. Instead they were deliberately planned to provide commentary and conversational support for comprehension, word study, and engagement by noting where students might need explanation, elaboration, or connection" (p. 377). I have modified their three-column chart as the basis for the stopping points in my approach. The following figure provides a glimpse of "The Think Aloud Chart" (see also Appendix E). Chapters 3, 4, and 5 walk you through exactly how to use it. In the first column, we write the text *exactly as it appears.* The last sentence in each row corresponds to the sentence indicating a stopping point. In the second column, we write a first-person narrative of exactly what we say to students. In the third column, we identify which comprehension strategy (or strategies!) our think aloud evokes.

Though this process may be time-consuming initially, the explicit nature of writing think alouds increases our confidence in implementing these lessons. I equate this process of writing the script of a think aloud to teaching a young child to ride a bike with training wheels. Just as training wheels provide stability and confidence in learning a new skill, so does the word-by-word script of a think aloud. Our end goal is to be able to think aloud with comfort, ease, and skill, just as a young child hopes to ride a bike independently.

The Think Aloud Chart

What the Text Says	What I Say	The Comprehension Strategy I Model

How to Use This Book

This book is the how-to guide for thinking aloud. In Chapter 2, I explore why think alouds work. I explore how think alouds build the motivational, attention, and comprehension skills of particular students. Here I also focus on the essential think aloud strategies: which strategies are of high priority in classrooms today? Chapters 3, 4, and 5 walk through the three steps to thinking aloud in detail. To demonstrate the three-step process, I showcase three texts spanning three grade levels. In these three think alouds, I apply the comprehension strategies presented in Chapter 2. I walk through a think aloud lesson with kindergartners using a Shel Silverstein poem ("Sick," 1974). I use the storybook *Enemy Pie* (Munson, 2000) to plan a think aloud for third graders. Lastly, I use Seymour Simon's *Eyes and Ears* (2003) for fifth graders. (Please keep in mind that the grade levels are mere suggestions. These texts span grade levels and can certainly be adapted to meet the needs of diverse readers. Although I use "Sick" for kindergarten, for example, it is certainly appropriate for the early elementary grades.) Chapter 6 describes my yearlong study, where I learned essential lessons from teachers who employed think alouds in their classroom practice. In the final chapter, I delineate the steps for transferring think alouds to students. Also included in this chapter are tips on honing your think aloud skills. The appendices—chock full of think aloud scripts—are organized according to grade level, with equal representation of narrative text, poetry, and expository text. These scripts are ready for immediate classroom application as you build your skills and confidence in thinking aloud.

At the conclusion of each chapter, you will find a brief element titled "Ready for a Trial Run?" Just as I used a think aloud to guide my daughter down a ski slope, I've provided a trial run for you to think through how each chapter's takeaways align with your instruction. I've included reflective questions and activities to get you ready to think aloud on your own. I encourage you to secure a blank notebook or start a new computer file that will afford you the space and time to write meaningful reflections in response to these questions. Some prompts ask you to generate lists; others ask you to make notes about your instructional process. In any case, you will most benefit from the "Ready for a Trial Run?" activities when the written reflection is done with careful observation and genuine thought. "Ready for a Trial Run?" also provides a fruitful place for teachers engaged in book clubs and students reading this text as a class assignment to begin conversations. Those conversations will be the richest, however, when every reader has had prior time and space to write independent reflections prior to group conversations.

Final Thoughts

Just as I began this chapter with the wisdom of literacy guru Doug Fisher, I'd like to end the chapter with some thoughts from his 2017 book, with Nancy Frey and John Hattie, *Teaching Literacy in the Visible Learning Classroom*. Fisher and colleagues write the following about think alouds:

> When teachers explain their expert thinking in a way that students can understand, students are better able to imitate the thinking of their

> teachers. We're not looking for students to simply replicate the work of the teacher but rather to explore the ways that other people think. Thinking is invisible, so teachers have to talk about their thinking. (p. 57)

By now, you're probably ready to open up a book you'd use in your classroom and hit the ground running with think alouds! While I appreciate your enthusiasm, I encourage you to read on. To further make my case for the importance of think alouds, I spend the next chapter examining how think alouds benefit all readers, particularly those who struggle. And because effective teachers are reflective practitioners who can link their instructional decisions to important research and theories, I touch upon the research base in reading comprehension. Enjoy, enjoy!

Ready for a Trial Run?

As teachers and proficient readers, we often forget what it feels like to struggle with a text. Reading and thinking about texts is second nature to us. We can navigate a variety of texts fluently without much cognitive effort. For the most part, our comprehension is not impeded by vocabulary, unfamiliar text structure, or a lack of background knowledge.

It is incredibly useful, however, to remind ourselves what it feels like to be a struggling reader (Afflerbach & Johnston, 1986). To remind you what it feels like to slog through difficult text, I've taken snippets of texts compiled by BuzzFeed's "25 Most Challenging Books You Will Ever Read" (Peitzman, 2013), as well as technical journals. My hunch is that well-intentioned teachers don't think aloud because they struggle to see where their students struggle in a text. As you attempt to navigate through the following texts, think through the following questions:

- What were the key points from this text? What were the essential takeaways?
- If a friend asked you to summarize the passage you just encountered, how would you respond?
- Where were your comprehension breakdowns?
- What prevented you from making meaning of the passage?
- What did you do to address your comprehension breakdowns? Evaluate how successful those strategies were.
- How did you feel as a reader while navigating this text?

Let's try some out. Read the following texts.

From *Gravity's Rainbow* by Thomas Pynchon (1973)

"Darkness invades the dreams of the glassblower. Of all the unpleasantries his dreams grab in out of the night air, an extinguished light is the worst. Light in his dreams, was always hope: the basic moral hope. As the contacts break helically away, hope turns to darkness, and the glassblower wakes sharply tonight crying, Who? Who?"

From *Moby-Dick* by Herman Melville (1851)

"This whale, among the English of old vaguely known as the Trumpa whale, and the Physeter whale, and the Anvil Headed whale, is the present Cachalot of the French, and the Pottsfich of the Germans, and the Macrocephalus of the Long Words. He is, without doubt, the largest inhabitant of the globe; the most formidable of all whales to encounter; the most majestic in aspect; and lastly, by far the most valuable in commerce; he being the only creature from which that valuable substance, spermaceti, is obtained."

From *The Corrections* by Jonathan Franzen (2001)

"By now it had been ringing for so many hours that the Lamberts no longer heard the message of 'bell ringing' but, as with any sound that continues for so long that you have the leisure to learn its component sounds (as with any word you stare at until it resolves itself into a string of dead letters), instead heard a clapper rapidly striking a metallic resonator, not a pure tone but a granular sequence of percussions with a keening overlay of overtones; ringing for so many days that it simply blended into the background except at certain early-morning hours when one or the other of them awoke in a sweat and realized that a bell had been ringing in their heads for as long as they could remember; ringing for so many months that the sound had given way to a kind of metasound whose rise and fall was not the beating of compression waves, but the much, much slower waxing and waning of their consciousness of the sound."

From the U.S. Court of Appeals:
***Jarkesy v. Securities and Exchange Commission* (2014)**

"We agree with the district court and affirm its judgment. In *Thunder Basin Coal Co. v. Reich*, 510 U.S. 200 (1994), the Supreme Court set forth a framework for determining when a statutory scheme of administrative and judicial review forecloses parallel district-court jurisdiction. The ultimate question is whether Congress intended exclusivity when it established the statutory scheme. Applying the considerations outlined in *Thunder Basin* and its progeny, we find the answer here is yes. The result is that Jarkesy, instead of obtaining judicial review of his challenges to the Commission's administrative proceeding now, can secure judicial review in a court of appeals when (and if) the proceeding culminates in a resolution against him."

From Chapter 1, "Organic Molecules and Chemical Bonding," in *Organic Chemistry* by Robert Neuman (1999)

"*H* and other atoms in column 1A, as well as those in columns 2A, and 3A of Figure [graphic 1.2] do not have enough outer shell electrons to achieve an octet when they form bonds so they have no unshared electron pairs in their compounds. *Si* (column 4a) typically has four bonds and no unshared electron pairs like C. The halogen atoms *Cl*, *Br*, and *I* have the same number of unshared electron pairs and preferred bonds as F because they are all in the same column. When *P* and S have 3 and 2 bonds, respectively, they have the same number of unshared electron pairs as N and O. However P and S sometimes form compounds where they have more than 8 outer valence shell electrons."

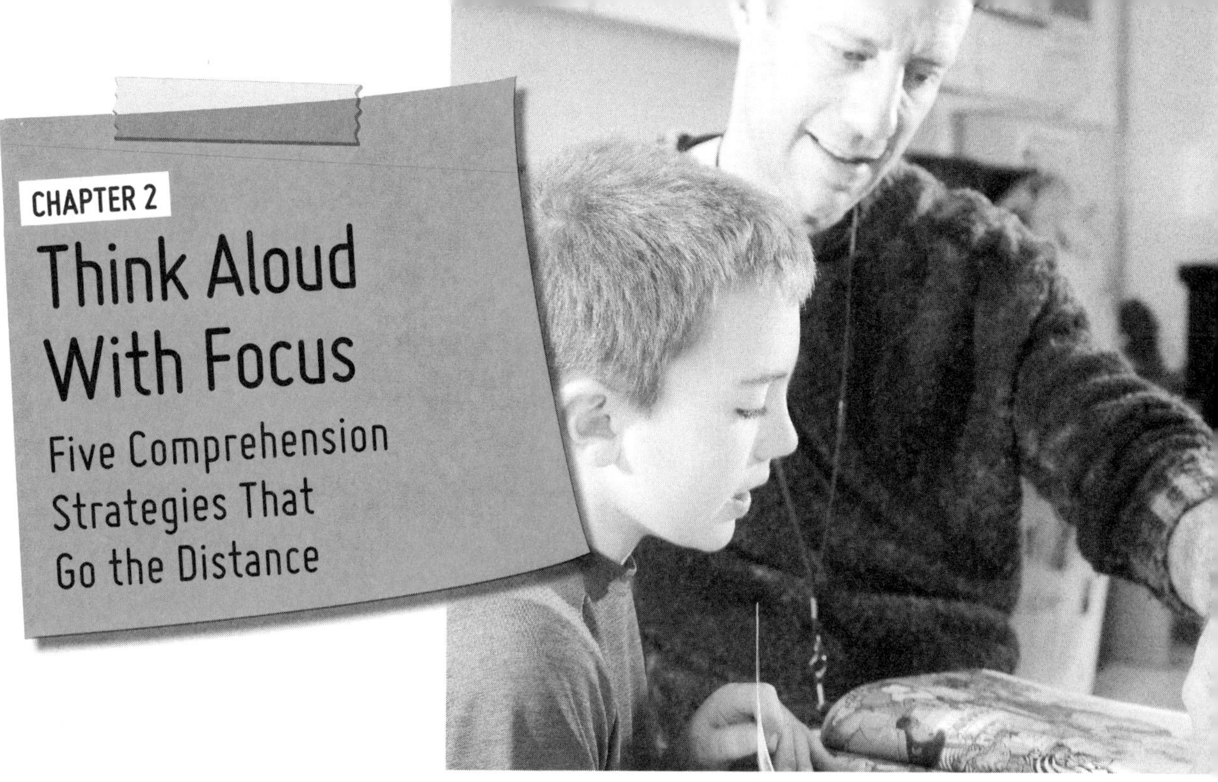

CHAPTER 2

Think Aloud With Focus

Five Comprehension Strategies That Go the Distance

© Rick Harrington Photography

Let me start this chapter with a golden oldie that taps into a teaching truth—"Time in a Bottle" by singer-songwriter Jim Croce. Though I was not yet born when it became a megahit, it somehow is in my emotional DNA. The line "But there never seems to be enough time to do the things you want to do once you find them" especially gets me. It is so darn true, and gets truer with each passing year. Time *is* the most valuable commodity. On a day-to-day work basis, teachers feel this especially acutely, with the needs of dozens of learners tugging at the instructional minutes each school day.

Add to that the long list of instructional priorities bombarding teachers and that "urgency" and "efficiency" and "accountability" are values du jour, and it's no wonder my pre-service and in-service teachers often say to me, "How do I find the time for this?"

The answer is: We make time by boldly, honestly jettisoning classroom practices and activities that don't have strong support from either published research or our own data. We prioritize the relevant, useful methods and strategies that yield positive outcomes for student learning. In my role as a teacher educator, I often say, "These are the ones that give the most instructional bang for our buck." By this, I mean strategies that are easy to plan and implement, that generate meaningful conversations and interactions around the classroom, and that leave a lasting impact on student learning. Think alouds fit all of these criteria.

How Think Alouds Benefit Our Readers

When teachers think aloud, students benefit. According to Lapp, Fisher, and Grant (2008),

> [a]n interactive think aloud provides a means for modeling, scaffolding, and practicing. It offers struggling readers the opportunity to see and hear how proficient readers approach a text, and it allows advanced students to engage in conversations that draw on their prior knowledge. (p. 378)

Effective teacher think alouds positively impact student achievement. The research spans three decades and is compelling (e.g., Anderson & Roit, 1993; Bereiter & Bird, 1985; Loxterman, Beck, & McKeown, 1994; Ortlieb & Norris, 2012; Schunk & Rice, 1985; Silvén & Vauras, 1992; Ward & Traweek, 1993). Think alouds are effective for children of all ages, from preschool (Dorl, 2007) to secondary levels (Coiro, 2011; Lapp et al., 2008). Think aloud instruction benefits students across text formats and genres: in online text (Coiro, 2008; Kymes, 2005), in narrative text (Dymock, 2007), and in informational text (Coiro, 2011; Lapp et al., 2008; Ortlieb & Norris, 2012). Equally promising are the effects of think alouds on struggling readers (Anderson & Roit, 1993; Migyanka, Policastro, & Lui, 2005; Smith, 2006) and on English language learners (Ghaith & Obeid, 2004; McKeown & Gentilucci, 2007). More specifically, there are three patterns among the research into how readers benefit from teacher-generated think alouds.

Think alouds prepare students to apply reading comprehension strategies to independent reading. Perhaps the most obvious reason that teachers think aloud is to model their reading moves and steps so that readers will adopt similar strategies in their independent reading. Just as I model good table manners at a restaurant, in hopes that my daughter will see my choices and emulate my behavior, teachers can do the same with their reading behaviors in their classrooms. Block (2004) surveyed 630 second through sixth graders, asking them what their teachers could do to help them better comprehend. Students most frequently responded that they wanted teachers to better explain their reading processes. More specifically, they wanted teachers to explain "just about everything that they did in their minds to comprehend." Similarly, English language learners and struggling readers requested think alouds from their teachers (Garcia, 2002). While conducting think alouds in a science text with kindergartners, Ortlieb and Norris (2012) found that students who received think aloud instruction outperformed their peers in the control group on reading comprehension scores. When teachers model how they address unfamiliar vocabulary, challenging concepts, and complicated text features, they build their students' ability to succeed in these challenges (Lapp et al., 2008).

Think alouds promote readers' self-efficacy and metacognition. Psychologist Albert Bandura defined self-efficacy as one's belief in one's ability to succeed in specific situations or accomplish a task. Bandura (1977) proposed that people with stronger efficacy beliefs are more likely to attempt novel tasks and experiences. A 2012 research article by Kadir Yoğurtçu posited that readers with high self-efficacy are more likely to develop reading strategies that are "effective, interactive, strategic, and quick" (p. 382). As our students witness us talking through the troublesome spots in a text, they increase in their ability to do the same. The more adept they are at applying comprehension strategies to text, the more confident in their reading skills our students become.

Think alouds help readers think about their own thinking. Readers who comprehend are metacognitive, or aware of their own processes. Flavell (1976) defined metacognition as "one's knowledge concerning one's own cognitive processes and products" (p. 232). In metacognitive reading experiences, readers are aware of any comprehension failures and which strategies they apply to comprehend a text. Inherently, successful readers are more metacognitive than less successful readers (Paris, Lipson, & Wixson, 1994). Furthermore, metacognition plays an important role in reading motivation. Logically, readers who struggle to comprehend lack an awareness of fix-it strategies to help repair their comprehension; poor comprehension can decrease students' motivation to read (Israel & Massey, 2005).

Think alouds build student engagement by turning passive readers into active readers. A 1996 article by Shelby J. Barrentine explains that "many teachers are dissatisfied with straight-through storybook readings that relegate listeners to a passive role" (p. 36). Another key point about think alouds: our students like them! Ivey and Broaddus (2001) reported that middle schoolers were more likely to stay engaged and motivated while listening to their teachers think aloud. In a survey of 1,765 middle schoolers and follow-up interviews, students reported that they enjoyed and were motivated by listening to the teacher reading and thinking aloud, and that such interaction provided "scaffolds to understanding."

Arming Yourself With the Five Essential Think Aloud Strategies

Instructional time is precious, so I offer a list of the five most essential comprehension strategies to model during think alouds. As I define each strategy, I explain how it contributes to reading comprehension. These strategies—as listed below—are rooted in the rigorous standards set forth by the collaboration between the International Literacy Association (founded as the International Reading Association) and the National Council of Teachers of English, as well as the anchor standards of the Common Core. I focus on a small number of strategies because, as suggested by Wilhelm (2001), it is "better to focus and really address a few goals rather than diffusing energy by trying to address too many" (p. 44). Additionally, multiple-strategy instruction is more effective than teaching strategies in total isolation; readers use more than one strategy as they encounter text (Duke & Pearson, 2002). For this reason, the think alouds in this book use multiple strategies concurrently. Should you want additional support in focusing on a single strategy, those transcripts are available in Appendix I.

Standing on the Shoulders of Giants

In my work with teachers, a question that I frequently encounter is "Which reading comprehension strategies should I incorporate into my think alouds?" Knowing the importance of depth over breadth, I focus on five strategies. In developing my list of strategies, I looked to the legends in the field of reading research. In his 2001 book *Improving Comprehension With Think-Aloud Strategies*, Jeffrey Wilhelm focused on the following reading comprehension strategies:

1. Set purposes for reading
2. Make predictions
3. Connect personally
4. Visualize
5. Monitor comprehension
6. Use fix-up strategies to address confusion and repair comprehension

In her 2009 book *Interactive Think-Aloud Lessons*, Lori Oczkus maps out the "Super Six" comprehension strategies incorporated by good readers: (1) connect, (2) predict, (3) question, (4) monitor/clarify, (5) summarize/synthesize, and (6) evaluate. I've modified Oczkus's list slightly to meet the demands of close reading and today's high-rigor expectations. For example, I've eliminated connections because too often I've seen this strategy veer readers off course. In addition, Oczkus lumps together predictions and inferences in her Super Six. In my experience, predictions come readily to most children, whereas making inferences is a struggle. While the two are certainly not the same strategy, they draw on the same skill set—as discussed below.

My top five strategies are as follows:

Five Essential Think Aloud Strategies

1. Asking questions
2. Making inferences
3. Synthesizing
4. Understanding the author's purpose
5. Monitoring and clarifying

I see these five strategies as the "path towards understanding and accessing complex texts" (Frey & Fisher, 2013, p. 17).

The remainder of this chapter is a detailed explanation of the five strategies that I rely on while thinking aloud. For each of the strategies, you'll find the following elements:

- A brief explanation of the strategy, as well as a bit of its research base
- A *student-friendly definition* of the strategy, written exactly as you'd give it to your students
- A strategy symbol, or quick image that visually represents the strategy
- Sentence starters, a framework to jump-start your think aloud

A Note About the Strategy Symbols

Next to each strategy, you'll find a visual image. I call these "strategy symbols"; each one represents a comprehension strategy. In the second step of my three-step process, I quickly sketch these strategy symbols on my sticky notes to denote which reading comprehension strategy I will incorporate. This way, I've made my work in the third step a bit easier as I have a reminder of what strategy to use. The symbols are meant to be quick sketches; by no means am I an artist!

For asking questions, the strategy symbol is obvious: a question mark.

For making inferences, I draw three vertical lines because making inferences is often described as "reading between the lines."

For synthesizing, I draw a circle with inner spirals, because this is a skill of continually intertwining strands of a text into a whole.

For understanding the author's purpose, I draw the letter A.

For monitoring and clarifying, I sketch two arrows, because so much of monitoring and clarifying is the process of rereading. The arrows represent how readers go back and forth in text to address their confusion.

A Note About the Sentence Starters

I've modified Oczkus's (2009) "strategy starters" into my *sentence starters* (also available in Appendix D). Sentence starters remove the difficulty of generating the correct academic language associated with each strategy. They are a crutch to rely on to get your creative juices flowing. As you become more adept at thinking aloud, you may come up with your own sentence starters. I encourage you to use my sentence starters at the beginning of the script that you say out loud to students as you think aloud.

The Five Essential Think Aloud Strategies

Asking Questions

Good readers are inquisitive. They ask questions both of the text and beyond the text. Rarely, if ever, does a reader pose a question for which there is one correct answer. Instead, authentic questions are those that can be explored—rather than definitively answered. The reader pursues them by simply reading on, perhaps by rereading, perhaps by discussing them with others, or even by having them come to mind hours, weeks, or years later! Our students must become amazing at being inquisitive and curious—not amazing at answering. In many schools and in our testing culture, this requires a significant shift in mindset.

The power of student-generated questions is indisputable. Key studies point out that proficient readers ask questions and that asking questions is a favorable strategy to enhance reading comprehension (Chin, Brown, & Bruce, 2002; Davey & McBride, 1986; King & Rosenshine, 1993; Ness, 2015; Nolte & Singer, 1985; Rosenshine, Meister, & Chapman, 1996; Taboada & Guthrie, 2006; Taylor, Alber, & Walker, 2002; Therrien & Hughes, 2008; Wong & Jones, 1982). As explained by Harvey and Goudvis (2000), asking questions pushes readers forward in their understanding of text. In their meta-analysis of question generation, Therrien and Hughes (2008) reported thirteen studies highlighted significant gains in reading comprehension scores with the use of question generation. Taboada and Guthrie (2006) noted that question generation contributes to the active reading comprehension process by helping students to initiate cognitive processes, concluding that "[w]hen asking questions, students are involved in multiple processes requiring deeper interactions with text" (p. 4). As they pose questions, students become focused readers with stronger understanding of the written text (Chin et al., 2002).

In addition to the reading comprehension benefits, question generation benefits children in other cognitive and motivational capacities. In posing questions, children think critically, activate higher-level thinking skills, and focus on essential information to synthesize their understandings. They learn not to accept information at its face value, but instead to extend their learning in a self-directed manner. A research team from the University of California, Davis (Singh, 2014), monitored brain activity to measure how engaged learners were in reading questions and their answers. When learners' curiosity was piqued by questions and their answers, the parts of the brain associated with pleasure, reward, and creation of memory underwent an increase in activity.

Fortunately, asking questions is a skill that comes naturally to young children. Any parent or teacher will attest to the sheer magnitude of questions generated by young children. On an average day, mothers typically are asked an average of 288 questions a day by their children aged two to ten (Frazier, Gelman, & Wellman, 2009). Chouinard, Harris, and Maratsos (2007) revealed that children ask between 400 and 1,200 questions each week!

The ability to ask questions is a high priority in today's classrooms. The Common Core State Standards (CCSS Initiative, 2010) emphasize question generation throughout the developmental spectrum of elementary grades. As readers rise in grade level, the questions that they are expected to ask become increasingly complex. Second graders are expected to ask journalistic-type questions (who, what, where, when, why, and how) about explicit information in a text. By the end of fourth grade, students are expected to ask both closed-ended and open-ended questions, requiring both inference skills and critical thinking.

Building Students' Skills in Asking Questions

To model question generation, teachers must demonstrate how they wonder before reading, during reading, and after reading. Teachers should model rich questions, both within and beyond the text. Not only should thinking aloud include the basic questions (who, what, where, when, why, and how), but it should also include higher-order and evaluative questions that push readers to engage beyond the surface level of a text (Oczkus, 2009). In my experience with young children, questions beget questions (Ness, 2015). The more they see their teachers and classmates wonder about possibilities within and beyond the text, the more likely students are to ask similar questions of their own.

© Rick Harrington Photography

A student adds to a collection of student-generated questions about *A Bad Case of Stripes.*

Classroom Spotlight on **ASKING QUESTIONS**

I recently had the pleasure of doing two different read alouds in a kindergarten classroom. For our first read aloud, I chose Tomie dePaola's Caldecott award winner *Strega Nona* (1975), which tells the story of an Italian witch doctor known for her successful remedies. By carving out instructional time to encourage question generation and by giving students simple questioning vocabulary (*who, what, where, when, why, how*), students eagerly share out a long list of questions:

- Will Big Anthony use the magic pasta pot?
- Why does Big Anthony never listen?
- What will Strega Nona do when she sees all of the pasta?
- Is there really magic?
- Where is Calabria? Italy?
- Could Big Anthony really eat all of that pasta?
- What is pasta made from?

In asking these questions, students become more engaged and purposeful in approaching the story. The same is true for a subsequent read aloud, with the picture book *Roller Coaster* by Marlee Frazee (2003). *Roller Coaster* begins with illustrations of a long line of people at a fairground. Ahead of them is a roller coaster named Rocket. As the line creeps slowly, passengers await anxiously. At last, twelve passengers—some calm and collected, others excited—climb into the cars. With vivid images and the typography mimicking the motion of the roller coaster, the illustrations depict the riders as they experience a variety of twists, turns, and loop-the-loops. Here, I encourage students to generate deeper questions—which cannot necessarily be answered within the pages of this book. They generate the following list:

- How does a roller coaster stay on the track? Does it ever fall off?
- What makes a roller coaster so noisy?
- Do you wear seatbelts on a roller coaster?
- Why do people put their hands in the air on a roller coaster? Aren't you supposed to hold on?
- I wonder why those riders are kissing in the back of the roller coaster.
- I wonder why that man is walking away from the roller coaster. Did he decide not to ride?
- How do you get to be a roller coaster ride operator?
- Why can't she open her eyes on the roller coaster?
- Why are most people dizzy after a roller coaster?
- I wonder if anyone threw up after riding.
- What do wobbly knees feel like? I wonder how a doctor might fix wobbly knees.

Defining Asking Questions for K–5 Readers

Purposeful readers are naturally curious. They ask questions about what happens in the text. Sometimes the answers to their questions are found in the text, and sometimes they are not.

The following sentence starters are useful to help generate the academic language associated with question generation:

- I wonder . . .
- I would like to ask the author . . .
- Who . . . ?
- What . . . ?
- When . . . ?
- Where . . . ?
- Why . . . ?
- How . . . ?
- This makes me wonder about . . .
- How is this different?
- How does this part here add to . . . ?

Making Inferences

When I was an elementary school student, my teacher often reminded the class that "good readers read between the lines to use clues in the text." Here, she laid the foundation for making inferences, the process of making educated guesses about a text based on what a reader already knows. Making inferences asks students to fill in information that was not directly presented to them. An inference is something that is probably true—probably something the author intends for us to think, feel, or know. The author and illustrator don't directly tell us everything in a story, but sometimes they give us clues to help us think about things that are probably true. In her pivotal text, Kylene Beers (2003) defines an inference as "the ability to connect what is in the text with what is in the mind to create an educated guess" (p. 62). An inference is the intersection of meaning; it is the product of clues from the text and background knowledge, or schema. To make an

Classroom Spotlight on **MAKING INFERENCES**

Let's examine an opportunity within the picture book *Thank You, Mr. Falker* (1998) by Patricia Polacco. This poignant narrative tells the story of Trisha, a struggling reader. Midway through the book is this essential event, which profoundly impacts Trisha's childhood:

> Trisha's grandma used to say that the stars were holes in the sky. They were the light of heaven coming from the other side. And she used to say that someday she would be on the other side, where the light comes from. One evening they lay on the grass together and counted the lights from heaven. "You know," her grandma said, "all of us will go there someday. Hang on to the grass, or you'll lift right off the ground, and there you'll be!" They laughed, and both hung on to the grass. But it was not long after that night that her grandma must have let go of the grass, because she went to where the lights were, on the other side. And not long after that, Trisha's grandpa let go of the grass, too.

A proficient reader would reach the inference that Trisha's grandparents have died. I observed a second-grade teacher tell her students to turn and talk about how Trisha might have felt about the death of her grandparents. After an awkward pause, students turned to their neighbors with puzzled looks. Finally, one brave boy raised his hand and said, "How are we supposed to know that Trisha's grandparents died? It doesn't say so in the book." He—and his classmates—entirely missed the inference about this pivotal event in the book and were unable to extract the significance of this event. What if the teacher had modeled her thinking to show her students how to reach this important inference? A think aloud might have looked like this.

What the Text Says	What the Teacher Says
Trisha's grandma used to say that the stars were holes in the sky. They were the light of heaven coming from the other side. And she used to say that someday she would be on the other side, where the light comes from. One evening they lay on the grass together and counted the lights from heaven. "You know," her grandma said, "all of us will go there someday. Hang on to the grass, or you'll lift right off the ground, and there you'll be!" They laughed, and both hung on to the grass.	*This evidence makes me think that Trisha's grandmother is talking about dying. On the other side of the stars is heaven—and someday she's going to go to heaven, meaning she will die. If you hang onto the grass, you will not be on the other side—where heaven is.*
But it was not long after that night that her grandma must have let go of the grass, because she went to where the lights were, on the other side. And not long after that, Trisha's grandpa let go of the grass, too.	*The author doesn't come right out and tell me, but I can figure out that Trisha's grandparents have both died. They let go of the grass and went to the other side—which I know is heaven.*

inference, students act like detectives to use facts, clues, observations, logic, and reasoning to come to an assumption or conclusion.

Inferences and predictions are not the same, though they are related. Whereas an inference asks, "What conclusions can you draw about what is happening now?," a prediction asks, "What will happen next?" Marzano (2010) encourages teachers to have students identify the information that they used to make an inference. This may include information directly from the text or the background information that a student brings to the context. An inference results from clues from the text and a reader's background knowledge.

Building Students' Skills in Making Inferences

Though we do it all the time, making inferences is a difficult skill. Students may struggle to make inferences because of the subtlety of a text or because of their limited background knowledge. To further complicate matters, inferences are not clearly confirmed or denied through reading. Yet without the ability to make inferences, students miss out on the subtleties of characters' feelings, underlying events and actions, and the nuances planted throughout a text.

Defining Making Inferences for K–5 Readers

Purposeful readers make inferences. An inference is something that is probably true. The author doesn't tell us exactly, but good readers take clues from the text and combine them with what they already know. An inference is made when a reader says, "This is probably true."

The following sentence starters are useful to help generate the academic language associated with inferences:

- From the text clues, I can conclude that . . .
- Based on what the text says and what I know, I think . . .
- This information makes me think . . .
- This evidence suggests . . .
- That is probably why . . .
- Although the author does not come right out and say it, I can figure out that . . .
- It could be that . . .

- Maybe/perhaps . . .
- This could mean . . .
- Based on what I know about these characters, I bet he/she is going to . . .
- With what just happened, I imagine this character is feeling . . .

Synthesizing

As readers wade through a text, their thinking changes as they read more and gain more information. A synthesis allows readers to reevaluate their schema to form new schema. Without synthesis, a reader's view of a text or topic may remain stagnant. Block and Duffy (2008) noted that synthesizing is critical to understanding the big ideas of informational text. Oczkus (2009) recommends that in a synthesis the reader ask, "How have I been changed by reading this book? What will I remember? What new ideas do I have about the topic, concept, the author, or genre? What is my new big idea to add to my background?" (p. 22). Synthesizing moves students away from simply recalling text-based facts toward how the author uses these facts to convey a central idea (Cummins & Stallmeyer-Gerard, 2011).

There is a logical fit between synthesizing as a reading comprehension strategy and expository text. Synthesizing requires readers to differentiate the main idea of a text from its supporting details, to put new material into their own words, and to combine new information with their prior knowledge. I'm specifically focusing on synthesizing as an extension of summarizing; whereas summarizing holds readers to restating the text's important points, synthesizing requires readers to input their ideas about the text to reach an evolving understanding of it.

Building Students' Skills in Synthesis

> **Defining Synthesis for K–5 Readers**
>
> Purposeful readers constantly change their minds as they read. They use the unfolding information or events in the book to adapt thoughts, opinions, and conclusions. In fiction, readers often synthesize to refine their understanding of characters and theme; in nonfiction, readers synthesize in order to get the most important points about parts of a text. As they continue to read and synthesize, they add up the bigger ideas in their mind. Ultimately, readers synthesize to draw a conclusion about what the author's perspective of a topic is, and what their own perspective is, based on the text.

The following sentence starters are useful to help generate the academic language associated with synthesizing:

- Before I read, I thought . . . , but now I think . . .
- My schema before I read was . . . , and now I understand . . .
- This part gives me an idea . . .
- When I put all these parts together, it seems the author is focusing on this big idea . . .
- My synthesis is . . .
- Mostly, . . .
- I learned . . .
- Now I understand . . .
- Now I think . . .
- The author keeps using these similar terms, so I think this whole section is really about this aspect of . . .
- Some of the most important ideas are . . .
- The text is mainly about . . .
- The text, pictures, and boxes all seem to point at informing me that . . .
- The author's most important ideas were . . .
- The details I need to include are . . .
- Some important concepts are . . .
- The most important evidence was . . .
- The basic gist is . . .
- The key information is . . .
- In a nutshell, this says that . . .
- If I asked the author to just tell me in one sentence what the big idea is, he/she would say . . .

Understanding the Author's Purpose

I love books that include an Author's Note before or after the text. Here I get the backstory—the rationale for the author's writing and the conscious explanation of how and why the author created the text. Most texts,

Here, students think aloud on sticky notes in response to Shel Silverstein's poem "Sick."

however, lack an Author's Note, leaving the reader to deduce why the author created the book. Proficient readers attempt to define the author's intention and to guess why the author was motivated to write this particular text. As readers understand the author's purpose, they can explore the effectiveness of the author's writing and message.

For understanding the author's purpose, I will introduce the three most common approaches, made memorable with the acronym PIE (persuade, inform, entertain). An author's purpose is

1. To persuade, or to convince the reader of an opinion
2. To inform, or to give information and teach
3. To entertain, or to capture and delight the reader with a story

In some cases, the author provides more than one purpose in the text; the PIE dichotomy begins to blur. For example, Jim Arnosky's *A Manatee Morning* (2000) informs young readers where manatees live, what they eat, and other facts. Also in the book is a deliberate persuasive element—encouraging children to be active in protecting these and other endangered animals. In fact, some of our most engaging high-quality children's books cannot be pigeonholed into a single category for understanding the author's purpose.

Building Students' Skills in Understanding the Author's Purpose

Reflective readers are able to analyze information more thoughtfully when they know an author's purpose.

> ### Defining Author's Purpose for K–5 Readers
>
> Purposeful readers try to figure out the reason that the author wrote a text. They want to know the purpose of the text. If a text gives a clear opinion or tries to convince the reader of something, the author's purpose is to persuade. If a text gives facts or tells a reader how to do something, the author's purpose is to inform. If the text is enjoyable, tells a story, or uses a story to teach a lesson, the author's purpose is to entertain.

The following sentence starters are useful to help generate the academic language associated with understanding the author's purpose:

- The author wants me to learn about . . . [specific to nonfiction]
- The author's purpose in writing this story was . . .
- I wonder why the author . . .
- I think the author's purpose is . . . because . . .
- The main character learns . . . in the end, so I wonder if the author wants me to reflect on . . .
- This story is set in history during [a famous event], so I think the author's purpose is to . . .
- I predict that the author's purpose is to inform/entertain/persuade because . . .
- After reading the selection, I believe the author's purpose is . . . because . . .
- The author's purpose is . . . based on . . .
- I am curious why the author . . .
- A golden line for me is . . .
- I like how the author uses . . . to show . . .
- This word/phrase stands out for me because . . .

Monitoring and Clarifying

Good readers are active; they monitor their own understanding and are cognizant of when they encounter troublesome spots in a text. Good readers engage in silent dialogues with the text. As they monitor their understanding, they are strategic in clarifying comprehension breakdowns. To be successful in this strategy, students first must be able to recognize the signals of when their comprehension is faltering. Cris Tovani (2000) outlines these signals of comprehension "red flags," or breakdowns:

- When the voice inside the reader's head is passive, or is not interacting with the text
- When the camera—which helps a reader to visualize what is happening in a text—inside a reader's head shuts off
- When the reader's mind is wandering, and not focusing on the text
- When the reader can't recall what he or she has read

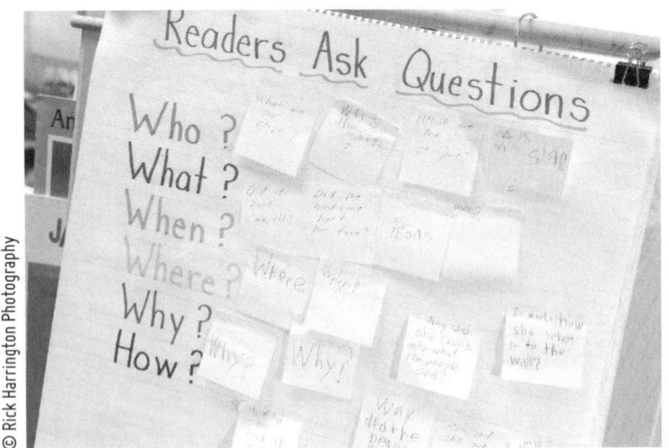

Students as young as kindergarten age can begin to jot down the questions that naturally arise in their heads as they hear and read stories and nonfiction.

- When the reader meets a character, event, or setting that has previously been introduced, but has no recollection of the person, event, or place

As readers begin to recognize the signals for when their comprehension breaks down, they understand the causes behind these breakdowns. Common reasons for comprehension breakdowns include fatigue, decrease in interest level, and lack of background knowledge. Knowing the cause of the comprehension breakdown allows a reader to more readily apply an appropriate fix-up strategy. Common fix-up strategies include the following:

- Reread
- Read on; move past the tricky passage
- Ask a question
- Use or seek out additional background knowledge
- Stop and refocus

Building Students' Skills in Monitoring and Clarifying

To model monitoring and clarifying, teachers must showcase both elements of metacognitive knowledge: the ability to evaluate their ongoing comprehension processes and the ability to take remedial action when needed (Baker, 1979; Baker & Brown, 1984).

> **Defining Monitoring and Clarifying for K–5 Readers**
>
> Purposeful readers know when they stop understanding what they are reading. Just as when a train is going too fast the conductor applies the brake, a reader slows down and takes steps to get back on track. A reader uses one or more "fix it" strategies for repairing his or her comprehension.

The following sentence starters are useful to help generate the academic language associated with monitoring and clarifying:

- I had to slow down when . . .
- It really surprised me, so I had to go back and reread because . . .

- I wonder what . . . means.
- Is this a different point in time?
- Is this a flashback?
- I wonder if this is a different narrator speaking, because . . .
- What is the author doing differently with the text here because I keep losing track . . . ?
- I need to know more about . . .
- This last part is about . . .
- I was confused by . . .
- I still don't understand . . .
- I had difficulty with . . .
- I used [name strategy] to help me understand this part.
- I can't really understand . . .
- I wonder what the author means by . . .
- I got lost here because . . .
- I need to reread the part where . . .

Final Thoughts

I started this chapter with the song lyrics of Jim Croce, so let me bring it full circle and end with more of his words. This time, let's turn to his 1974 "I'll Have to Say I Love You in a Song." So far in this book, I've worked to convince you of the need for and the power of think alouds. In this chapter, I've highlighted the academic benefits of think alouds and given you a concrete list of the five focal strategies. The next three chapters—which explicitly walk through the steps to planning think alouds—will steer you clear of any blunders, confusion, or mishaps in thinking aloud. Jim Croce sang, "Every time I tried to tell you, the words just came out wrong." With my direction and your careful planning, your think aloud words will surely not come out wrong.

Ready for a Trial Run?

Now, I want you to think about your own reading and about yourself as a reader. My aim here is to encourage you to become a metacognitive reader, as explained by Flavell's (1976) theory. Being metacognitive about your reading improves your ability to demonstrate think alouds with readers.

For instance, I know that my weakness as a reader is in making inferences and clarifying confusion. With that knowledge, I can devote extra attention to these strategies so that I further understand them, can engage with them, and, in turn, can model them. The more that we know ourselves as readers, the better prepared we are to teach our children to become readers. In order to effectively plan and implement think alouds, teachers must be metacognitive about themselves as readers; Duffy (2003) and Maria and Hathaway (1993) implored teachers to be aware of their own reading strategies so that they could conduct think alouds.

Think about the reading that you do on a daily basis: newspaper articles, recipes, social media posts, emails, blogs, pleasure reading. Spend some time thinking about these reflective questions:

- What is the purpose of each text?
- What do you as the reader bring to a text?
- What processes do you as a reader use in navigating the text? What reading strategies do you tend to favor?
- What reading strategies do you gloss over?

If these questions are novel to you, or you are unsure how to begin examining metacognitive reading processes, the Metacognitive Awareness of Reading Strategies Inventory (MARSI) may be a useful tool. The MARSI (Mokhtari & Reichard, 2002) is a thirty-question reading strategies inventory. Readers evaluate their frequency of reading strategies such as "I preview the text to see what it's about before reading it" and "I try to guess what the material is about when I read." As you complete and score the MARSI, think through these questions:

- What did you learn about yourself as a reader?
- What are your strengths as a reader? What habits and strategies do you commonly use?
- What are your weaknesses as a reader? How does knowing your weaknesses as a reader help inform your instruction?

The MARSI can be accessed at dayofreading.org/DOR10HO/MARSI_2002.pdf.

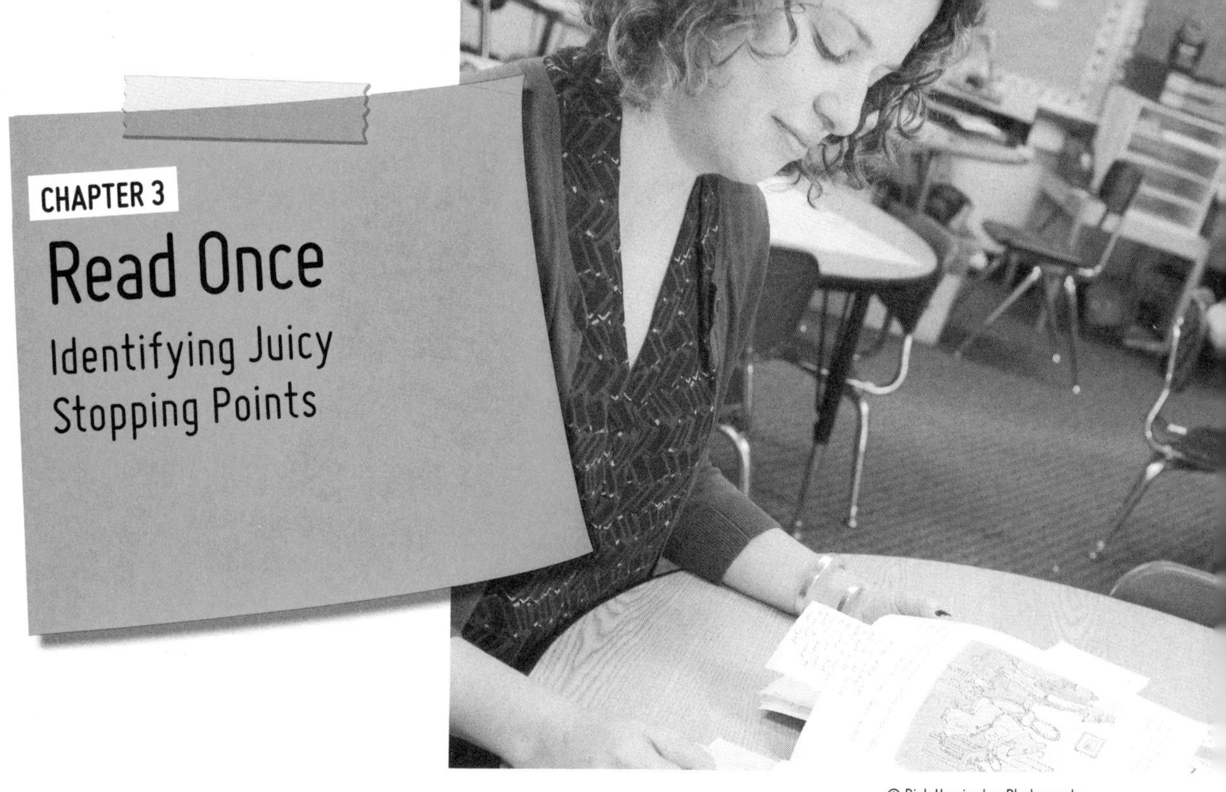

CHAPTER 3

Read Once

Identifying Juicy Stopping Points

© Rick Harrington Photography

Ready to dive in? In the next chapters, I walk you through the three-step process in detail, explaining both the purpose of each step and its key to-dos—and to-don'ts! I'll use three sample texts to demonstrate what planning looks like across a span of genres and grade levels: (1) a poem to use with kindergartners, (2) a narrative text to use with third graders, and (3) an informational text to use with fifth graders.

Because my end goal in thinking aloud is to *apply the most relevant comprehension strategy at the most opportune stopping point*, you will see that I employ multiple strategies as I approach these three texts. For those readers who need to focus on one comprehension strategy at a time, Appendix I provides multiple transcripts with a singular focus.

An Overview

I begin planning my think aloud with a stack of sticky notes in hand. The purpose of this first reading is to quickly mark portions of text that provide a "juicy stopping point" for a reader. My only aim is to identify the places I *might* stop and think aloud, though I do number each sticky note to match the number of the stopping point. I am not yet thinking about what to say or making final decisions on which comprehension strategies I want to demonstrate.

A juicy stopping point offers a range of possibilities, either comprehension opportunities or likely stumbling blocks for student readers. More specifically, juicy stopping points stir a reader to puzzle, ponder, feel, or react. A stopping point is

- When the reader asks questions about unknown things and wants to try to find the answer
- When the reader uses clues to make educated guesses and predictions about the text
- When the reader stops because of confusion
- When the reader thinks about the text in relation to his or her life, the world, or other texts
- When the reader gives him- or herself an additional chance to make sense of the text
- When the reader creates pictures in his or her mind connected to the text
- When the reader takes important information from the text and puts it into his or her own words
- When the reader has a general comment, question, or reaction, or simply wants to say something about the text
- When the reader notices imagery-rich details or any details that are designed to stir deeper pondering or investigation
- When the reader notices a cliffhanger opportunity, or a suspenseful or action-driven point in the text to make a guess about what happens next

In the list above, I phrased each point as "When the reader . . ." to emphasize that it's the reader's role to notice the text, and it's that active reading one models in a think aloud. In other words, for the sake of clarity, I'm deliberately downplaying the author's role in intentionally creating the juicy stopping points. The author creates some of the low-hanging fruit; then, each reader notices other juicy stopping points. This is what Rosenblatt (1994) described in her transactional theory of reading. It's a two-way transaction between writer and reader.

This first step of sticky-noting is kind of a brainstorming session, so I adhere to a few principles of brainstorming: (1) go for quantity, (2) withhold criticism, and (3) welcome wild ideas. Thus, in the first step of thinking aloud, I identify far more stopping points than I will actually use in the lesson.

After this first reading, I may have identified as many as twelve to fifteen juicy stopping points. In my first reading of the storybook *Enemy Pie* (Munson, 2000), I flagged more than twenty potential stopping points! I withhold judgment or reflection about the usefulness of or rationale for stopping. Instead, I merely say to myself, "Aha! This might be a fruitful stopping point" because of the reasons listed above.

Using Poetry in Kindergarten

The poetry of Shel Silverstein resonated with me as a young child and does the same many years later in my roles as a parent and teacher. Silverstein's poetry is devoid of inaccessible themes, complicated vocabulary, and elusive metaphors. His work offers comical twists on relatable characters and situations. Silverstein's rhythm and rhyme build students' understanding of phonological awareness and word patterns. Douglas Florian, Lee Bennett Hopkins, Rebecca Kai Dotlich—there are so many terrific poets writing for children whose collections deserve space in our classroom libraries, but what I like about Shel Silverstein for think alouds is that his poems are so readable, and offer challenge but avoid frustration-level complexity.

I've selected the poem "Sick" from Silverstein's volume *Where the Sidewalk Ends* (1974), which introduces the narrator Peggy Ann McKay. This young girl gives a lengthy list of her ailments that prevent her from going to school. The humor in this poem lies in the excuses that the narrator gives, as well as the twist at the end. Upon hearing that it's Saturday, Peggy Ann hops out of bed to go play. Children—who are familiar with making excuses to avoid something—relate easily to this poem.

As I approach "Sick" with my sticky notes, I know that my initial reading will yield more stopping points than I will actually use. For a relatively short poem, twelve stopping points may be too many; if my stopping points are too many and not purposeful, they may actually impede comprehension. For the most part, I hold my stopping points until the end of the sentence so as to not unnaturally interrupt the flow of the text. In the table on the next page, I present the rationale behind my selection of each stopping point. My rationale will be useful in the next chapter, when I determine the usefulness of each stopping point.

Here, I'm completing Step 1 with a nonfiction text. Remember to consider both words and graphics when planning your think alouds.

Write what you think on sticky notes!

Kindergarten: Possible Stopping Points in "Sick" by Shel Silverstein

What the Text Says	What I Think
"Sick"	*This title leads to several questions.*
"I cannot go to school today," Said little Peggy Ann McKay.	*As I read this first sentence, I've got an immediate question.*
"I have the measles and the mumps, A gash, a rash and purple bumps.	*I've chosen this as a stopping point because I'm creating pictures in my mind. I also recognize that some of these unknown terms might elicit confusion from young readers.*
My mouth is wet, my throat is dry, I'm going blind in my right eye. My tonsils are as big as rocks, I've counted sixteen chicken pox And there's one more—that's seventeen, And don't you think my face looks green?	*Several questions come to mind here as Peggy Ann lists her ailments and appears to speak to someone within the text.*
My leg is cut—my eyes are blue— It might be instamatic flu.	*I'm flagging this unfamiliar term; surely students won't know it.*
I cough and sneeze and gasp and choke, I'm sure that my left leg is broke— My hip hurts when I move my chin, My belly button's caving in, My back is wrenched, my ankle's sprained,	*I've gotten a lot of information in this poem so far, so it might be prudent to see what sense I can make of it all together.*
My 'pendix pains each time it rains. My nose is cold, my toes are numb. I have a sliver in my thumb.	*This stopping point might lead to questions, and I'm also starting to think about why this author has written this poem.*
My neck is stiff, my voice is weak, I hardly whisper when I speak. My tongue is filling up my mouth,	*More questions naturally occur here, about her illnesses and about Peggy Ann as a character.*
I think my hair is falling out. My elbow's bent, my spine ain't straight, My temperature is one-o-eight. My brain is shrunk, I cannot hear, There is a hole inside my ear.	*At this point, I might be able to piece together all of the parts of the poem in a synthesis. I've got a reaction to the questions Peggy Ann is posing at this point.*
I have a hangnail, and my heart is—what? What's that? What's that you say?	*I'm noting a cliffhanger ending, a perfect place to stop.*
You say today is . . . Saturday?	*I'm identifying this point as a suspenseful twist, and it is a logical place for me to model my thinking.*
G'bye, I'm going out to play!"	*With this turn of events, I most certainly will want to stop and model my thinking.*

In my next step, which I outline in the following chapter, I will look at each of these stopping points and decide if it truly matches my overarching objective.

Using Narrative Text in Third Grade

There's so much to love about the popular picture book *Enemy Pie* by Derek Munson (2000): the subtle humor, the author's implied message, and the charming illustrations. *Enemy Pie* tells the story of an unnamed school-aged narrator who anticipates the perfect summer. His plans are foiled when his number-one enemy moves next door. Luckily, the narrator's father knows a surefire way to get rid of enemies—Enemy Pie! But one of its secret ingredients is spending an entire day with the enemy. This funny and endearing book teaches life lessons about friendship. Furthermore, because of the implied messages and subtle nuances within the text, opportunities for making inferences abound. The table starting on the next page gives my rationale for selecting each stopping point.

Using Informational Text in Fifth Grade

Informational text—which conveys factual information about the natural and real world—presents a unique set of challenges to readers. Informational texts are often replete with technical, content-specific vocabulary words. Not only may students lack firm understandings of these unfamiliar terms, but they may also struggle to derive the meanings of these words because of the lack of background knowledge to support their efforts (Hall & Sabey, 2007). The complex text structures embedded in informational text are an additional source of difficulty. In addition to complex text structures, informational texts contain unique features including headings and subheadings, typography, and graphics; children may not understand how these features provide essential information to help readers navigate the text.

Furthermore, too often our students miss out on informational text. In her yearlong study of twenty first-grade classrooms, Duke (2000) pointed out an alarming dearth of informational text; during written language activities, students were exposed to only 3.6 minutes of informational text per day. Yopp and Yopp (2006) reported that only 14 percent of primary-grade read alouds during an average instructional day involved informational text.

Despite its potential sources of confusion, students can be successful with informational text, and think alouds are a key scaffold for students. More specifically, young children can successfully explore written language (Richgels, 2002), learn about informational book language

Write what you think on sticky notes!

Third Grade: Possible Stopping Points in *Enemy Pie* by Derek Munson

What the Text Says	What I Think
Enemy Pie	*This title is a logical place to generate questions.*
It should have been a perfect summer.	*I'm stopping here because the word should seems like an important clue.*
My dad helped me build a tree house in our backyard. My sister was at camp for three whole weeks. And I was on the best baseball team in town. It should have been a perfect summer. But it wasn't.	*This seems like a stopping point where I could restate what I already know.*
It was all good until Jeremy Ross moved into the neighborhood, right next door to my best friend Stanley. I did not like Jeremy Ross.	*I might generate a question here.*
He laughed at me when he struck me out in a baseball game. He had a party on his trampoline, and I wasn't even invited. But my best friend Stanley was.	*Stopping points arise when the reader takes important information from the text and puts it into his or her words. Here I can certainly take what the author is saying and associate it with some of my thoughts about Jeremy.*
Jeremy Ross was the one and only person on my enemy list.	*I don't understand what an enemy list is; it surely will cause confusion for my students.*
I never even had an enemy list until he moved into the neighborhood. But as soon as he came along, I needed one. I hung it up in my tree house, where Jeremy Ross was not allowed to go. Dad understood stuff like enemies. He told me that when he was my age, he had enemies, too. But he knew of a way to get rid of them.	*Here is a logical place that I could ask questions about the dad and his experiences with enemies.*
I asked him to tell me how. "Tell you how? I'll show you how!" he said. He pulled a really old recipe book off the kitchen shelf. Inside, there was a worn-out scrap of paper with faded writing. Dad held it up and squinted at it. "Enemy Pie," he said, satisfied.	*The author is giving me clues about this recipe by how his dad hunts for this recipe. This stopping point may lend itself to inferences.*
You may be wondering what exactly is in Enemy Pie. I was wondering, too. But Dad said the recipe was so secret, he couldn't even tell me. I decided it must be magic. I begged him to tell me something—anything.	*The author has built up suspense here. There is a bit of a cliffhanger, leading me to wonder about Enemy Pie. I might ask questions or make predictions.*
"I will tell you this," he said. "Enemy Pie is the fastest known way to get rid of enemies."	*The word fastest seems like a deliberate choice by the author. The author's word choice leads me to ask questions or to dig into the author's purpose.*
Now, of course, this got my mind working. What kinds of things—disgusting things—would I put into a pie for an enemy?	*The character generates a question, and stopping here might be beneficial to modeling additional question generation.*

What the Text Says	What I Think
I brought Dad some weeds from the garden, but he just shook his head. I brought him earthworms and rocks, but he didn't think he'd need those. I gave him the gum I'd been chewing on all morning. He gave it right back to me.	*As the father goes to work making this Enemy Pie, there are several questions that come into my head.*
I went out to play, alone. I shot baskets until the ball got stuck on the roof. I threw a boomerang that never came back to me. And all the while, I listened to the sounds of my dad chopping and stirring and blending the ingredients of Enemy Pie.	*The author seems to be giving us clues about how the boy is feeling. This would be a logical point to make inferences.*
This could be a great summer after all.	*I'm reacting to this because it seems like a big change from the story's opening sentence.*
Enemy Pie was going to be awful. I tried to imagine how horrible it must smell, or worse yet, what it would look like. But when I was in the backyard, looking for ladybugs, I smelled something really, really, really good. And as far as I could tell, it was coming from our kitchen. I was a bit confused.	*Stopping points arise when a reader is confused. In this instance, the character is confused, so I might model here what is confusing to the character.*
I went in to ask Dad what was wrong. Enemy Pie shouldn't smell this good. But Dad was smart. "If Enemy Pie smelled bad, your enemy would never eat it," he said. I could tell he'd made Enemy Pie before. The buzzer rang, and Dad put on the oven mitts and pulled the pie out of the oven. It looked like plain, old pie. It looked good enough to eat! I was catching on.	The expression catching on *might be a source of confusion for some students, so this seems to be an opportune time to clarify.*
But still. I wasn't really sure how this Enemy Pie worked. What exactly did it do to enemies? Maybe it made their hair fall out, or their breath stinky. Maybe it made bullies cry. I asked Dad but he was no help. He wouldn't tell me a thing. But while the pie cooled, he filled me in on my job. He talked quietly. "There is one part of Enemy Pie that I can't do. In order for it to work, you need to spend a day with your enemy. Even worse, you have to be nice to him. It's not easy. But that's the only way that Enemy Pie can work. Are you sure you want to go through with this?"	*I can anticipate that my students would have strong reactions to the character having to spend a day being nice to his enemy. I can seize on this opportunity to model my reactions to this portion of the text.*
Of course I was. It sounded horrible. It was scary. But it was worth a try. All I had to do was spend one day with Jeremy Ross, then he'd be out of my hair for the rest of my life.	*I'd pause here to ask some questions and make some inferences about the narrator's feelings and motivations.*
I rode my bike to his house and knocked on the door. When Jeremy opened the door, he seemed surprised. He stood on the other side of the screen door and looked at me, waiting for me to say something. I was nervous. "Can you play?" I asked. He looked confused. "I'll go ask my mom," he said.	*As we see Jeremy's reaction to the narrator, I'd use context clues to model making inferences.*

continued . . .

. . . from previous

What the Text Says	What I Think
He came back with his shoes in his hand. His mom walked around the corner to say hello. "You boys stay out of trouble," she said, smiling.	*As we get a glimpse of Jeremy's mother, I'm questioning her motivation and her involvement in the Enemy Pie plan.*
We rode bikes for a while and played on the trampoline. Then we made some water balloons and threw them at the neighbor girls, but we missed. Jeremy's mom made us lunch. After lunch we went over to my house.	*The author presents the facts about what the boys did, but does not indicate anything about how either boy is feeling. I'd model how to understand the author's purpose.*
It was strange, but I was kind of having fun with my enemy. He almost seemed nice.	*I'm taking a clue from the text—the word* almost*—to predict what might happen.*
Jeremy Ross knew how to throw a boomerang. He threw it and it came right back to him. I threw it and it went over my house and into the backyard. When we climbed over the fence to find it, the first thing Jeremy noticed was my tree house. My tree house was *my* tree house. I was the boss. If my sister wanted in, I didn't have to let her. If my dad wanted in, I didn't have to let him. And if Jeremy wanted in . . .	*The author has used the ellipsis to create a cliffhanger ending, so I'll seize on the chance to predict.*
"Can we go in it?" he asked. I knew he was going to ask me that! But he was the top person, the ONLY person, on my enemy list. And enemies aren't allowed in my tree house. But he did teach me to throw a boomerang. And he did have me over for lunch. And he did let me play on his trampoline. He wasn't being a very good enemy.	*I can certainly generate a comment here about the narrator's internal conflict. This last sentence is also particularly intriguing, so I'd stop to think through its implications.*
"Okay," I said, "but hold on." I climbed up ahead of him and tore the enemy list off the wall.	*This was a provocative gesture by the narrator, and I'd model making inferences about the character's motivations and feelings.*
I had a checkerboard and some cards in the tree house, and we played games until my dad called us down for dinner. We pretended we didn't hear him, and when he came out to get us, we tried to hide from him. But somehow he found us. Dad made us macaroni and cheese for dinner—my favorite. It was Jeremy's favorite too! Maybe Jeremy Ross wasn't so bad after all. I was beginning to think that maybe we should just forget about Enemy Pie.	*I'd use context clues to notice a shift in the narrator's feelings about Jeremy.*
But sure enough, after dinner, Dad brought out the pie. I watched as he cut the pie into eight thick slices. "Dad," I said, "it sure is nice having a new friend in the neighborhood." I was trying to get his attention and trying to tell him that Jeremy Ross was no longer my enemy. But Dad only smiled and nodded.	*I'm curious about the dad's reaction. I'd likely generate a question here.*

What the Text Says	What I Think
I think he thought I was just pretending. Dad dished up three plates, side by side, with big pieces of pie and giant scoops of ice cream. He passed one to me and one to Jeremy. "Wow!" Jeremy said, looking at the pie, "my dad never makes pies like this." It was at this point that I panicked. I didn't want Jeremy to eat Enemy Pie! He was my friend! I couldn't let him eat it!	*As the narrator becomes very animated, I'm curious as to how he will handle the situation.*
"Jeremy, don't eat it! It's bad pie! I think it's poisonous or something!" Jeremy's fork stopped before reaching his mouth. He crumpled his eyebrows and looked at me funny.	*The author gives us a hint about how Jeremy might be feeling here, so the point lends itself to making inferences or asking questions.*
I felt relieved. I had saved his life. I was a hero. "If it's so bad," Jeremy asked, "then why has your dad already eaten half of it?" I turned to look at my dad. Sure enough, he was eating Enemy Pie! "Good stuff," he mumbled through a mouthful.	*The last line presents a twist—and any unexpected event makes for a productive stopping point.*
And that was all he said. I sat there watching them eat Enemy Pie for a few seconds. Dad was laughing. Jeremy was happily eating. And neither of them was losing any hair! It seemed safe enough, so I took a tiny taste. Enemy Pie was delicious! After dessert, Jeremy rode his bike home but not before inviting me over to play on his trampoline in the morning. He said he'd teach me how to flip. As for Enemy Pie, I still don't know how to make it. I still wonder if enemies really do hate it or if their hair falls out or their breath turns bad. But I don't know if I'll ever get an answer, because I just lost my best enemy.	*Modeling the author's purpose would allow readers to get a better understanding of the central message about the book.*

(Pappas, 1993), retell informational text (Moss, 1997; Pappas, 1993), learn content from informational text (Duke & Kays, 1998; Leal, 1994), understand author's craft (Farest, Miller, & Fewin, 1995), participate in sophisticated discussions of informational text (Heller, 2006), draw intertextual connections in informational text (Oyler & Barry, 1996), produce higher numbers of comprehension discourse moves from informational text read alouds than storybook read alouds (Donovan & Smolkin, 2002), examine the purposes and features of informational text structures (Maloch, 2008), and construct written responses to informational text (Moss & Leal, 1994). In sum, the reasons to support the use of informational text in elementary classrooms far outweigh any potential obstacles that impede it.

© Rick Harrington Photography

Talk about high-level thinking about texts! When we think aloud with a riveting read aloud, our students get the double benefit of the author's engaging text and their teacher's process of enjoying it.

To model this process, I've selected Seymour Simon's *Eyes and Ears* (2003). Simon is a prolific author who began his career as a middle school science teacher. His books are highly regarded informational texts, earning recognition by the National Science Teachers Association. Unlike many informational texts, Simon does not use many of the common text structures (including subtitles, bold print, and glossary) to help the reader navigate the text. I've selected *Eyes and Ears* for this exact reason—the reader does not have any crutches on which to rely. Though Simon's work includes highly technical vocabulary, his works are well organized and succinct. His graphics are largely displayed and few in number, forcing the reader to interact deeply with the text rather than wandering around numerous diagrams, photographs, illustrations, and charts.

I find it particularly important for readers to preview an expository text as a prereading strategy. Often called a *text feature walk*, this step shows students how the features in informational text support comprehension (Kelley & Clausen-Grace, 2010). Just as the pictures help a reader while navigating fiction texts, the charts, diagrams, titles and subtitles, and typography support readers in making sense of informational text. Immediately in a text feature walk in a Seymour Simon book, readers would notice the lack of subtitles and the absence of italics or bold print to showcase vocabulary terms. Furthermore, readers might notice the page layout—a consistent use of top-to-bottom text boxes with one or two very prominent photographs per page.

To begin my work with *Eyes and Ears*, I search for the juicy stopping points that present comprehension opportunities. In the table on the next page, I present the rationale behind my selection of each stopping point.

Final Thoughts

The point of this chapter was to share my process of flagging potential teaching opportunities within a text so that you get a sense for how it's an intuitive blending of what I, as a reader, noticed and what I anticipate my students will notice and need. Ultimately, what we want our students to take away from a think aloud is to slow down and savor. Often, as readers, we are so engaged with a text that we plow through it to find out what happens next or what information we will acquire. In noticing the juicy stopping points,

Write what you think on sticky notes!

Fifth Grade: Possible Stopping Points in *Eyes and Ears* by Seymour Simon

What the Text Says	What I Think
Eyes and Ears	*This title leads me to question the relationship between eyes and ears. Why might the author lump these two things together in one book?*
Light travels from objects and passes into our eyes. Light comes from many different sources, including the sun and electric bulbs. When light hits an object, light waves bounce off in all directions.	*I'd stop here to ensure that students are noting the repetition of words.*
Special light-sensitive cells in our eyes sense the light and send signals to our brain.	*The author is introducing the brain's role in vision here. This stopping point might be a place to integrate previous knowledge with new knowledge.*
Sound waves move through the air and enter our ears. Sound is made when objects move back and forth, or vibrate. The vibrations travel through the air in invisible ripples called sound waves. Sound-sensitive cells in our ears sense the vibrations and send signals to our brain.	*This is a potential stopping point to discuss how the first two paragraphs are structured in the same format. I might be able to analyze why the author did that.*
We see and hear when our brain makes sense out of the messages it gets from our eyes and our ears.	*This sentence stands alone—it is the only one in the paragraph. It makes for an opportune time to question why the author wrote a paragraph with just one sentence.*
Your eye is also called an eyeball. It is shaped like a small ball about one inch across. Two eyeballs sit in cuplike sockets in the front of your head. Your eyelids cover parts of your eyes and make them appear more oval than round.	*I've identified this as a clear opportunity to demonstrate how to summarize a brief paragraph. I might also stop here to make a mental image, or visualize.*
Six tiny muscles hold each eyeball steady in the sockets of your head. The muscles work in teams. One team of muscles swivels the eye toward or away from your nose. Another team of muscles moves the eye upward or downward. Still another team moves the eye at an angle down and outward or up and outward.	*Here is another opportunity to model summarization.*
Rays of light enter the eyeball through a clear, round layer of cells called the cornea. The cornea acts like a camera lens and bends light into the eye.	*This would be a good place to model how I not only summarize what the text says, but combine it with previous knowledge to synthesize.*
The colored part of your eye just behind the cornea is called the iris. What color are *your* eyes? The opening in the central part of the iris is called the pupil. The size of the pupil is controlled by the muscles in the iris. The muscles tighten to make the pupil smaller in bright light and relax to make the pupil larger in dim light.	*This stopping point lends itself to several questions.*

continued . . .

. . . from previous

What the Text Says	What I Think
Light goes through the pupil and passes into the eye through the aqueous humor and then through the eye lens. The center of the eyeball contains a fluid called the vitreous humor. The vitreous humor fills the eyeball so that it has a rounded shape. The lens focuses light through the vitreous humor onto the back of the eye, the retina. Light-sensitive cells in the retina are connected to the brain by a large optic nerve.	*I'd stop here to touch on the author's purpose in this paragraph.*
Here's what happens when you look at something, say a tree. Light reflected from the tree enters your eye through the pupil. The lens forms the light into an image that is a small picture of a tree. The image falls upside down on your retina. In people with normal vision, light rays from an object are focused by the eye's lens exactly on the retina. But some people are nearsighted. They can see close objects clearly, but distance objects look blurred.	*The structure of this paragraph lends itself to predictions. I might stop and predict what the author will tell us about in the next paragraphs.*
The reason for nearsightedness is that the eyeball in some people is a bit too long, front to back. Light rays from a distant object form an image in front of the retina. Nearsightedness, also called myopia, is corrected by wearing glasses or contact lenses. The lenses change the focal point so that the image falls exactly on the retina. . . .	*I see this as an opportunity to connect my background knowledge—about people who wear glasses—with the information from the text to synthesize this portion.*
The retina contains two different kinds of light-sensitive nerve cells: rods and cones.	*The structure of this sentence sets the reader up for what we are about to read next, so I'd model how the text structure provides a clue to my reading.*
They get their names because of the way they are shaped. Rod cells are sensitive to shades of brightness and are used to see in black and white. There are over one hundred million rod cells.	*This information naturally leads to questions.*
Cone cells work best in bright light and let us see color. There are about seven million cone cells in your retina. A tiny spot in the center of your eye contains only cones. It gives you the sharpest image. Around the edges of the retina are fewer cones and more and more rods. We use the cones more during the day and the rods more at night.	*This stopping point is an opportunity to model how the author differentiates the two different types of cells.*

What the Text Says	What I Think
Every rod and cone cell in your retina is connected by its own nerve cell to the brain. When light strikes your retina, the cells respond. They send out tiny electric impulses. All the nerve cells collect at the back of the eye. They form a main cable called the optic nerve. The optic nerve runs back from the eyeball through a tunnel in the skull to a crossover in the brain. The information from the right eye crosses over and goes to the left back of the brain. The information from the left eye crosses over and goes to the right back of the brain.	*I might stop here to summarize the essential points about how these cells interact with the optic nerve and brain.*
We still do not know exactly how the brain works.	*A statement like this leaves me with many questions.*
However,	*I might stop to draw my readers' attention to this signal word, to ensure they understand the role it plays.*
we do know that it is in your brain that seeing finally takes place. The brain puts together the nerve impulses from your eyes along with other brain impulses. The image is turned right side up, and you see what's out there.	*With a focus of synthesis, I might demonstrate how this text confirms or changes my preexisting knowledge.*
There is one spot on the retina that is not sensitive to light. It is called the blind spot. It has no rods and cones because it is just at the point where the optic nerve goes out to the brain. Each of your eyes has its own blind spot.	*Most readers will have heard the term* blind spot *as they often ride in cars. Here is an opportunity to integrate new knowledge with my previous understanding.*
Usually you are not aware of the blind spot in your eyes. Your eyes are always moving around. You can get enough light images about what you are looking at so that you never notice the blind spot. But here's a way of checking the blind spot in your right eye. Close your left eye and look at the X below with your right eye. Keep staring straight at the X while bringing the book closer to your eye. At about six to ten inches from your eye, you will no longer see the black dot to the side of the X. If you bring the book closer, the dot will appear again. At the point where you can't see the dot, the light from it just falls on the blind spot. If you want to check the blind spot in your left eye, turn the book over. Close your right eye and follow the same directions as above.	*Here, I have the opportunity to draw my readers' attention to a graphic that is needed to understand the term* blind spot.
Sunlight is more than one hundred thousand times brighter than moonlight. That's why you can see colors in the daylight but not in moonlight. The light of the moon looks silvery because you're seeing it with the color-blind rods in your retina. The color-sensing cones of your retina do not respond to the dim light of the moon.	*I might take this information and synthesize it with my previous question about why rods matter so much.*

continued...

. . . from previous

What the Text Says	What I Think
As with everything else you see, your brain is involved in sensing color. Here's how you can show how your brain is involved in seeing color. Cut out a circle of white cardboard about four inches across. Color half green and the other half red. Push a two-inch nail through the center of the cardboard disk and trim the opening so that the disk spins freely on the nail. Spin it as rapidly as you can. Your brain will combine the colors sensed by your eyes, and you will see a greyish tint instead of the green and red.	*I can think about this portion of the text in relation to the people I know who are color blind. I might ask questions about how this portion of the text relates to color blindness.*
The ear is an amazing and important sense organ.	*I've read so much about the eye that this is a big shift.*
We can hear all kinds of sounds, from the loud sound of a door slamming to the soft sound of tree leaves rustling in the wind. We can tell the sound of one friend's voice from that of another friend's voice. We use our ears to listen to radio and television and all of the everyday sounds around us.	*This is an opportunity to synthesize what the author is suggesting about the sounds around us.*
An ear has three parts: the outer ear, the middle ear, and the inner ear.	*This sentence might lead me to visualize and infer what parts of the ear are visible externally and what are internal.*
The earflaps on each side of your head are called pinnae. The pinnae are made of flexible cartilage and covered by a layer of skin. The bottom part of each pinna is called the earlobe. Some people have long and curved earlobes while others have small and flat earlobes.	*I might tease out the author's message about the shape and appearance of ears.*
The pinnae act as a kind of sound catcher. They channel the sound waves down a short tube called the auditory canal to the eardrum.	*This is a logical place to activate my background knowledge to clarify that sound waves are invisible. I don't want my readers to think that I can see them—like waves on the beach.*
The eardrum separates the outer ear from the middle ear. The eardrum is a thin flap of skin that stretches tightly across the end of the auditory canal. Sound waves cause the eardrum to vibrate just like the top of a drum when it is hit by a drumstick.	*I could stop here to have my readers make inferences about why it is called the eardrum.*
The middle ear is a tiny space behind the eardrum. Inside the middle ear are the three smallest bones in the body, linked together.	*I might point out that this is new information to me—that we have bones in our ears! I might generate a question about whether it is possible to break one of these bones, like you can break other bones.*
They are called the hammer, the anvil, and the stirrup because of their shapes. These three bones together are called the ossicles. The vibrations of the eardrum cause the ossicles to move. The movements are transmitted to another tight, thin flap of skin called the oval window.	*This is a fair amount of information in this dense paragraph, so I'd stop to monitor my understanding of it.*

What the Text Says	What I Think
The middle ear is linked to the back of your throat by the Eustachian tube. This narrow tube is usually closed. But when you swallow, chew, or yawn, the entrance to the tube opens and air travels in and out of your middle ear.	*I'd pause here to focus on how the tube opens and closes as needed.*
That keeps the air pressure on either side of your eardrum the same. Sometimes your ears "pop" when the tubes suddenly open.	*I'd illustrate the idea of this pop with examples that I've noticed—airplanes, chewing gum, etc.*
Your inner ear lies in a bony hollow within your skull. The inner ear has a maze of spaces called the labyrinth. At the end of the labyrinth is a spiral, coiled tube shaped like a snail shell. It is called the cochlea from the Latin word for snail. Inside the cochlea is a strip of skin covered with tiny hairs. The cochlea is filled with a fluid. When vibrations travel through the ear, they set off waves in the fluid. The waves cause the hairs to ripple like fields of grass in the wind.	*This is another dense paragraph, so I'd stop to monitor my understanding of how the cochlea, hairs, and fluid work together.*
At the bottom of each hair is a nerve cell. Each ear has about twenty thousand nerve cells. The cells send a message through the auditory nerve to the hearing centers of the brain.	*This last phrase gives us important clues about the complexity of the brain. It also reminds me of what the text said about the brain's role in vision.*
The brain tells you what the vibrations mean: your teacher talking, a car honking, or a paper rustling. Finally, you hear. The ears do another job.	*I'd generate a question, since this last sentence might present unfamiliar information to my readers.*
Next to the cochlea are three semicircular canals. These help you to keep your balance when you sit still, walk about, or jump and bend. The curved tubes of the semicircular canals point in three directions. Like the cochlea, the canals are filled with a fluid and lined with a hairy skin. When you move your head in any direction, the fluid moves in at least one of the canals. Nerve cells in the canals send signals to the brain: You are moving up or down, to the side or another, backward or forward. The signals let your brain know how you are moving and help keep you steady. Even with your eyes closed, you know the position of your head. However, if you whirl around and around, the fluid in the canals keeps moving for a few seconds even after you stop. Then you may get dizzy and lose your balance.	*In this information-packed paragraph, I would clarify confusion by rereading and retracing what the text says to me. I might focus on what happens after I spin to make me feel dizzy.*
Some people may have difficulty hearing. Sometimes hearing loss is caused by a sticky material made inside the ears called earwax. Earwax can build up and collect dirt and dust. Then the outer ears have to be carefully cleaned to remove the blockage. You should never try to do this yourself because of the danger of hurting your eardrums.	*I might point out how the author set up this paragraph—telling us that some people have trouble hearing. I'd predict some other causes of hearing difficulty.*

continued . . .

...from previous

What the Text Says	What I Think
As people get older, some will gradually become hard of hearing. They may use a hearing aid that fits inside their outer ear. Hearing aids make sounds louder to help people with this kind of deafness.	*Here is an opportunity to make inferences about how hearing aids work—based on what the author told us previously about how our ears work.*
Some people are born with a severe hearing loss or lose their hearing as a result of an injury. They often use hearing aids as well as other machines to alert them to sounds. For example, special telephones can be made to flash a light instead of ringing a bell. Then the message can be seen on a screen instead of being heard through an earpiece. Many hard-of-hearing people can understand what other people say by lip reading.	*There are some fruitful points here to generate questions about how people learn to lip read, the term* hard of hearing, *and injuries that might cause people to lose their hearing.*
We use our senses to learn what is happening in the world around us.	*Here is a point to clarify that hearing and vision—as covered in this book—are only two of our five senses.*
Our eyes and ears sense light and sound and send nerve signals to the brain. The brain puts the information together to let us see and hear.	*I'd point out the synthesizing that the author does in these last lines and evaluate them.*

we slow our reading down so that we can truly interact, appreciate, question, understand, and clarify all of the complexities of text. Kylene Beers and Robert Probst (2013) might call this noticing and noting. These juicy stopping points mark the times that I, as the reader, am most engaged, most inquisitive, and most purposeful. By simply being aware of the opportunities embedded within the high-quality poems, narratives, and expository text we incorporate into everyday classroom instruction, we become more metacognitive as readers ourselves and better prepared to model our thinking to our students.

Ready for a Trial Run?

In Appendix B, you will find three sample texts: a poem called "The Owl and the Pussy-Cat" (Lear, 1871), a narrative text called *The Sandwich Swap* (Al-Abdullah & DiPucchio, 2010), and an expository text called *The William Hoy Story* (Churnin, 2016). Using the principles from this chapter, work through each of the texts and determine where you'd stop. Use a pencil to draw an asterisk at each potential point, or mark it with a sticky note. Then, as I have modeled, think through why you've identified this as a stopping point. Your challenge here is merely to identify where you've stopped and why you've stopped—don't rush yourself into thinking of what your think aloud will be or what strategies you'll incorporate. Adhere to the principles of brainstorming! No judgments. Overidentify stopping points—in the next steps, you will scale back to a more manageable number. Then think through these questions and prompts:

- How did this step go for you?
- What did you notice about yourself as a reader while trying out this step?
- Did anything surprise, intrigue, confuse, or stump you in this step?

CHAPTER 4

Read Twice

Determining Where and When to Think Aloud

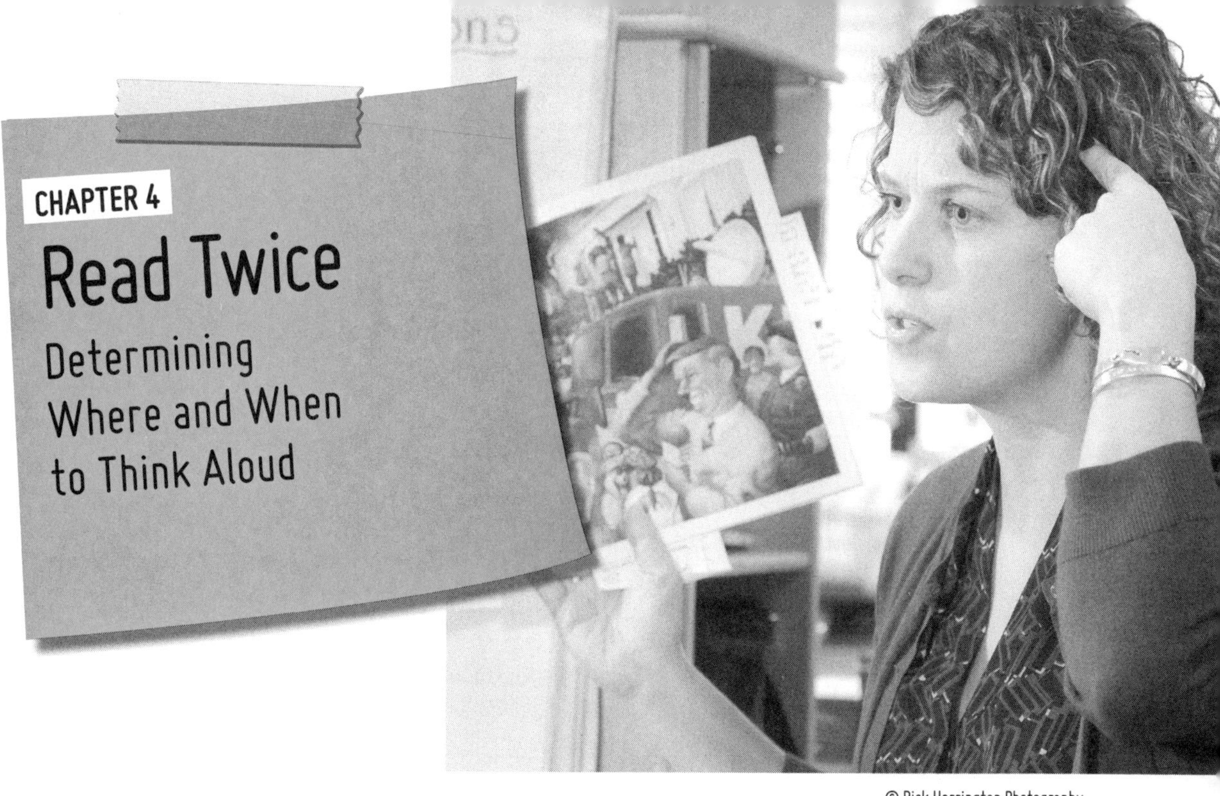

© Rick Harrington Photography

Now we are on to Step 2, when you look at the flurry of sticky notes and prune them down to stopping points that seem poised to have the biggest instructional impact. When I embark on Step 2, I literally look at each of my sticky notes, read the text again, and ask myself questions like these to see if it will make the cut:

- As a reader, what does this stopping point invite me to do?
- Is this stopping point especially ripe for demonstrating a particular reading comprehension strategy?
- In what ways is this stopping point effective or ineffective for showing young readers my metacognitive processes?
- What exactly would young readers gain from hearing me think aloud at this stopping point?

What I'm after are the junctures in a text that most authentically lend themselves to modeling metacognitive processes; I don't want to overwhelm students by stopping too often or thinking aloud in ways that actually complicate the comprehension process. If something seems forced or I can't envision my students following my train of thought, I drop it.

In my second reading, I have the advantage of knowing the entire text. I use that knowledge to help me consolidate my stopping points. For example, in my initial reading, I might break up a single paragraph into several stopping points. But on the second go-around, I might find it disruptive to break the flow of the paragraph and so eliminate a stopping point to create a tighter think aloud. As a general rule of thumb, I generally end up with ten to fifteen stopping points for a storybook or an informational text, and six to eight for a poem, and I renumber the sticky notes accordingly.

Quick Tips

- Aim for 10–15 stopping points for storybooks and informational text
- Aim for 6–8 stopping points for poems and chapters in chapter books
- Ask yourself, "Can I combine portions into larger texts?"
- Try to hold stopping points for the text's natural breaks—like the end of a paragraph or a page
- Eliminate stopping points that focus on minor details, occur after very short portions of text, or don't align with your central objective for this think aloud

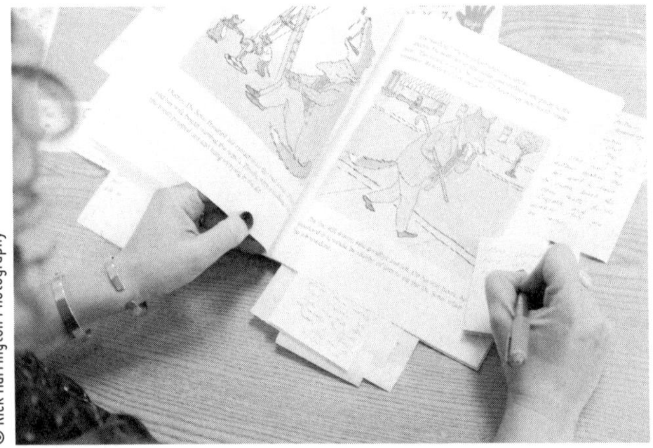

In Step 2, I delete some sticky notes and home in on the most authentic questions that the text and images stir up.

As you make these decisions, be mindful of your overall purpose for selecting this particular text, your learning objectives in this lesson, and which comprehension strategies are familiar or unfamiliar to your students prior to reading this text.

Let's walk through this second step using the same texts from the previous chapter, beginning with Shel Silverstein's poem "Sick" (1974). In this second reading, my aim is to finalize five or six strong stopping points since it is such a short poem. In the following chart, you will see that for each stopping point I identified I ask myself the reflective questions above and use the answers to determine my next direction.

Examining the Original Stopping Points in "Sick" by Shel Silverstein

What the Text Says	What I'm Thinking Now	My Decisions for This Stopping Point
"Sick"	*Initially, I thought that the title would be a great place to model asking questions, but as I look forward, I think it would be more powerful to ask questions with more of the poem.*	**I will eliminate this stopping point and combine it with the next lines.**
"I cannot go to school today," Said Little Peggy Ann McKay.	*This point logically aligns to some questions that I want my young readers to see.*	**I think it's better to collapse the first and second stopping points into one think aloud.**
"I have the measles and the mumps, A gash, a rash and purple bumps.	*I originally flagged this because of the unfamiliar vocabulary, but I'm not sure it's necessary to define measles and mumps for kids to understand the poem.*	**I can eliminate this stopping point and move forward.**
My mouth is wet, my throat is dry, I'm going blind in my right eye. My tonsils are as big as rocks, I've counted sixteen chicken pox And there's one more—that's seventeen, And don't you think my face looks green?	*I'm stopping after that last line because I really want my students to see me try to figure out whom Peggy Ann is talking to. If I don't model making an inference about whom Peggy Ann is talking to, the poem loses its humor.*	**I'm going to stop here and model making inferences.**
My leg is cut—my eyes are blue— It might be instamatic flu.	*I originally thought instamatic flu was a place to monitor and clarify unknown vocabulary, but I see now that the author doesn't give me any more information on clarifying. Plus, not knowing what the instamatic flu is does not detract from my comprehension of the overall poem.*	**I'm eliminating this stopping point.**
I cough and sneeze and gasp and choke, I'm sure that my left leg is broke— My hip hurts when I move my chin, My belly button's caving in, My back is wrenched, my ankle's sprained,	*I might showcase some questions here, but I'm thinking that stopping here does not correspond logically with a comprehension strategy.*	**I'm eliminating this stopping point.**
My 'pendix pains each time it rains. My nose is cold, my toes are numb. I have a sliver in my thumb.	*This would be an effective place to stop—merge this long list of ailments into one long chunk—and try to make sense of this new information.*	**I'm combining three stopping points into one—an important place to synthesize information.**
My neck is stiff, my voice is weak, I hardly whisper when I speak. My tongue is filling up my mouth,	*I originally had a question here, but I'm not sure this is a fruitful stopping point.*	**I'm eliminating this stopping point.**

continued...

. . . from previous

What the Text Says	What I'm Thinking Now	My Decisions for This Stopping Point
I think my hair is falling out. My elbow's bent, my spine ain't straight, My temperature is one-o-eight. My brain is shrunk, I cannot hear, There is a hole inside my ear.	*I can combine the previous point from above with this one to think through the reasons behind Peggy Ann's ailments.*	III **I want to showcase to my readers how I might deduce the reason for all of Peggy Ann's excuses through making inferences.**
I have a hangnail, and my heart is—what? What's that? What's that you say?	*I originally stopped at this cliffhanger ending, but I think it would be more effective to combine it with the golden line below.*	**I'm eliminating this stopping point.**
You say today is . . . Saturday?	*My intent here is to show readers how much this one word changes the meaning of the text!*	**I will stop here and focus on this golden word, *Saturday*, which holds so much meaning!**
G'bye, I'm going out to play!"	*A crucial stopping point, this spot helps me to understand the author's purpose.*	A **I will stop here and focus on understanding the author's purpose.**

In Step 3, which I outline in the following chapter, I will closely examine each stopping point and question its importance and relation to my overarching objective. As noted in Chapter 3, if my stopping points are too many and not purposeful, they may actually impede comprehension. I will revisit which stopping points are essential and which are extraneous in the next chapter.

Let's move on to the narrative text, *Enemy Pie* by Derek Munson (2000). In my first reading, I placed thirty sticky notes on possible stopping points—I want to cut that number in half while still addressing multiple comprehension strategies. I also noticed in my first reading that there are unique opportunities in *Enemy Pie* for making inferences, so I'll privilege stopping points that invite this strategy. By third grade, students are expected to read closely to determine what a text says explicitly and to make logical inferences from it. A difficult strategy for many students to master, making inferences requires readers to draw on their schema and clues embedded within the text.

I follow the same process, in which I examine each stopping point to determine its purpose and necessity, in the following chart. My end result is narrowing my initial thirty sticky notes into nineteen points rich with opportunities to model making inferences, synthesizing, and monitoring and clarifying.

Examining the Original Stopping Points in *Enemy Pie* by Derek Munson

What the Text Says	What I'm Thinking Now	My Decisions for This Stopping Point
Enemy Pie	*My original intent here was to ask questions, but upon review I don't envision this being particularly beneficial.*	**This stopping point is unnecessary. I will collapse its text into the next portion.**
It should have been a perfect summer.	*I wanted to focus on the meaning of the word should and what it implies, but if I include this sentence with the next portion, the stopping point will be more meaningful.*	**Instead of stopping after this one sentence, I will lump this line in with the next stopping point.**
My sister was at camp for three whole weeks. And I was on the best baseball team in town. It should have been a perfect summer. But it wasn't.	*By combining the two stops above with this one, I have an important chance to synthesize.*	**I will stop here to synthesize.**
It was all good until Jeremy Ross moved into the neighborhood, right next door to my best friend Stanley. I did not like Jeremy Ross.	*Originally this seemed like an opportunity to question the narrator's reasons for disliking Jeremy. But as this question is explicitly answered in the next lines, it seems unnecessary.*	**I will eliminate this stopping point.**
He laughed at me when he struck me out in a baseball game. He had a party on his trampoline, and I wasn't even invited. But my best friend Stanley was.	*By combining this portion with the lines above, I can think through what I've learned so far.*	**I will stop here to synthesize.**
Jeremy Ross was the one and only person on my enemy list.	*This is such a powerful single line that evokes questions and possible confusion that it is necessary to address.*	**I will stop here to monitor and clarify.**
I never even had an enemy list until he moved into the neighborhood. But as soon as he came along, I needed one. I hung it up in my tree house, where Jeremy Ross was not allowed to go. Dad understood stuff like enemies. He told me that when he was my age, he had enemies, too. But he knew of a way to get rid of them.	*As I kept reading, I got additional information that clarified my confusion above, so I will be sure to mention that. This is also an effective spot to ask questions about "a way to get rid of" enemies.*	**?** **I will stop here to clarify my previous confusion and to ask a question.**
I asked him to tell me how. "Tell you how? I'll show you how!" he said. He pulled a really old recipe book off the kitchen shelf. Inside, there was a worn-out scrap of paper with faded writing. Dad held it up and squinted at it. "Enemy Pie," he said, satisfied.	*I see this as an opportunity to make inferences about both the dad as a character and this recipe.*	**I will stop here to make an inference.**

continued...

. . . from previous

What the Text Says	What I'm Thinking Now	My Decisions for This Stopping Point
You may be wondering what exactly is in Enemy Pie. I was wondering, too. But Dad said the recipe was so secret, he couldn't even tell me. I decided it must be magic. I begged him to tell me something—anything.	*I originally saw this as a cliffhanger that makes me want to generate questions about what Enemy Pie is. I think the sentence below would be a prudent inclusion as well.*	? **I will stop here to ask questions.**
"I will tell you this," he said. "Enemy Pie is the fastest known way to get rid of enemies."	*This single sentence does not seem to be worthy in itself for a think aloud, so I'll include it above.*	**I'm eliminating this stopping point.**
Now, of course, this got my mind working. What kinds of things—disgusting things—would I put into a pie for an enemy?	*Although I originally thought I'd stop here to ask questions, I now see that the question explicitly included in the text is powerful enough.*	**I will eliminate this stopping point.**
I brought Dad some weeds from the garden, but he just shook his head. I brought him earthworms and rocks, but he didn't think he'd need those. I gave him the gum I'd been chewing on all morning. He gave it right back to me.	*My sticky note from the first reading suggested a place to ask questions, but the relative simplicity of this text makes me think that my time is better spent on other comprehension strategies.*	**I will eliminate this stopping point.**
I went out to play, alone. I shot baskets until the ball got stuck on the roof. I threw a boomerang that never came back to me. And all the while, I listened to the sounds of my dad chopping and stirring and blending the ingredients of Enemy Pie.	*Because of the amount of action here, young readers will benefit from hearing me combine all this information into a synthesis.*	**I will combine the eliminated points above and stop to model synthesizing.**
This could be a great summer after all.	*I originally used a sticky note because of this sentence's parallels to earlier statements about how "it should have been the perfect summer." But I'm eliminating this point because it does not logically correspond to any of my focal comprehension strategies.*	**I will eliminate this stopping point.**
Enemy Pie was going to be awful. I tried to imagine how horrible it must smell, or worse yet, what it would look like. But when I was in the backyard, looking for ladybugs, I smelled something really, really, really good. And as far as I could tell, it was coming from our kitchen. I was a bit confused.	*If a character states that he or she is confused, it is only logical to note that confusion by monitoring.*	**I will model monitoring and clarifying.**

What the Text Says	What I'm Thinking Now	My Decisions for This Stopping Point
I went in to ask Dad what was wrong. Enemy Pie shouldn't smell this good. But Dad was smart. "If Enemy Pie smelled bad, your enemy would never eat it," he said. I could tell he'd made Enemy Pie before. The buzzer rang, and Dad put on the oven mitts and pulled the pie out of the oven. It looked like plain, old pie. It looked good enough to eat! I was catching on.	*At first, I identified catching on as a potential source of confusion for young readers, but upon a second reading I think it's more important to highlight the important information here.*	**I will model synthesizing this key point from his dad.**
But still. I wasn't really sure how this Enemy Pie worked. What exactly did it do to enemies? Maybe it made their hair fall out, or their breath stinky. Maybe it made bullies cry. I asked Dad but he was no help. He wouldn't tell me a thing. But while the pie cooled, he filled me in on my job. He talked quietly. "There is one part of Enemy Pie that I can't do. In order for it to work, you need to spend a day with your enemy. Even worse, you have to be nice to him. It's not easy. But that's the only way that Enemy Pie can work. Are you sure you want to go through with this?"	*I had originally thought that I might ask my students to react to the idea of having to spend a day with their enemies, but I now recognize that a turn and talk does not model what I—as a proficient reader—do. My time would be better spent by modeling my potential confusion.*	**I will stop to monitor and clarify confusion over the idea of spending a day with an enemy.**
Of course I was. It sounded horrible. It was scary. But it was worth a try. All I had to do was spend one day with Jeremy Ross, then he'd be out of my hair for the rest of my life.	*I initially marked this with a sticky note to make inferences about the narrator's feelings, but I now see that this opportunity would be richer if I included a portion from below about Jeremy's reaction.*	**I will eliminate this stopping point.**
I rode my bike to his house and knocked on the door. When Jeremy opened the door, he seemed surprised. He stood on the other side of the screen door and looked at me, waiting for me to say something. I was nervous. "Can you play?" I asked.	*I see Jeremy's reaction as an opportunity for me to model making inferences about Jeremy's reaction and feelings toward the narrator.*	**I will model making inferences about how Jeremy feels here.**
He came back with his shoes in his hand. His mom walked around the corner to say hello. "You boys stay out of trouble," she said, smiling.	*When I first read this, I thought that Jeremy's mother might be a part of the Enemy Pie plan, so I saw this as an opportunity to make an inference about her. Upon rereading, I saw this was the only glimpse of her, so she's not an essential character.*	**I will eliminate this stopping point.**
We rode bikes for a while and played on the trampoline. Then we made some water balloons and threw them at the neighbor girls, but we missed. Jeremy's mom made us lunch. After lunch we went over to my house.	*I originally saw this as an opportunity to model understanding the author's purpose, but now that I know the whole text, I see the book's message really becomes clearer later.*	**I will eliminate this stopping point and move this portion up with the portion above.**

continued . . .

. . . from previous

What the Text Says	What I'm Thinking Now	My Decisions for This Stopping Point
It was strange, but I was kind of having fun with my enemy. He almost seemed nice.	*I first saw this as an opportunity for predicting, but this is not a focal comprehension strategy.*	**I'm eliminating this point and moving this portion to a larger section from above.**
Jeremy Ross knew how to throw a boomerang. He threw it and it came right back to him. I threw it and it went over my house and into the backyard. When we climbed over the fence to find it, the first thing Jeremy noticed was my tree house. My tree house was *my* tree house. I was the boss. If my sister wanted in, I didn't have to let her. If my dad wanted in, I didn't have to let him. And if Jeremy wanted in . . .	*I originally envisioned the ellipsis as a cliffhanger spot to make a prediction, but I'm more inclined to include this portion with a richer stopping point later.*	**I am eliminating this point and moving this portion of text.**
"Can we go in it?" he asked. I knew he was going to ask me that! But he was the top person, the ONLY person, on my enemy list. And enemies aren't allowed in my tree house. But he did teach me to throw a boomerang. And he did have me over for lunch. And he did let me play on his trampoline. He wasn't being a very good enemy.	*As a proficient reader, I can recognize the internal conflict that the narrator is feeling in his decision to let Jeremy into his tree house, so my readers will benefit from my modeling the inferences inherent in reaching that conclusion. This last sentence is so important that my students need to see me make sense of it.*	**I will model making inferences here as well as synthesizing.**
"Okay," I said, "but hold on." I climbed up ahead of him and tore the enemy list off the wall.	*My gut was to stop and think through why the narrator took this action. Since its meaning is implied, it's a perfect opportunity for making an inference.*	**I will model making inferences.**
I had a checkerboard and some cards in the tree house, and we played games until my dad called us down for dinner. We pretended we didn't hear him, and when he came out to get us, we tried to hide from him. But somehow he found us. Dad made us macaroni and cheese for dinner—my favorite. It was Jeremy's favorite too! Maybe Jeremy Ross wasn't so bad after all. I was beginning to think that maybe we should just forget about Enemy Pie.	*My original plan was to comment on the narrator's change of opinion, but that observation does not lend itself readily to one of the focal comprehension strategies.*	**I will eliminate this point and combine it with the text below.**
But sure enough, after dinner, Dad brought out the pie. I watched as he cut the pie into eight thick slices. "Dad," I said, "it sure is nice having a new friend in the neighborhood." I was trying to get his attention and trying to tell him that Jeremy Ross was no longer my enemy. But Dad only smiled and nodded.	*The author has given a lot of information in this passage, so my readers will gain insight into how the new information is making the narrator rethink Jeremy as an enemy.*	**I will stop here to synthesize key information.**

What the Text Says	What I'm Thinking Now	My Decisions for This Stopping Point
I think he thought I was just pretending. Dad dished up three plates, side by side, with big pieces of pie and giant scoops of ice cream. He passed one to me and one to Jeremy. "Wow!" Jeremy said, looking at the pie, "my dad never makes pies like this." It was at this point that I panicked. I didn't want Jeremy to eat Enemy Pie! He was my friend! I couldn't let him eat it!	*Originally I thought I'd ask a question here because I was curious about what the narrator would do. I now see that this maneuver is more of a prediction, and not required.*	**I will eliminate this stopping point and move this passage to be included below.**
"Jeremy, don't eat it! It's bad pie! I think it's poisonous or something!" Jeremy's fork stopped before reaching his mouth. He crumpled his eyebrows and looked at me funny.	*It's unclear what the author means with the line "looked at me funny," so this presents an opportunity to talk through potential sources of confusion.*	⇄ **I will combine the text from above into this point to monitor and clarify.**
I felt relieved. I had saved his life. I was a hero. "If it's so bad," Jeremy asked, "then why has your dad already eaten half of it?" I turned to look at my dad. Sure enough, he was eating Enemy Pie! "Good stuff," he mumbled through a mouthful.	*I flagged this as a point of confusion—the narrator does not expect the dad to be eating Enemy Pie, and thus it's an opportunity for monitoring comprehension.*	⇄ **This is an additional spot for monitoring and clarifying.**
And that was all he said. I sat there watching them eat Enemy Pie for a few seconds. Dad was laughing. Jeremy was happily eating. And neither of them was losing any hair! It seemed safe enough, so I took a tiny taste. Enemy Pie was delicious! After dessert, Jeremy rode his bike home but not before inviting me over to play on his trampoline in the morning. He said he'd teach me how to flip. As for Enemy Pie, I still don't know how to make it. I still wonder if enemies really do hate it or if their hair falls out or their breath turns bad. But I don't know if I'll ever get an answer, because I just lost my best enemy.	*In my experience, young readers often need help deducing the implied message of a book. This author clearly is sending a message with Enemy Pie, a point that requires modeling.*	**A** **The message of the book is an obvious place to model understanding the author's purpose.**

Finally, *Eyes and Ears* is a complex informational text chock full of facts, explanation, and domain-specific vocabulary. In Step 1, I identified over forty potential stopping points—clearly way too many! So, in my Step 2 reading, my aim is to consolidate the number. And because of the nature of this informational text, much of my thinking aloud will likely focus on the strategy of synthesizing.

Examining the Original Stopping Points in *Eyes and Ears* by Seymour Simon

What the Text Says	What I'm Thinking Now	My Decisions for This Stopping Point
Eyes and Ears	*I originally viewed the title as a place to generate questions, but instead I think I'd more likely do a prereading strategy like a KWL (Know, Want to Know, Learned) chart where I have students generate their background knowledge about the topic.*	**This is an unnecessary stopping point.**
Light travels from objects and passes into our eyes. Light comes from many different sources, including the sun and electric bulbs. When light hits an object, light waves bounce off in all directions.	*As I see the sentence below about how our eyes sense light, I think it's best to group these two sections together.*	**I will combine this section with the portion below.**
Special light-sensitive cells in our eyes sense the light and send signals to our brain.	*This sentence—along with the portion from above—seems to be a fruitful point to stop to synthesize new information.*	**I will stop and generate a synthesis.**
Sound waves move through the air and enter our ears. Sound is made when objects move back and forth, or vibrate. The vibrations travel through the air in invisible ripples called sound waves. Sound-sensitive cells in our ears sense the vibrations and send signals to our brain.	*Originally I had stopped throughout this paragraph to think about the similar structures of these paragraphs. I believe it's better to include the line below.*	**I will eliminate this point and combine it with the portion below.**
We see and hear when our brain makes sense out of the messages it gets from our eyes and our ears.	*This sentence is an important summary that explains the relationship of the brain to our two senses, so it's worth focusing on.*	**As I did with the introductory paragraph about eyes, I will stop to synthesize new information about ears.**
Your eye is also called an eyeball. It is shaped like a small ball about one inch across. Two eyeballs sit in cuplike sockets in the front of your head. Your eyelids cover parts of your eyes and make them appear more oval than round.	*My purpose is to consolidate stopping points, so I will group together all the text about the structure and muscles of the eyeball together. That means I will not stop here.*	**I will eliminate this stopping point and stop after the description of the eyeball.**

What the Text Says	What I'm Thinking Now	My Decisions for This Stopping Point
Six tiny muscles hold each eyeball steady in the sockets of your head. The muscles work in teams. One team of muscles swivels the eye toward or away from your nose. Another team of muscles moves the eye upward or downward. Still another team moves the eye at an angle down and outward or up and outward.	*This seems to be the end of the information about the structure and muscles of the eyeball, so it's a logical place to stop for a synthesis.*	**I will stop here and synthesize the new information about the eyeball's structures and muscular function.**
Rays of light enter the eyeball through a clear, round layer of cells called the cornea. The cornea acts like a camera lens and bends light into the eye.	*This portion—along with the portion below—describes the cornea and the iris. I will combine these two interrelated portions together.*	**I will eliminate this stopping point.**
The colored part of your eye just behind the cornea is called the iris. What color are *your* eyes? The opening in the central part of the iris is called the pupil. The size of the pupil is controlled by the muscles in the iris. The muscles tighten to make the pupil smaller in bright light and relax to make the pupil larger in dim light.	*Originally I had seen this as an opportunity to ask questions, but this portion is dense with new information. Thus, I think a synthesis would be more appropriate. Also, I had to reread this portion slowly to ensure I understood, so I might think aloud about monitoring.*	**I will stop here to clarify potential confusion and to synthesize this new information.**
Light goes through the pupil and passes into the eye through the aqueous humor and then through the eye lens. The center of the eyeball contains a fluid called the vitreous humor. The vitreous humor fills the eyeball so that it has a rounded shape. The lens focuses light through the vitreous humor onto the back of the eye, the retina. Light-sensitive cells in the retina are connected to the brain by a large optic nerve.	*As I'm reading here, I am aware that the author is describing normal eye function. But so many people need glasses or contacts! I'm curious about what happens there, so I see this portion as a chance to ask questions.*	? **I will keep this as a stopping point, with the opportunity to ask questions.**
Here's what happens when you look at something, say a tree. Light reflected from the tree enters your eye through the pupil. The lens forms the light into an image that is a small picture of a tree. The image falls upside down on your retina. In people with normal vision, light rays from an object are focused by the eye's lens exactly on the retina. But some people are nearsighted. They can see close objects clearly, but distance objects look blurred.	*This section is a shift in tone—we are not just getting information. Instead the author is really giving us an everyday example to clarify a complicated process. It's worthy of focusing on the author's purpose.*	A **I will keep this stopping point and use it as a chance to focus on the author's choices in giving this example.**

continued . . .

...from previous

What the Text Says	What I'm Thinking Now	My Decisions for This Stopping Point
The reason for nearsightedness is that the eyeball in some people is a bit too long, front to back. Light rays from a distant object form an image in front of the retina. Nearsightedness, also called myopia, is corrected by wearing glasses or contact lenses. The lenses change the focal point so that the image falls exactly on the retina. . . .	*It's logical to group together the sentences about normal vision and myopia—from the section above. I'll adjust my stopping point to include both.*	**I'm going to include the portion about people with normal vision and myopia into one stopping point to synthesize.**
The retina contains two different kinds of light-sensitive nerve cells: rods and cones.	*Originally I saw this as a place to model text structure, but I think it's worth including more elaboration on the rods and cones.*	**I will eliminate this stopping point.**
They get their names because of the way they are shaped. Rod cells are sensitive to shades of brightness and are used to see in black and white. There are over one hundred million rod cells.	*I'm trying to reduce my stopping points, so I can cut out this one and include it with a larger description below of rods and cones.*	**I will eliminate this stopping point.**
Cone cells work best in bright light and let us see color. There are about seven million cone cells in your retina. A tiny spot in the center of your eye contains only cones. It gives you the sharpest image. Around the edges of the retina are fewer cones and more and more rods. We use the cones more during the day and the rods more at night.	*The author really wants me to understand the difference between rods and cones, so I think I will stop after one paragraph that includes a description of both.*	**I will stop here to synthesize this new information about rods and cones.**
Every rod and cone cell in your retina is connected by its own nerve cell to the brain. When light strikes your retina, the cells respond. They send out tiny electric impulses. All the nerve cells collect at the back of the eye. They form a main cable called the optic nerve. The optic nerve runs back from the eyeball through a tunnel in the skull to a crossover in the brain. The information from the right eye crosses over and goes to the left back of the brain. The information from the left eye crosses over and goes to the right back of the brain.	*I agree with my initial thought that this is an important paragraph worthy of a synthesis.*	**I will stop here to synthesize.**
We still do not know exactly how the brain works.	*Upon a second reading, I still have questions about this statement, but it's useful to combine it into a larger portion.*	**I will eliminate this stopping point.**

What the Text Says	What I'm Thinking Now	My Decisions for This Stopping Point
However,	*Though however is an important signal word that shows a shift, I may disrupt the larger flow of the text by stopping after only one word.*	**I don't want to stop and think aloud after only one word, so I will cut out this stopping point.**
we do know that it is in your brain that seeing finally takes place. The brain puts together the nerve impulses from your eyes along with other brain impulses. The image is turned right side up, and you see what's out there.	*I appreciate the author telling me what we do know about the brain, but I want to know more about what we don't know about the brain!*	**?** **I'm going to combine this with the two stopping points above and ask some questions.**
There is one spot on the retina that is not sensitive to light. It is called the blind spot. It has no rods and cones because it is just at the point where the optic nerve goes out to the brain. Each of your eyes has its own blind spot.	*As I revisit this portion, I can see that it really belongs with the portion below. I'll combine it into a description and illustration about our blind spots.*	**I'm going to eliminate this stopping point.**
Usually you are not aware of the blind spot in your eyes. Your eyes are always moving around. You can get enough light images about what you are looking at so that you never notice the blind spot. But here's a way of checking the blind spot in your right eye. Close your left eye and look at the X below with your right eye. Keep staring straight at the X while bringing the book closer to your eye. At about six to ten inches from your eye, you will no longer see the black dot to the side of the X. If you bring the book closer, the dot will appear again. At the point where you can't see the dot, the light from it just falls on the blind spot. If you want to check the blind spot in your left eye, turn the book over. Close your right eye and follow the same directions as above.	*These descriptions and text features show me something important about the retina's blind spot, so this is an important stopping point.*	**A** **This graphic and description exemplifies how the author purposefully included this portion to explain a complicated process. It's worth stopping here to synthesize and think about the author's purpose.**
Sunlight is more than one hundred thousand times brighter than moonlight. That's why you can see colors in the daylight but not in moonlight. The light of the moon looks silvery because you're seeing it with the color-blind rods in your retina. The color-sensing cones of your retina do not respond to the dim light of the moon.	*This was entirely new information to me, and it relates to the previous portion about the function of cones and rods. It's a useful stopping point.*	**I will stop here to synthesize this new information.**

continued...

. . . from previous

What the Text Says	What I'm Thinking Now	My Decisions for This Stopping Point
As with everything else you see, your brain is involved in sensing color. Here's how you can show how your brain is involved in seeing color. Cut out a circle of white cardboard about four inches across. Color half green and the other half red. Push a two-inch nail through the center of the cardboard disk and trim the opening so that the disk spins freely on the nail. Spin it as rapidly as you can. Your brain will combine the colors sensed by your eyes, and you will see a greyish tint instead of the green and red.	*I agree with my initial thoughts that this is a useful spot to ask questions.*	? **I will stop and ask questions.**
The ear is an amazing and important sense organ.	*Since I'm condensing my original number of stopping points, I think it's best to think aloud with more than one sentence.*	**I will eliminate this point.**
We can hear all kinds of sounds, from the loud sound of a door slamming to the soft sound of tree leaves rustling in the wind. We can tell the sound of one friend's voice from that of another friend's voice. We use our ears to listen to radio and television and all of the everyday sounds around us.	*I'm noticing a subtle message here about how much hearing contributes to our lives, so I see this as a place for making inferences.*	**I will stop here to make an inference.**
An ear has three parts: the outer ear, the middle ear, and the inner ear.	*This is a topic sentence that leads to a description of the three parts of the ear. I know it leads into a brief description of the three parts, so I will group this sentence in with additional text.*	**I will eliminate this stopping point.**
The earflaps on each side of your head are called pinnae. The pinnae are made of flexible cartilage and covered by a layer of skin. The bottom part of each pinna is called the earlobe. Some people have long and curved earlobes while others have small and flat earlobes.	*This portion describes the outer ear. But it belongs with the text below, so I will group them together.*	**I will eliminate this stopping point.**
The pinnae act as a kind of sound catcher. They channel the sound waves down a short tube called the auditory canal to the eardrum.	*It's useful to check in to make sure students understand the description of the first portion—the outer ear.*	**I will synthesize the information about the outer ear.**

What the Text Says	What I'm Thinking Now	My Decisions for This Stopping Point
The eardrum separates the outer ear from the middle ear. The eardrum is a thin flap of skin that stretches tightly across the end of the auditory canal. Sound waves cause the eardrum to vibrate just like the top of a drum when it is hit by a drumstick.	*In my initial reading of the text, I did not realize there were so many elements in the middle ear. I don't want to separate this portion of the middle ear from the information further below.*	**I will eliminate this point to make way for one stopping spot for synthesis about the middle ear.**
The middle ear is a tiny space behind the eardrum. Inside the middle ear are the three smallest bones in the body, linked together.	*These bones are in the middle ear, so this should be grouped with the entire portion about the middle ear.*	**I will eliminate this point to make way for one stopping spot for synthesis about the middle ear.**
They are called the hammer, the anvil, and the stirrup because of their shapes. These three bones together are called the ossicles. The vibrations of the eardrum cause the ossicles to move. The movements are transmitted to another tight, thin flap of skin called the oval window.	*I'm still getting information here about the middle ear.*	**I will eliminate this point to make way for one stopping spot for synthesis about the middle ear.**
The middle ear is linked to the back of your throat by the Eustachian tube. This narrow tube is usually closed. But when you swallow, chew, or yawn, the entrance to the tube opens and air travels in and out of your middle ear.	*More about the middle ear!*	**I will eliminate this point to make way for one stopping spot for synthesis about the middle ear.**
That keeps the air pressure on either side of your eardrum the same. Sometimes your ears "pop" when the tubes suddenly open.	*Finally, I've reached a logical conclusion to the information about the middle ear, so although this is a lengthy portion, it all belongs together.*	**I will stop and think aloud while synthesizing the information about the middle ear.**
Your inner ear lies in a bony hollow within your skull. The inner ear has a maze of spaces called the labyrinth. At the end of the labyrinth is a spiral, coiled tube shaped like a snail shell. It is called the cochlea from the Latin word for snail. Inside the cochlea is a strip of skin covered with tiny hairs. The cochlea is filled with a fluid. When vibrations travel through the ear, they set off waves in the fluid. The waves cause the hairs to ripple like fields of grass in the wind.	*This is the third of the three parts of the ear. As originally planned, I will stop here to synthesize this dense paragraph.*	**I will focus my synthesis on how the cochlea, hairs, and fluid work together.**
At the bottom of each hair is a nerve cell. Each ear has about twenty thousand nerve cells. The cells send a message through the auditory nerve to the hearing centers of the brain.	*I had originally planned to stop and think through the brain's complexity, but now I see that the section below needs to go with this chunk to construct meaning about the brain's role.*	**I will eliminate this point and move it to later in the text.**

continued...

. . . from previous

What the Text Says	What I'm Thinking Now	My Decisions for This Stopping Point
The brain tells you what the vibrations mean: your teacher talking, a car honking, or a paper rustling. Finally, you hear. The ears do another job.	*I'll combine the portion above into one stopping point where I synthesize and read between the lines about the function of the brain.*	**I will stop here to make an inference and to synthesize about the function of the brain.**
Next to the cochlea are three semicircular canals. These help you to keep your balance when you sit still, walk about, or jump and bend. The curved tubes of the semicircular canals point in three directions. Like the cochlea, the canals are filled with a fluid and lined with a hairy skin. When you move your head in any direction, the fluid moves in at least one of the canals. Nerve cells in the canals send signals to the brain: You are moving up or down, to the side or another, backward or forward. The signals let your brain know how you are moving and help keep you steady. Even with your eyes closed, you know the position of your head. However, if you whirl around and around, the fluid in the canals keeps moving for a few seconds even after you stop. Then you may get dizzy and lose your balance.	*In the first reading, I identified the correct stopping point and purpose. This is a dense paragraph that needs to be monitored and synthesized.*	**I will think aloud here with synthesis and monitoring.**
Some people may have difficulty hearing. Sometimes hearing loss is caused by a sticky material made inside the ears called earwax. Earwax can build up and collect dirt and dust. Then the outer ears have to be carefully cleaned to remove the blockage. You should never try to do this yourself because of the danger of hurting your eardrums.	*Now that I'm familiar with the text, I know that there is a long paragraph that provides the various reasons that people have difficulty hearing. I think it's wise to combine all of that related text into one stopping point.*	**I will eliminate this stopping point.**
As people get older, some will gradually become hard of hearing. They may use a hearing aid that fits inside their outer ear. Hearing aids make sounds louder to help people with this kind of deafness.	*As this deals with the hearing loss, I'll combine it with the portion below.*	**I will eliminate this stopping point to allow for one think aloud dealing with hearing loss.**

What the Text Says	What I'm Thinking Now	My Decisions for This Stopping Point
Some people are born with a severe hearing loss or lose their hearing as a result of an injury. They often use hearing aids as well as other machines to alert them to sounds. For example, special telephones can be made to flash a light instead of ringing a bell. Then the message can be seen on a screen instead of being heard through an earpiece. Many hard-of-hearing people can understand what other people say by lip reading.	*I think it's okay to combine this all into one section—the central takeaway of this book is not about hearing loss, so I can address these sections somewhat briefly.*	**I will combine the above stopping points into one large section about hearing loss. This provides an opportunity to synthesize.**
We use our senses to learn what is happening in the world around us.	*I'm now realizing that this line goes along with the final paragraph to serve as a conclusion.*	**I will eliminate this stopping point.**
Our eyes and ears sense light and sound and send nerve signals to the brain. The brain puts the information together to let us see and hear.	*This conclusion also will work as a point to think aloud about the author's purpose.*	**A** **I will think aloud about the author's purpose.**

Final Thoughts

Don't be intimidated by Step 2! The charts above are models of the process that I use. I have written them out simply to be as explicit as possible in teaching this process; in reality, this stage occurs as an internal thought process, not in a written-out chart. Be prepared to spend about fifteen minutes to reread the book and winnow down your stopping points. No doubt you will get faster and more adept at this process with practice!

Ready for a Trial Run?

Now, with the same three sample texts provided in Appendix B, think through the stopping points you identified on your first reading of each text. As you examine each sticky note, use these questions to evaluate the need for and purpose of each stopping point:

- As a reader, what does this stopping point invite me to do?
- Is this stopping point especially ripe for demonstrating a particular reading comprehension strategy?
- In what ways is this stopping point effective or ineffective for showing young readers my metacognitive processes?
- What exactly would young readers gain from hearing me think aloud at this stopping point?

It's as simple as this: good stories and nonfiction stir children's curiosity. What *you* think aloud becomes what your students wonder about, too.

Remember that your goal is to reduce the stopping points you originally identified to the ones that you will use in your final script writing. After you've narrowed down your stopping points, reflect on the questions below.

- How did this step go for you?
- What did you notice about yourself as a reader while trying out this step?
- Did anything surprise, intrigue, confuse, or stump you in this step?

CHAPTER 5

Read Three Times

Writing the Scripts on Sticky Notes

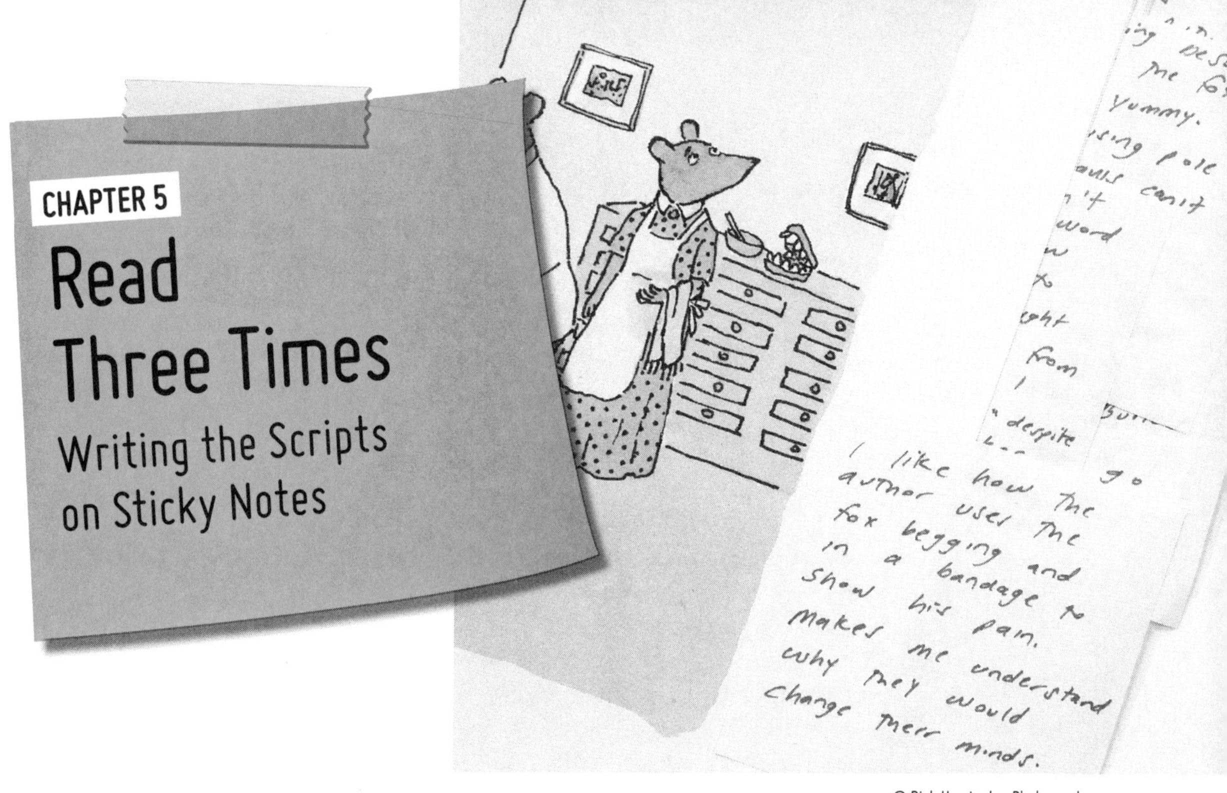

© Rick Harrington Photography

Scriptwriting, huh? Kind of Hollywood, right? Who knew it was the stuff of a reading teacher? But when you think about it, it makes perfect sense that the most effective think alouds are planned performances. And just like you wouldn't wing a TED Talk or a cameo with Denzel Washington, a well-prepared teacher goes into the think aloud knowing just what to say, when to say it, and why. So, the third reading, Step 3, requires you to draft a first-person "script." As a teacher, you do a version of this all the time—let's face it, good teachers are good stand-up performers—but I know it may sound intimidating. Your work will pay off with huge rewards: significant progress in your readers' comprehension as a result of your think alouds.

I wish I had bought stock in sticky notes—after all, they are a teacher's best friend! As I plan my think alouds, I begin with a stack of sticky notes. Any shape and size will do—I'm particularly partial to the ones that look like word bubbles. In the first reading, I slap down sticky notes wherever I have identified a potential stopping point. In the second reading, I reduce the sticky notes; at the end of this step, I have sticky notes placed exactly in the text where I will stop and think aloud. In the third reading, I use those same sticky notes as a place to write out exactly what I will say.

I want to underscore the importance—in Step 3—of writing out exactly what you will say. It is tempting to scribble down the strategy that you will employ—like "make an inference"—rather than the actual first-person

© Rick Harrington Photography

Here, I fill out the chart so I will know just what to say during my think aloud lesson.

script. As you begin this process, fight the urge to cut corners! These sticky notes are your crutch—they tell you exactly what to say at the right point. Too many times, I vowed that I would remember what I had intended to say, but in the split-focus nature of the classroom, I would lose my train of thought and had to ad-lib. As a result, my think alouds were not nearly as powerful as I had initially planned. Without the scripts, it really is far too easy to go off the rails, and look up to a sea of perplexed expressions on students' faces. And as I learned from my research study—further explained in Chapter 6—without writing a script, we run the risk of improvising our think alouds.

Another tried-and-true trick of mine: As I conduct the read aloud in front of my students, I often pick the sticky note up and place it on the back cover of the text. This is just a simple system to remind me of the comprehension moves I've made throughout the think aloud. I also find that it is easier to look at my students and deliver the think aloud with gusto if I'm holding the sticky note in my hand, rather than reading it as it's placed on the page. I also number the sticky notes so that I can still follow their order, even if I've moved the sticky note during the read aloud to the back cover.

Let's walk through an example. In my first reading, I identify twenty-three potential stopping points. I've got twenty-three sticky notes. I number each sticky note to match the number of the stopping point. In my second reading, I go through those twenty-three sticky notes and reduce them to a more manageable number, the juicy stopping points that are essential places to think aloud. In this go-around, I reach twelve places to stop and think aloud. I discard the extra sticky notes, and I'm now left with a pile of twelve sticky notes. I simply erase the old numbers, and renumber the remaining notes—hence the importance of a pencil! In my third reading, I use the sticky notes I numbered in Step 2 to write out exactly what I will say.

A Recap of the First Two Steps

Reading Step 1: Slap a sticky note on any possible stopping point in a text. Number each point.

Reading Step 2: Reduce your stopping points, and discard the unused sticky notes. Renumber the sticky notes.

What kind of time commitment is involved? In writing the numerous transcripts I produced for field-testing in K–5 classrooms and including in this book, I found that this process was time-consuming at first, but as with any skill, I got faster at it as I got into the groove of it. And more importantly, the very process of writing built my confidence and skill in delivering the think aloud. I became more fluent in the language of the sentence starters. I could more easily spot the ripe opportunities in text to think aloud. I equate this process of writing the script of a think aloud to teaching a young child to ride a bike with training wheels. Just as training wheels provide stability and confidence in learning a new skill, so does the word-by-word script of a think aloud. I also think back to my early years as a novice teacher, where I spent late nights writing detailed lesson plans. Over time, I gained the confidence and skill to plan lessons without explicitly writing out each step in lengthy detail. The same is true for the think aloud process. As you become more adept at thinking aloud, you will likely get to the point where you can mark where you will stop to think aloud, along with a brief note about which strategy you will apply. In other words, the three-column chart I showcase here (and in Appendix E) is your training wheels. My end goal is for you to be able to think aloud with comfort, ease, and skill, just as one learns to ride a bike independently—and never forgets how.

Signaling for Think Alouds

As I think aloud, I provide an explicit gesture that helps students differentiate between when I am reading from the text and when I am thinking about the text. For some readers, the internal thought process during reading will be unfamiliar, as they may be used to simply reading a book and not thinking beyond the words on the page. Therefore, using a signal is essential. One technique I use is to alert my students that *when I am reading*, the book is open to them so I can show them the illustrations. Many young students are used to sitting on the classroom rug for a read aloud while looking at the pictures, so this may be comfortable for them. *When I am thinking aloud*, the book is flat on the table or flat in my lap. Another signal for when I'm thinking aloud is to point my index finger to my temple or to tap on the side of my head, as shown in the Chapter 4 opening photo on page 59. With this gesture, students readily get that the words I'm saying are not found in the book, but rather are in my head. I tend to use the "finger to my temple"

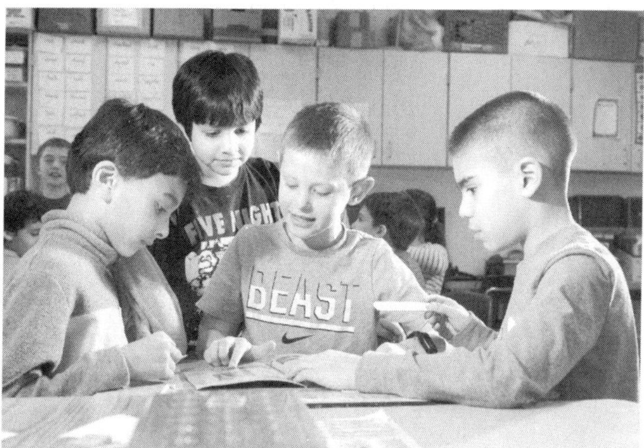

© Rick Harrington Photography

Students use Popsicle stick prompts to think aloud with a nonfiction text.

signal more than the other one, as I can more easily see my sticky note scripts on the book's back cover.

I encourage you to try my signals or to develop some of your own (and share them with me at www.drmollyness.com). Regardless of what signal you choose, it is essential to alert readers to the signals and then to continuously remind them of each signal's significance. Feel free to borrow from my explanation below:

> As I read, you're going to hear me telling you exactly what I'm thinking throughout the book. I want you to see all of the things I do to understand the book and to figure out the parts that are tricky for me. I want you to be really clear on when I am reading and when I am thinking, so you will see me use this cue to show the difference. When my finger is pointing to my head, that means I'm thinking. If you don't see my finger on my head, I'm reading the *author's* words, directly from the book.

From time to time over the school year, I might remind my students of the purpose of the signals with a brief explanation like this:

> As I read, pay attention for those times when you see my finger on my head. That signal means those words are not in the book; they are the words I'm thinking in my head—it's kind of like an inside dialogue all readers do as they work to understand. I want you to hear my thinking so you can try this thinking too when you read.

I talk to students about how I use sentence starters to help me think aloud effectively.

Think Aloud Sentence Starters

A key ingredient in the think aloud process is sentence starters. Originally devised to help generate academic language, sentence starters provide a partial frame to begin a sentence. Sentence starters give us the jump start to an idea. I use them as a springboard to my thinking; they remove the difficulty of "What will I say?" As you look at the sentence starters I've provided on pages 84–85 (and in Appendix D), you may notice a range of academic levels among them. For example, a less sophisticated sentence starter for synthesizing might be "I learned . . ." versus a more sophisticated one like "Some important concepts are . . ." The variation among the sentence starters allows for differentiation.

As you use these sentence starters, you will likely rely on a couple of safe favorites. I encourage you to dabble among all the sentence starters so that your students can see all of the different types of academic language to synthesize or make inferences. I also encourage you to use these sentence starters with your students. Post them in your classroom. Provide copies to paste into students' reading notebooks.

Big Possibilities for Creative Uses of Sentence Starters

- Use the template on page 82 to make a die. Write a different sentence starter on each side. As students roll the die, they must use the face-up sentence starter to generate a think aloud.
- Use the template on page 83 to make a game spinner with a brad or paper clip. Write a different sentence starter on each section of the spinner. Model taking a turn on the wheel, and use the prompt you land on for your think aloud.
- Buy an inflatable beach ball and use a permanent marker to write sentence starters on the colors of the ball. Toss the ball around the room; when students catch the ball, they must use the sentence starter that their right thumb lands on to generate an appropriate think aloud.

Eventually, you may come to a place where the sentence starters feel forced or inauthentic. By all means, push them aside! The sentence starters are meant to be a small step toward building your skills and confidence in thinking aloud. If you are more comfortable independently generating the language behind a think aloud, don't let the frames stunt your progress. I encourage you to make the sentence starters accessible to students, as they are a reliable and predictable safety net. They will be particularly important for students who are English language learners as they build the academic language needed to get to the higher-order thinking skills of reading comprehension.

Die Template for Using Sentence Starters

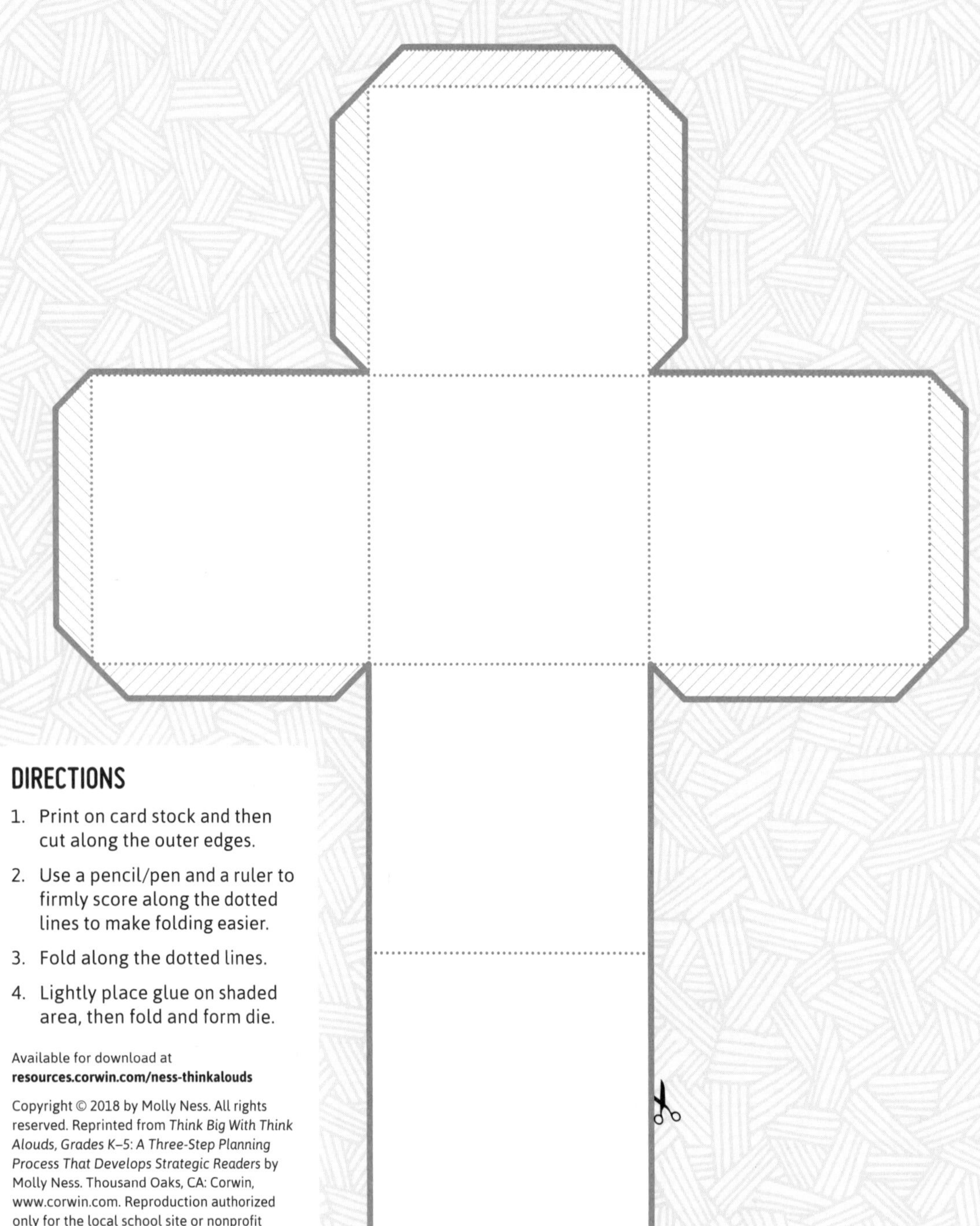

DIRECTIONS

1. Print on card stock and then cut along the outer edges.
2. Use a pencil/pen and a ruler to firmly score along the dotted lines to make folding easier.
3. Fold along the dotted lines.
4. Lightly place glue on shaded area, then fold and form die.

Available for download at
resources.corwin.com/ness-thinkalouds

Spinner Template for Using Sentence Starters

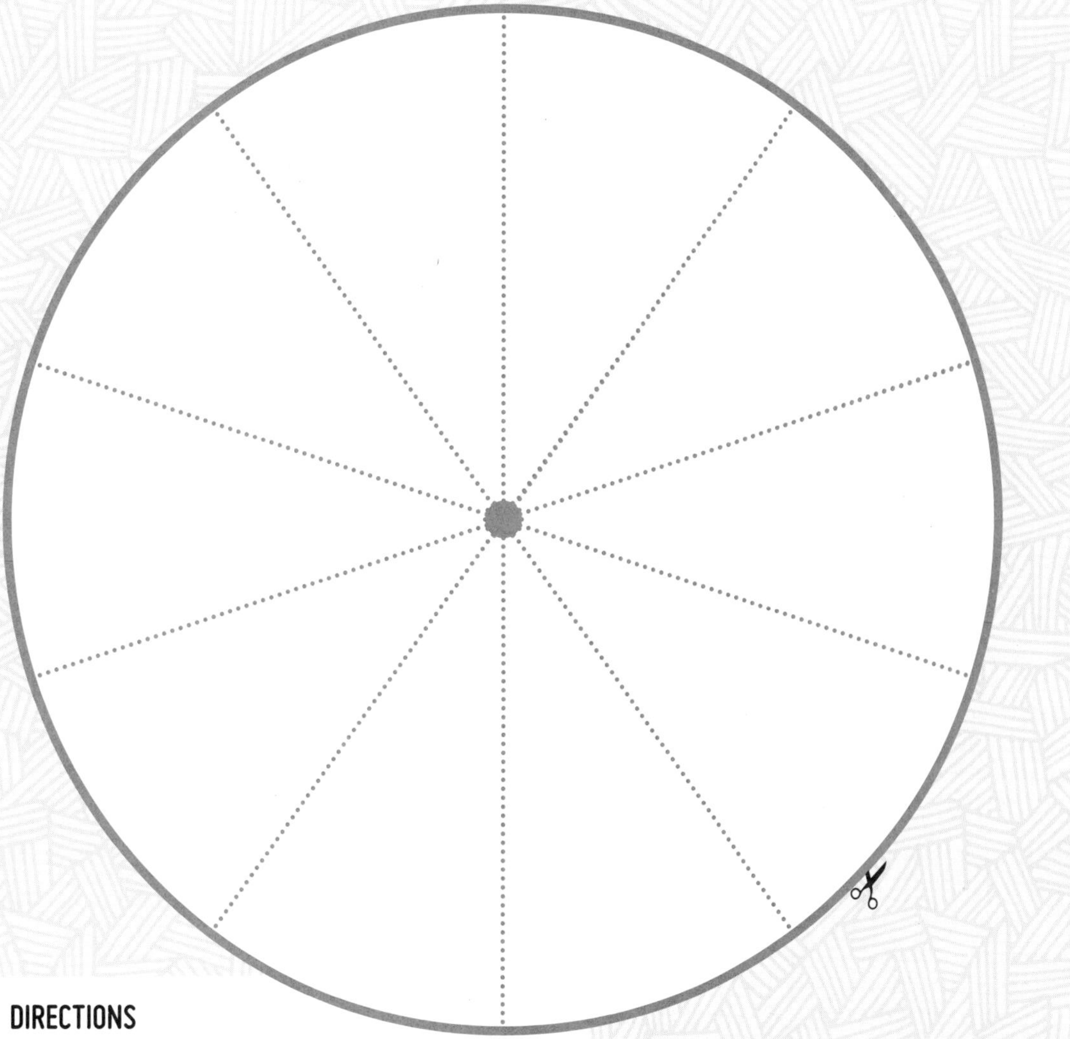

DIRECTIONS

1. Print on cardstock and then cut out spinner and arrow along the outer edges.
2. With orange side facing up, fold up back edge of arrow at dotted line.
3. Punch a hole in the center and use a brad, a fastener, or a paper clip to make a spinner.

Available for download at **resources.corwin.com/ness-thinkalouds**

Think Aloud Sentence Starters

Comprehension Strategy	Sentence Starters
Asking Questions Purposeful readers are naturally curious. They ask questions about what happens in the text. Sometimes the answers to their questions are found in the text, and sometimes they are not.	• I wonder . . . • I would like to ask the author . . . • Who . . . ? • What . . . ? • When . . . ? • Where . . . ? • Why . . . ? • How . . . ? • This makes me wonder about . . . • How is this different? • How does this part here add to . . . ?
Making Inferences Purposeful readers make inferences. An inference is something that is probably true. The author doesn't tell us exactly, but good readers take clues from the text and combine them with what they already know. An inference is made when a reader says, "This is probably true."	• From the text clues, I can conclude that . . . • Based on what the text says and what I know, I think . . . • This information makes me think . . . • This evidence suggests . . . • That is probably why . . . • Although the author does not come right out and say it, I can figure out that . . . • It could be that . . . • Maybe/perhaps . . . • This could mean . . . • Based on what I know about these characters, I bet he/she is going to . . . • With what just happened, I imagine this character is feeling . . .
Synthesizing Purposeful readers constantly change their minds as they read. They use the unfolding information or events in the book to adapt thoughts, opinions, and conclusions. In fiction, readers often synthesize to refine their understanding of characters and themes; in nonfiction, readers synthesize in order to get the most important points about parts of a text.	• Before I read, I thought . . . , but now I think . . . • My schema before I read was . . . , and now I understand . . . • This part gives me an idea . . . • When I put all these parts together, it seems the author is focusing on this big idea . . . • My synthesis is . . . • Mostly, . . . • I learned . . . • Now I understand . . . • Now I think . . . • The author keeps using these similar terms, so I think this whole section is really about this aspect of . . . • Some of the most important ideas are . . . • The text is mainly about . . . • The text, pictures, and boxes all seem to point at informing me that . . . • The author's most important ideas were . . .

Comprehension Strategy	Sentence Starters
Readers may also synthesize to draw a conclusion about what the author's perspective of a topic is, and what their own perspective is, based on the text.	• The details I need to include are . . . • Some important concepts are . . . • The most important evidence was . . . • The basic gist is . . . • The key information is . . . • In a nutshell, this says that . . . • If I asked the author to just tell me in one sentence what the big idea is, this is what he/she would say . . .
A Understanding the Author's Purpose Purposeful readers try to figure out the reason that the author wrote a text. They want to know the purpose of the text. If a text gives a clear opinion or tries to convince the reader of something, the author's purpose is to persuade. If a text gives facts or tells a reader how to do something, the author's purpose is to inform. If the text is enjoyable, tells a story, or uses a story to teach a lesson, the author's purpose is to entertain.	• The author wants me to learn about . . . [specific to nonfiction] • The author's purpose in writing this story was . . . • I wonder why the author . . . • I think the author's purpose is . . . because . . . • The main character learns . . . in the end, so I wonder if the author wants me to reflect on . . . • This story is set in history during [a famous event], so I think the author's purpose is to . . . • I predict that the author's purpose is to inform/entertain/persuade because . . . • After reading the selection, I believe the author's purpose is . . . because . . . • The author's purpose is . . . based on . . . • I am curious why the author . . . • A golden line for me is . . . • I like how the author uses . . . to show . . . • This word/phrase stands out for me because . . .
Monitoring and Clarifying Purposeful readers know when they stop understanding what they are reading. Just as when the train is going too fast the conductor applies the brake, a reader slows down and takes steps to get back on track. A reader uses one or more "fix it" strategies for repairing his or her comprehension.	• I had to slow down when . . . • It really surprised me, so I had to go back and reread because . . . • I wonder what . . . means. • Is this a different point in time? • Is this a flashback? • I wonder if this is a different narrator speaking, because . . . • What is the author doing differently with the text here because I keep losing track . . . ? • I need to know more about . . . • This last part is about . . . • I was confused by . . . • I still don't understand . . . • I had difficulty with . . . • I used [name strategy] to help me understand this part. • I can't really understand . . . • I wonder what the author means by . . . • I got lost here because . . . • I need to reread the part where . . .

Introducing the Three-Column Chart

From this point in the book, you will see my think alouds occur in a three-column chart (see the Think Aloud Chart on the next page and in Appendix E). In the first column (*What the Text Says*), I write the text *exactly as it appears*. The last sentence in each row indicates a stopping point. In the second column (*What I Say*), I write a first-person narrative of exactly what I say to students. In the third column (*The Comprehension Strategy I Model*), I identify which comprehension strategy (or strategies!) the think aloud evokes. As you work through the third column when writing your own think alouds, keep in mind that some think alouds use a combination of strategies.

I am including this chart so that I can present my three-step process with as much support and scaffolding as possible. No teachers have the time to type out the words for every text that they will use in their classroom instruction! As you get familiar with the process, you may swap the chart for just sticky notes as a place both to mark your stopping point and to jot down your transcript. If you are just beginning this practice or need additional support, I encourage you to try the charts. You may be able to copy and paste the text from the Internet to save yourself the time of the laborious part of typing out words. Regardless of which route you take, I encourage you to devote the bulk of your time to the work found in the middle column. It is incredibly helpful to practice writing out exactly what you will say, using the sentence starters on pages 84–85. As you will see from my yearlong study with teachers (see Chapter 6), most teachers were surprised to find that quality think alouds needed meaningful preparation and did not come extemporaneously.

The Think Aloud Scripts for Our Model Texts

By now, you are quite familiar with our three model texts: "Sick" (Silverstein, 1974), *Enemy Pie* (Munson, 2000), and *Eyes and Ears* (Simon, 2003). In the previous chapter, I narrowed down many potential stopping points to the ones that I will definitely use. Keep in mind that I am employing multiple comprehension strategies here to showcase how proficient readers rely on a variety of strategies to make meaning from text. With "Sick," I largely rely on asking questions, making inferences, and synthesizing. With *Enemy Pie*, I frequently synthesize and monitor and clarify. As this narrative text has an implied message from the author, I end the think aloud by thinking through the author's purpose. Finally, *Eyes and Ears* is a quintessential informational text that presents a myriad of facts and processes. It is a natural place to synthesize.

The Think Aloud Chart

Write what you plan to say on sticky notes!

What the Text Says	What I Say	The Comprehension Strategy I Model

Available for download at **resources.corwin.com/ness-thinkalouds**

Thinking Aloud in Kindergarten With "Sick" by Shel Silverstein

What the Text Says	What I Say	The Comprehension Strategy I Model
"Sick" "I cannot go to school today," Said little Peggy Ann McKay.	*Who is Peggy Ann McKay? How old is she? Why can't she go to school?*	? **Asking questions**
"I have the measles and the mumps, A gash, a rash and purple bumps. My mouth is wet, my throat is dry, I'm going blind in my right eye. My tonsils are as big as rocks, I've counted sixteen chicken pox And there's one more—that's seventeen, And don't you think my face looks green?	*What are the measles? What are the mumps? I'm thinking that they are kinds of illnesses that Peggy Ann has that make it so she can't go to school. Can kids get the chicken pox anymore? I thought there was a shot to prevent kids from getting it. Who is the you in this poem? Who is Peggy Ann talking to? I'm thinking it is her parent, and she's trying to convince her mom or dad that she's just too sick for school.*	? **Asking questions** **Making inferences**
My leg is cut—my eyes are blue— It might be instamatic flu. I cough and sneeze and gasp and choke, I'm sure that my left leg is broke— My hip hurts when I move my chin, My belly button's caving in, My back is wrenched, my ankle's sprained, My 'pendix pains each time it rains. My nose is cold, my toes are numb. I have a sliver in my thumb.	*I got confused about what the instamatic flu is—I've never heard of that. But I don't think I really need to look it up—I think it's just another way she's saying she's sick, so I will keep reading. As I read all of her ailments, I'm starting to wonder if she's faking these ailments. I'm thinking that there's just no way one little girl can have so much wrong with her! Let's keep reading to see if my thoughts are right.*	**Monitoring and clarifying**
My neck is stiff, my voice is weak, I hardly whisper when I speak. My tongue is filling up my mouth. I think my hair is falling out. My elbow's bent, my spine ain't straight, My temperature is one-o-eight. My brain is shrunk, I cannot hear, There is a hole inside my ear.	*The author is giving us even more ailments, and now I'm thinking that this whole list of what is wrong with her is kind of funny! There's no way she could have a fever of one hundred and eight! And our elbows always are bent! I'm thinking that Peggy Ann is faking all of these things just to get out of school.*	**Synthesizing** **Making inferences**
I have a hangnail, and my heart is—what? What's that? What's that you say? You say today is . . . Saturday?	*When Peggy Ann keeps repeating "What?" it makes me think that someone is interrupting her to tell her something important. And a golden line here is that it's Saturday—there's no school on Saturday!*	**Synthesizing**

What the Text Says	What I Say	The Comprehension Strategy I Model
G'bye, I'm going out to play!"	*The author doesn't come right out and tell me, but I'm getting the sense that this poem is meant to be funny. We hear this huge list of everything that is wrong with Peggy Ann, but when she finds out there is no school, all of a sudden she's cured! I think the author understands that sometimes kids make up excuses to get out of things they don't want to do, like go to school.*	**Making inferences** **Understanding the author's purpose**

Thinking Aloud in Third Grade With *Enemy Pie* by Derek Munson

What The Text Says	What I Say	The Comprehension Strategy I Model
It should have been a perfect summer. My dad helped me build a tree house in our backyard. My sister was at camp for three whole weeks. And I was on the best baseball team in town. It should have been the perfect summer. But it wasn't.	*A golden line for me is "But it wasn't." I can tell I'm about to read a story about why this was not the perfect summer, even with all of the great things—a tree house, being away from a sister, the best baseball team.*	**Synthesizing**
It was all good until Jeremy Ross moved into the neighborhood, right next door to my best friend Stanley. I did not like Jeremy Ross. He laughed at me when he struck me out in a baseball game. He had a party on his trampoline, and I wasn't even invited. But my best friend Stanley was.	*I'm thinking that this character feels left out and bullied by Jeremy Ross.*	**Synthesizing**
Jeremy Ross was the one and only person on my enemy list.	*I'm a bit confused about what an enemy list is. I've never heard of it. Maybe the author will tell me more if I read on.*	**Monitoring and clarifying**
I never even had an enemy list until he moved into the neighborhood. But as soon as he came along, I needed one. I hung it up in my tree house, where Jeremy Ross was not allowed to go. Dad understood stuff like enemies. He told me that when he was my age, he had enemies too. But he knew of a way to get rid of them.	*So now I see that this boy made a list of his enemies—mainly Jeremy Ross—and hung it up in a special place. But what is a way to get rid of enemies?*	**Monitoring and clarifying** **Asking questions**

continued . . .

. . . from previous

What The Text Says	What I Say	The Comprehension Strategy I Model
I asked him to tell me how. "Tell you how? I'll show you how!" he said. He pulled a really old recipe book off the kitchen shelf. Inside, there was a worn-out scrap of paper with faded writing. Dad held it up and squinted at it. "Enemy Pie," he said, satisfied.	*I'm getting the sense that this dad is really supportive and involved. My clues to this are how he builds a tree house and how he offers to show how to get rid of enemies. I'm also thinking that this recipe must be really valuable—my clues here are that it was old and faded and hidden somewhere safe.*	**Making inferences**
You may be wondering what exactly is in Enemy Pie. I was wondering, too. But Dad said the recipe was so secret, he couldn't even tell me. I decided it must be magic. I begged him to tell me something—anything. "I will tell you this," he said. "Enemy Pie is the fastest known way to get rid of enemies."	*I have so many questions about Enemy Pie. What is it made of? Why is it so secret? What makes it work so fast?*	? **Asking questions**
Now, of course, this got my mind working. What kinds of things—disgusting things—would I put into a pie for an enemy? I brought Dad some weeds from the garden, but he just shook his head. I brought him earthworms and rocks, but he didn't think he'd need those. I gave him the gum I'd been chewing on all morning. He gave it right back to me. I went out to play, alone. I shot baskets until the ball got stuck on the roof. I threw a boomerang that never came back to me. And all the while, I listened to the sounds of my dad chopping and stirring and blending the ingredients of Enemy Pie.	*The key information here is that his dad rejects the gross stuff for Enemy Pie but he is working really hard on making this recipe.*	**Synthesizing**
This could be a great summer after all. Enemy Pie was going to be awful. I tried to imagine how horrible it must smell, or worse yet, what it would look like. But when I was in the backyard, looking for ladybugs, I smelled something really, really, really good. And as far as I could tell, it was coming from our kitchen. I was a bit confused.	*I'm confused, too! At first, I thought that Enemy Pie was going to taste and smell terrible, but then the author tells me about a really good smell coming from the kitchen. I need to keep reading to see what's behind this Enemy Pie.*	**Monitoring and clarifying**

What The Text Says	What I Say	The Comprehension Strategy I Model
I went in to ask Dad what was wrong. Enemy Pie shouldn't smell this good. But Dad was smart. "If Enemy Pie smelled bad, your enemy would never eat it," he said. I could tell he'd made Enemy Pie before. The buzzer rang, and Dad put on the oven mitts and pulled the pie out of the oven. It looked like a plain, old pie. It looked good enough to eat! I was catching on.	*A key phrase for me is* catching on. *It makes me think that there is some trick to Enemy Pie. His dad confirms this, because he says that Enemy Pie has to look and smell good to make your enemies want to eat it.*	**Synthesizing**
But still, I wasn't really sure how this Enemy Pie worked. What exactly did it do to enemies? Maybe it made their hair fall out, or their breath stinky. Maybe it made bullies cry. I asked Dad, but he was no help. He wouldn't tell me a thing. But while the pie cooled, he filled me in on my job. He talked quietly. "There is one part of Enemy Pie that I can't do. In order for it to work, you need to spend a day with your enemy. Even worse, you have to be nice to him. It's not easy. But that's the only way that Enemy Pie can work. Are you sure you want to go through with this?"	*Now I'm really stumped. I don't understand how spending time and being nice to Jeremy can help the problem. Maybe if I keep reading the author will tell me more, and help me see the trick to Enemy Pie.*	**Monitoring and clarifying**
Of course I was. It sounded horrible. It was scary. But it was worth a try. All I had to do was to spend one day with Jeremy Ross, then he'd be out of my hair for the rest of my life. I rode my bike to his house and knocked on the door. When Jeremy opened the door, he seemed surprised. He stood on the other side of the screen door and looked at me, waiting for me to say something. I was nervous. "Can you play?" I asked. He looked confused. "I'll go ask my mom," he said.	*I'm getting the sense that Jeremy isn't too fond of this boy either—my clues are that he seems surprised and confused by his invitation to play.*	**Making inferences**
He came back with his shoes in his hand. His mom walked around the corner to say hello. "You boys stay out of trouble," she said, smiling. We rode bikes for a while and played on the trampoline. Then we made some water balloons and threw them at the neighbor girls, but we missed. Jeremy's mom made us lunch. After lunch, we went over to my house. It was strange, but I was kind of having fun with my enemy. He almost seemed kind of nice.	*Before I thought Jeremy and the narrator would always be enemies, but now I'm thinking that they might start getting along. They are enjoying each other's company and have things in common.*	**Synthesizing**

continued...

. . . from previous

What The Text Says	What I Say	The Comprehension Strategy I Model
Jeremy Ross knew how to throw a boomerang. He threw it and it came right back to him. I threw it and it went over my house and into the backyard. When we climbed over the fence to find it, the first thing Jeremy noticed was my tree house. My tree house was my tree house. I was the boss. If my sister wanted in, I didn't have to let her in. If my dad wanted in, I didn't have to let him in. And if Jeremy wanted in . . . "Can we go in it?" he asked. I knew he was going to ask me that! But he was the top person, the ONLY person, on my enemy list. And enemies aren't allowed in my tree house. But he did teach me to throw a boomerang. And he did let me play on his trampoline. He wasn't being a very good enemy.	*From the clues, I can tell that the narrator is really torn about what to do. He is the boss of his tree house, and Jeremy is his only enemy. When the author uses the word but and tells me about the fun he had with Jeremy, I think he's reconsidering whether Jeremy is his enemy. I wonder what his decision will be. A golden line is "He wasn't being a very good enemy"—it really shows me the conflict he is feeling about Jeremy being in his tree house.*	**Synthesizing** **Making inferences**
"Okay," I said, "but hold on." I climbed up ahead of him and tore the enemy list off the wall.	*Wow. This is a big deal that he took this list down! I'm guessing he did it to try to protect Jeremy's feelings, and to be kind. That makes me think that he doesn't see Jeremy as his enemy anymore.*	**Making inferences**
I had a checkerboard and some cards in the tree house, and we played games until my dad called us down for dinner. We pretended we didn't hear him, and when he came out to get us, we tried to hide from him. But somehow he found us. Dad made us macaroni and cheese for dinner—my favorite. It was Jeremy's favorite too! Maybe Jeremy Ross wasn't so bad after all. I was beginning to think that maybe we should just forget about Enemy Pie. But sure enough, after dinner, Dad brought out the pie. I watched as he cut the pie into eight thick slices. "Dad," I said, "it sure is nice having a new friend in the neighborhood." I was trying to get his attention and trying to tell him that Jeremy Ross was no longer my enemy. But Dad only smiled and nodded.	*The key information is that Jeremy is no longer his enemy. They play together and like the same foods, and the narrator even tries to protect him!*	**Synthesizing**

What The Text Says	What I Say	The Comprehension Strategy I Model
I think he thought I was just pretending. Dad dished up three plates, side by side, with big pieces of pie and giant scoops of ice cream. He passed one to me and one to Jeremy. "Wow!" Jeremy said, looking at the pie. "My dad never makes pies like this." It was at this point that I panicked. I didn't want Jeremy to eat Enemy Pie! He was my friend! I couldn't let him eat it! "Jeremy, don't eat it! It's bad pie! I think it's poisonous or something!" Jeremy's fork stopped before reaching his mouth. He crumpled his eyebrows and looked at me funny.	*I'm having difficulty understanding the line about how Jeremy looked funny. Does that mean funny like he's about to be sick or die from Enemy Pie? Or does it mean funny because Jeremy doesn't understand? I have to keep reading to find my answer!*	**Monitoring and clarifying**
I felt relieved. I had saved his life. I was a hero. "If it's so bad," Jeremy asked, "then why has your dad already eaten half of it?" I turned to look at my dad. Sure enough, he was eating Enemy Pie! "Good stuff," he mumbled through a mouthful.	*What is going on here? I don't understand why his dad is eating Enemy Pie! Let me keep reading.*	**Monitoring and clarifying**
And that was all he said. I sat there watching them eating Enemy Pie for a few seconds. Dad was laughing. Jeremy was happily eating. And neither of them was losing any hair! It seemed safe enough, so I took a tiny taste. Enemy Pie was delicious!	*Although the author doesn't come right out and say it, I'm thinking the narrator's father pulled a trick on him! Enemy Pie is really delicious, and I think the trick was that by spending the day with his enemy, the narrator realizes how much fun Jeremy is. There's not really any such thing as Enemy Pie—the real trick is spending time with your enemy so that he is not your enemy anymore.*	**Making inferences**
After dessert, Jeremy rode his bike home but not before inviting me over to play on his trampoline in the morning. He said he'd teach me how to flip. As for Enemy Pie, I still don't know how to make it. I still wonder if enemies really do hate it or if their hair falls out or their breath turns bad. But I don't know if I'll ever get an answer, because I just lost my best enemy.	*A golden line here is "I just lost my best enemy." I'm getting the idea that the author wrote this book to show me that the best way to get rid of our enemies is to spend time with them and get to know them.*	A **Understanding the author's purpose**

Thinking Aloud in Fifth Grade With *Eyes and Ears* by Seymour Simon

What the Text Says	What I Say	The Comprehension Strategy I Model
Light travels from objects and passes into our eyes. Light comes from many different sources, including the sun and electric bulbs. When light hits an object, light waves bounce off in all directions. Special light-sensitive cells in our eyes sense the light and send signals to our brain.	*Some of the most important ideas here are that light waves bounce off things and that our brain helps our eyes to sense the light. Right away, I can see that there is a lot of information that the author wants me to learn here, so I can guess he wrote this book to inform.*	**Synthesizing** **A** **Understanding the author's purpose**
Sound waves move through the air and enter our ears. Sound is made when objects move back and forth, or vibrate. The vibrations travel through the air in invisible ripples called sound waves. Sound-sensitive cells in our ears sense the vibrations and send signals to our brain. We see and hear when our brain makes sense out of the messages it gets from our eyes and our ears.	*I'm noticing that this paragraph follows the same format as the one above it. I think the author did that on purpose—to show me that seeing and hearing are really similar. Just like our brain helps our eyes to interpret light waves, our brain helps our ears to hear sound waves.*	**A** **Understanding the author's purpose** **Synthesizing**
Your eye is also called an eyeball. It is shaped like a small ball about one inch across. Two eyeballs sit in cuplike sockets in the front of your head. Your eyelids cover the parts of your eyes and make them appear more oval than round. Six tiny muscles hold each eyeball steady in the sockets of your head. The muscles work in teams. One team of muscles swivels the eye toward or away from your nose. Another team of muscles moves the eye upward or downward. Still another team moves the eye at an angle down and outward or up and outward.	*The basic gist here is that muscles are really necessary for our eyes to work.*	**Synthesizing**
Rays of light enter the eyeball through a clear, round layer of cells called the cornea. The cornea acts like a camera lens and bends light into the eye. The colored part of your eye just behind the cornea is called the iris. What color are your eyes? The opening in the central part of the iris is called the pupil. The size of the pupil is controlled by the muscles in the iris. The muscles tighten to make the pupil smaller in bright light and relax to make the pupil larger in dim light.	*I had to slow down when I got all the information about the cornea, the iris, and the pupil. When I reread, I saw how important those muscles were to control how much light comes into the pupil.*	**Monitoring and clarifying** **Synthesizing**

What the Text Says	What I Say	The Comprehension Strategy I Model
Light goes through the pupil and passes into the eye through the aqueous humor and then through the eye lens. The center of the eyeball contains a fluid called the vitreous humor. The vitreous humor fills the eyeball so that it has a rounded shape. The lens focuses light through the vitreous humor onto the back of the eye, the retina. Light-sensitive cells in the retina are connected to the brain by a large optic nerve.	*I want to know more about the job of the retina and the lens. In people who have to wear glasses, is there something wrong with their retina or their lens?*	? **Asking questions**
Here's what happens when you look at something, say a tree. Light reflected from the tree enters your eye through the pupil. The lens forms the light into an image that is a small picture of a tree. The image falls upside down on your retina.	*So the author really wants me to understand that light reflections from the things I see come in through my pupil. The lens takes that light to make an image that is projected by my retina.*	**Synthesizing**
In people with normal vision, light rays from an object are focused by the eye's lens exactly on the retina. But some people are nearsighted. They can see close objects clearly, but distance objects look blurred. The reason for nearsightedness is that the eyeball in some people is a bit too long, front to back. Light rays from a distant object form an image in the front of the retina. Nearsightedness, also called myopia, is corrected by wearing glasses or contact lenses. The lenses change the focal point so that the image falls exactly on the retina. . . .	*Earlier I was wondering why people had to wear glasses. Here I learn that the glasses help to change the focal point for people who have an irregularly shaped eye.*	**Monitoring and clarifying** **Synthesizing**
The retina contains two different kinds of light-sensitive nerve cells: rods and cones. They get their names because of the way they are shaped. Rod cells are sensitive to shades of brightness and are used to see in black and white. There are over one hundred million rod cells. Cone cells work best in bright light and let us see color. There are about seven million cone cells in your retina. A tiny spot in the center of your eye contains only cones. It gives you the sharpest image. Around the edges of the retina are fewer cones and more and more rods. We use the cones more during the day and the rods more at night.	*It's essential that I remember the two kinds of cells in the retina: the rods help me see black and white, and the cones help me see color.*	**Synthesizing**

continued . . .

...from previous

What the Text Says	What I Say	The Comprehension Strategy I Model
Every rod and cone cell in your retina is connected by its own nerve cell to the brain. When light strikes your retina, the cells respond. They send out tiny electric impulses. All the nerve cells collect at the back of the eye. They form a main cable called the optic nerve. The optic nerve runs back from the eyeball through a tunnel in the skull to a crossover in the brain. The information from the right eye crosses over and goes to the left back of the brain. The information from the left eye crosses over and goes to the right back of the brain.	*It's important to understand here that the optic nerve helps deliver light waves to our brain.*	**Synthesizing**
We still do not know exactly how the brain works. However, we do know that it is in your brain that seeing finally takes place. The brain puts together the nerve impulses from your eyes along with other brain impulses. The image is turned right side up, and you see what's out there.	*I wonder what the author means when he says we don't know how the brain works. What do we not know about the brain? And how can we find out the answers to what we don't know?*	? **Asking questions**
There is one spot on the retina that is not sensitive to light. It is called the blind spot. It has no rods and cones because it is just at the point where the optic nerve goes out to the brain. Each of your eyes has its own blind spot. Usually you are not aware of the blind spot in your eyes. Your eyes are always moving around. You can get enough light images about what you are looking at so that you never notice the blind spot. But here's a way of checking the blind spot in your right eye. Close your left eye and look at the X below with your right eye. Keep staring straight at the X while bringing the book closer to your eye. At about six to ten inches from your eye, you will no longer see the black dot to the side of the X. If you bring the book closer, the dot will appear again. At the point where you can't see the dot, the light from it just falls on the blind spot. If you want to check the blind spot in your left eye, turn the book over. Close your right eye and follow the same directions as above.	*This example shows me exactly how the blind spot works—a spot that has no rods or cones and is not sensitive to light. I like how the author gives me a picture to show me exactly how the blind spot works. It really makes me understand it. The author wants me to be as informed as he is.*	**Synthesizing** A **Understanding the author's purpose**

What the Text Says	What I Say	The Comprehension Strategy I Model
Sunlight is more than one hundred thousand times brighter than moonlight. That's why you can see colors in the daylight but not in the moonlight. The light of the moon looks silvery because you're seeing it with the color-blind rods in your retina. The color-sensing cones of your retina do not respond to the dim light of the moon.	*Before I thought that things at night looked silvery because of silver light from the moon, but now I realize that it is because I'm using my rods.*	**Synthesizing**
As with everything else you see, your brain is involved in sensing color. Here's how you can show how your brain is involved in seeing color. Cut out a circle of white cardboard about four inches across. Color half green and the other half red. Push a two-inch nail through the center of the cardboard disk and trim the opening so that the disk spins freely on the nail. Spin it as rapidly as you can. Your brain will combine the colors sensed by your eyes, and you will see a greyish tint instead of the green and red.	*Here I'm learning about how my brain helps sense color, but I've heard that some people are color blind. I wonder what that means. Does it mean that your brain can't sense colors? Does it mean you can only see in black and white?*	? **Asking questions**
The ear is an amazing and important sense organ. We can hear all kinds of sounds, from the loud sound of a door slamming to the soft sound of tree leaves rustling in the wind. We can tell the sound of one friend's voice from that of another friend's voice. We use our ears to listen to radio and television and all of the everyday sounds around us.	*The author doesn't come right out and say it, but I'm getting the sense that it would be really hard to live in this world without hearing—not only hard to hear phones ring, car horns, and all that, but hard emotionally because you can't hear the nice sound of a good friend or family member's voice to make you feel connected.*	**Making inferences**
An ear has three parts: the outer ear, the middle ear, and the inner ear. The earflaps on each side of your head are called pinnae. The pinnae are made of flexible cartilage and covered by a layer of skin. The bottom part of each pinna is called the earlobe. Some people have long and curved earlobes while others have small and flat earlobes. The pinnae act as a kind of sound catcher. They channel the sound waves down a short tube called the auditory canal to the eardrum.	*This part is about the three parts of the ear. I learned here about the first part—the outer ear—which catches sound waves. Let me keep reading to find out about the other two parts.*	**Synthesizing**

continued...

. . . from previous

What the Text Says	What I Say	The Comprehension Strategy I Model
The eardrum separates the outer ear from the middle ear. The eardrum is a thin flap of skin that stretches tightly across the end of the auditory canal. Sound waves cause the eardrum to vibrate just like the top of a drum when it is hit by a drumstick. The middle ear is a tiny space behind the eardrum. Inside the middle ear are the three smallest bones in the body, linked together. They are called the hammer, the anvil, and the stirrup because of their shapes. These three bones together are called the ossicles. The vibrations of the eardrum cause the ossicles to move. The movements are transmitted to another tight, thin flap of skin called the oval window. The middle ear is linked to the back of your throat by the Eustachian tube. This narrow tube is usually closed. But when you swallow, chew, or yawn, the entrance to the tube opens and air travels in and out of your middle ear. That keeps the air pressure on either side of your eardrum the same. Sometimes your ears "pop" when the tubes suddenly open.	*Okay, so the second part of the ear—the middle ear—has your eardrum and three tiny bones that vibrate with sound.*	**Synthesizing**
Your inner ear lies in a bony hollow within your skull. The inner ear has a maze of spaces called the labyrinth. At the end of the labyrinth is a spiral, coiled tube shaped like a snail shell. It is called the cochlea from the Latin word for snail. Inside the cochlea is a strip of skin covered with tiny hairs. The cochlea is filled with a fluid. When vibrations travel through the ear, they set off waves in the fluid. The waves cause the hairs to ripple like fields of grass in the wind.	*And here I found out about the third part of the ear—the inner ear with the cochlea in it. The first part is the outer ear, which picks up the sound waves, the second part is the middle ear, which has the eardrum, and now this third part, the inner ear, has the cochlea.*	**Synthesizing**
At the bottom of each hair is a nerve cell. Each ear has about twenty thousand nerve cells. The cells send a message through the auditory nerve to the hearing centers of the brain. The brain tells you what the vibrations mean: your teacher talking, a car honking, or a paper rustling. Finally, you hear.	*Here I discovered that the tiny hairs have nerve cells that send messages to the brain. I'm getting the sense that the brain helps so many of our body functions, and that is why it is so important. Maybe that is why we protect our brains by wearing helmets, because we'd really be in trouble if our brains got hurt!*	**Synthesizing** **Making inferences**

What the Text Says	What I Say	The Comprehension Strategy I Model
The ears do another job. Next to the cochlea are three semicircular canals. These help you to keep your balance when you sit still, walk about, or jump and bend. The curved tubes of the semicircular canals point in three directions. Like the cochlea, the canals are filled with a fluid and lined with a hairy skin. When you move your head in any direction, the fluid moves in at least one of the canals. Nerve cells in the canals send signals to the brain: You are moving up or down, to the side or another, backward or forward. The signals let your brain know how you are moving and help keep you steady. Even with your eyes closed, you know the position of your head. However, if you whirl around and around, the fluid in the canals keeps moving for a few seconds even after you stop. Then you may get dizzy and lose your balance.	*At first when I read that the ears do another job, I couldn't think of what else they would do, so I was confused. But as I kept reading, I learned about the fluid in my ear helping me maintain my balance. I used to think I got dizzy because my eyes were spinning around and around, but now I know it is because of the fluid in my ears.*	**Monitoring and clarifying** **Synthesizing**
Some people may have difficulty hearing. Sometimes hearing loss is caused by a sticky material made inside the ears called earwax. Earwax can build up and collect dirt and dust. Then the outer ears have to be carefully cleaned to remove the blockage. You should never try to do this yourself because of the danger of hurting your eardrums. As people get older, some will gradually become hard of hearing. They may use a hearing aid that fits inside their outer ear. Hearing aids make sounds louder to help people with this kind of deafness. Some people are born with a severe hearing loss or lose their hearing as a result of an injury. They often use hearing aids as well as other machines to alert them to sounds. For example, special telephones can be made to flash a light instead of ringing a bell. Then the message can be seen on a screen instead of being heard through an earpiece. Many hard-of-hearing people can understand what other people say by lip reading.	*In a nutshell, this part tells me that there are a few ways people can lose their hearing or have a hard time hearing. But, there are ways that people who have a hard time hearing can get help—just like how glasses and contacts help people who have a hard time seeing.*	**Synthesizing**
We use our senses to learn what is happening in the world around us. Our eyes and ears sense light and sound and send nerve signals to the brain. The brain puts the information together to let us see and hear.	*I really like how the author gives me these final sentences to summarize the most important ideas of the book—that our eyes and ears sense things and our brain helps us interpret this information. It seems like the author wants us to appreciate that our bodies are pretty amazing, and that all the systems work together to help us live in the world.*	A **Understanding the author's purpose** III **Making inferences**

Final Thoughts

So now you've got three complete think aloud transcripts ready to be used right away in your classroom instruction. These transcripts are by no means set in stone; instead, I encourage you to understand the process by which I created these, rather than focus solely on the product. Each transcript can be modified and adapted to the needs of your diverse learners. As you read on in this book, I will coach you on replicating this process across a variety of genres and content areas.

Ready for a Trial Run?

Now, with the same three sample texts provided in Appendix B, work on using the three-column chart (Appendix E) to write a think aloud. Use the sentence starters (Appendix D) to write out the scripts in the first-person narrative exactly as you'd say it to your students. After you've completed the scripts, reflect on the questions below.

- How did this step go for you?
- What did you notice about yourself as a reader while trying out this step?
- Did anything surprise, intrigue, confuse, or stump you in this step?

How Did They Go?

Teachers Share Successes and Challenges

So here we are. You've used the three-step process to write think aloud scripts. If you're like Billy Crystal's character in *When Harry Met Sally*, who reads the last page of a book first, you might be reading this chapter before trying out your own think alouds. Maybe you're off and running in thinking aloud in front of students. Chances are you could use some time to reflect on what went well and what still seems shaky in your execution of the strategy. The truth is, even with all the careful planning, think alouds never go exactly as planned in terms of how students "catch" them and apply them to their independent reading. Learners are wonderfully changeable and unpredictable. In the next chapter we will look more closely at student ownership of thinking aloud, but for now I'm going to share some of the ups and downs of teachers' journeys with think alouds. Their successes and stumbling blocks will help you to anticipate any challenges and to exploit tips and insights that lead to success.

First, I'll review the professional learning study that informed this book. As I briefly explained in Chapter 1, the ideas that I present in this book emerged from a yearlong study. As a teacher educator and a professor at a graduate school of education, I often have the pleasure of engaging in research projects. In this particular one, my aim was to improve teachers' abilities to think aloud in their routine classroom instruction. In this chapter, I explore the lessons I've learned from this project and its impact on the book that you currently hold.

Inside K–5 Classrooms: A Yearlong Study

In the fall of 2014, I formed a research team composed of K–5 classroom teachers. All participants were early-career teachers, in their first five years of classroom teaching, and volunteered to be a part of the research project because of their desire to improve their reading comprehension instruction. I also invited students in my literacy methods courses and reflective seminars to join the team. In this yearlong collaboration, volunteers participated in both face-to-face and online meetings. As researchers, we aimed to answer the following questions:

1. What happens when early-career teachers plan, implement, and reflect on multiple think aloud lessons?
2. What successes and challenges do early-career teachers encounter in thinking aloud?

As a part of the research team, I provided extensive training and professional development on think alouds. Teachers read several practitioner-appropriate journal articles about how, when, and why to use think alouds (Barrentine, 1996; Block & Israel, 2004; Oster, 2001; Walker, 2005). I modeled think alouds with poetry, nonfiction text, and storybooks. We watched video clips of think alouds and critically analyzed the lessons. We planned think alouds collaboratively, while I provided assistance and feedback. As a part of the research team, teachers planned, implemented, and reflected on three think aloud lesson plans.

In the lesson plans, teachers selected a K–5 children's book appropriate for their students. These lesson plans required teachers to complete the three-column chart, including clearly identified stopping points where they would pause and think aloud, a transcript of what they planned to verbalize to the class at each predetermined stopping point, and the associated comprehension strategies. In these lesson plans, participants were not directed to include a particular number of stopping points for think alouds or to incorporate any specific reading comprehension strategies; rather, they were left to determine both what kind of and how many strategies were appropriate for their students and their chosen text. Participants also were expected to teach these lessons in their classrooms. We came together to reflect on these lessons. The topics of conversation included what worked and what did not work in thinking aloud, some of the lingering questions (further discussed in the remainder of this chapter), and ways to improve future think alouds.

At the culmination of the project, teachers audiotaped or videotaped themselves while teaching their think aloud lesson. The intent here was to transcribe their lessons, to examine how closely they followed the planned think aloud script, to be metacognitive about their instructional choices, and to evaluate the appropriateness of the think alouds they provided during their read alouds.

At the conclusion of the project, participants completed a written questionnaire. They reflected on the process of planning and implementing several think aloud lesson plans with the following questions:

- What was the think aloud process like for you? What about thinking aloud worked for you? What about thinking aloud didn't work?
- What about thinking aloud was easy for you? What about thinking aloud was hard for you?
- Evaluate your own level of comfort in thinking aloud with K–5 students. How ready do you feel to incorporate think alouds in future teaching?
- As you move forward in thinking aloud, what instructional support would be useful for you? What activities, if any, helped build your confidence in your think aloud skills?

Lessons Learned From the Yearlong Study

I cannot overestimate how much I learned in the collaboration with this research team. The key findings were as follows:

The Takeaways From Our Yearlong Investigation

Lesson 1: Planning a think aloud requires a clear structure and process.

Lesson 2: Teachers' abilities to think aloud and confidence in the strategy grow tremendously over time.

Lesson 3: Teachers are eager for additional and ongoing support in thinking aloud.

Each of these lessons is further discussed below.

Lesson 1: Planning a think aloud requires a clear structure and process.

Time and time again, participants were surprised to realize that effective think alouds do not simply emerge naturally and spontaneously, as described by a third-grade teacher:

> I thought that these think alouds would emerge off the cuff, but I was surprised by how much I struggled with what to say and when to say it when I didn't meticulously plan.

The big takeaway was that successful think alouds require careful preparation, advance planning, and intimate knowledge of relevant text selections.

During our yearlong period, the Think Aloud Chart evolved and went through several iterations. In their first lesson plans, teachers were not given any form for their lesson plan. Instead, they were simply asked to select an appropriate book and to write a script of what they would say. I presented the following steps outlined by Wilhelm (2001):

1. Select a short section of text.
2. Select a few relevant and purposeful strategies.
3. State the purpose for reading and deliberately focus on particular strategies.
4. Read the text aloud to students while modeling the chosen strategies.
5. Have students annotate the text.
6. Brainstorm cues and strategies used.
7. Teach students to generalize the strategies.
8. Reinforce the think aloud with follow-up lessons.

This format was too ambiguous for my early-career teachers, who craved more direction, more prescriptive steps to follow in planning, and a template to use. Simply put, my participants wanted a graphic organizer to help them plan their think alouds. I kept returning to the comments of a fourth-grade teacher, who explained, "I truly had to plan out exactly what I wanted to say and where I wanted to say it, and almost write a script on a sticky note at each stopping point." Thus, the Think Aloud Chart, in its three-column version, was born—giving teachers a structure of when to stop, what to say, and how their script links to comprehension strategies.

Lesson 2: Teachers' abilities to think aloud and confidence in the strategy grow tremendously over time.

Over the year, I saw a significant evolution of teachers' think aloud lessons. More specifically, teachers grew in both the number and the variety of reading comprehension strategies they incorporated. In their first lesson plans, teachers most frequently relied on three basic reading comprehension strategies: making predictions, activating prior knowledge, and making connections. Let's examine the following table to see which reading comprehension strategies were incorporated into the three lesson plans.

Reading Comprehension Strategies Incorporated in Teachers' Think Aloud Lesson Plans

Commonly Used Metacognitive Strategies	Overall Percentage of Teachers Including the Strategy in Lesson Plan 1	Overall Percentage of Teachers Including the Strategy in Lesson Plan 2	Overall Percentage of Teachers Including the Strategy in Lesson Plan 3
Overviewing the text	2%	8%	14%
Visualizing	10%	18%	60%
Activating prior knowledge	48%	62%	78%
Asking questions	24%	22%	42%
Understanding the author's purpose	0%	4%	8%
Making inferences	0%	2%	10%
Making connections	74%	86%	100%
Making and revising predictions	82%	88%	78%
Determining the most important ideas	10%	14%	28%
Synthesizing	0%	6%	10%
Monitoring	6%	12%	20%
Clarifying	8%	10%	22%
Restating	10%	20%	40%
Backtracking or rereading	8%	14%	16%

Though activating prior knowledge, making connections, and making and revising predictions remained the most favored comprehension strategies, teachers demonstrated a willingness to include all of the reading comprehension strategies in some capacity. By the final lesson plan, teachers demonstrated growth in including some of the more difficult comprehension strategies, such as making inferences (from 0 percent in the first lesson plan to 10 percent in the third lesson plan), synthesizing (from 0 percent in the first lesson plan to 10 percent in the third lesson plan), and understanding the author's purpose (from 0 percent in the first lesson plan to 8 percent in the third lesson plan).

Upon recognizing that their think alouds were fairly limited in the repertoire of strategies, teachers included a wider diversity of reading comprehension strategies in subsequent lessons. A fourth-grade teacher noted in a written reflection, "I couldn't believe that in my lesson I used the same two strategies time and time again. Next time around, I need to expand my comfort zone and include some others!"

I also want to comment on the five strategies I focus on in this book: asking questions, making inferences, synthesizing, understanding the author's purpose, and monitoring and clarifying. I have selected these as the focal strategies for this book largely because of my yearlong study. Even after many layers of support and professional development, the participants in my research group still used these five strategies with relative infrequency. Let's examine the data below:

- By the end of their third lesson plan, only 42 percent of participants included asking questions in their think alouds.
- By the end of their third lesson plan, only 10 percent of participants included making inferences in their think alouds.
- By the end of their third lesson plan, only 10 percent of participants included synthesizing in their think alouds.
- By the end of their third lesson plan, only 8 percent of participants included understanding the author's purpose in their think alouds.
- By the end of their third lesson plan, only 20 percent of participants included monitoring and 22 percent included clarifying in their think alouds.

These data suggest that participants had not yet reached the point where they could incorporate these five strategies readily and confidently into their think alouds; with this realization in mind, I determined the focal strategies for the book you are now holding.

Lesson 3: Teachers are eager for additional and ongoing support in thinking aloud.

Just as teachers grew in their ability to think aloud, they also sought additional support to continue their ongoing professional development. Naturally, some members of the research team asked for additional support to better prepare them for thinking aloud. A third-grade teacher explained:

> Just as we expect with our young readers, we as teachers need a lot of exposure to a topic in order to internalize it and be ready to try it out. It's not enough to read an article about how to think aloud; I needed to watch teachers trying it, to debrief with my colleagues on the process, and to collaboratively plan a lesson all just to get me ready to try it out myself.

To me, these sentiments were particularly encouraging. They revealed the ever-curious, reflective nature of my research team—eager to continue learning and growing. To answer their calls for ongoing support, I am providing more suggestions below.

Ideas to Hone Your Thinking Aloud

One of the common sentiments that I heard pertained to the difficulty of identifying students' sources of confusion. Because many teachers are avid and proficient readers, they may be unfamiliar with the process and feelings of struggling (Maria & Hathaway, 1993). A second-grade teacher explained:

> As a proficient reader, it's sometimes difficult to see where in a text my students are likely to struggle and how I can help model what to do when a comprehension breakdown arises. How can I verbalize the processes that are so inherent to me?

In other words, it's hard to put ourselves in our students' shoes and identify their sources of confusion. In the first chapter of this book (see "Ready for a Trial Run?" on page 19), I delineate an activity recommended by Afflerbach and Johnston (1986), in which teachers practice thinking aloud through confusion in a frustrating text. By requiring teachers to think aloud with Renaissance literature, a college chemistry textbook, and a legal document, for example, we simulate the experience of struggling with a text so that we can empathize with students and better understand potential comprehension breakdowns.

In the classroom, I recommend a game that I call Stump the Chump. Here, I challenge students to bring in a piece of text that they find particularly difficult. Wilhelm (2001) explains, "Students enjoy trying to stump me and enjoy watching me sweat! This is good. It shows them that I struggle too and that I know what strategies to use" (p. 108). This activity is particularly effective for several reasons. First, it is highly motivating for students. As they search for the most difficult text in order to make their teacher "sweat," they become metacognitive about the sources of their confusion. Is this text confusing because of its structure? Its complicated vocabulary? Its assumed background knowledge? Additionally, the activity helps me understand the stumbling blocks for students—which as pointed out by my research team is often difficult for teachers. Finally, monitoring and clarifying is often one of the trickiest strategies to model for teachers, since we are unsure of the wheres and whys for students' confusion. One teacher explained, "It would have been helpful for me to have more explicit modeling on how to think aloud around comprehension breakdowns and applying fix-up strategies, my biggest source of confusion." Stump the Chump is a perfect way to provide such modeling.

Evaluating Your Own Thinking Aloud

Another common question from my research team was "How do I evaluate my own think alouds?" My answer was always an enthusiastic "Videotape yourself teaching!" When I was a novice teacher in the 1990s, this was a cumbersome process involving a tripod and a camcorder. The videotaping capacities of today's smartphones and tablets have simplified the process. I find watching and evaluating one's own teaching so valuable that it is the focus of this chapter's "Ready for a Trial Run?"

Let me show you how I evaluate my own thinking aloud. I will begin with a transcript from a think aloud I did with my first-grade daughter, Callie.

The proof is in the pudding, as they say. That is, you should be able to hear the "big think" of your think alouds as you listen to your readers discuss what they read.

My aim was to model making inferences, and I selected the picture book *The Bear Ate Your Sandwich* (2015). Written by Julia Sarcone-Roach, this mischievous book tells the story of what happened to a sandwich. The surprise ending introduces readers to an unlikely narrator, and offers opportunities for the reader to make inferences about who really ate the sandwich. My aim in this think aloud was to model my inference-making skills so that Callie would be able to derive the source of humor in the book.

Let me be the first to confess that this is a totally ineffective think aloud! Admittedly, this was one of my earliest attempts at thinking aloud. As you read through this transcript, ask yourself why I see this as an ineffective example. What did I do well? What could I have done better? I will reflect on these questions after the transcript.

Note: The italicized portions reflect the text directly.

Molly: This book is called *The Bear Ate Your Sandwich*. We have a dog that eats our sandwiches, right?

Callie: Yeah.

Molly: *By now, I think you know what happened to your sandwich. But you may not know how it happened. So let me tell you. It all started with the bear.* So the author's giving us a clue about a bear and a sandwich. What do you think might have happened?

Callie: The bear ate the sandwich.

Molly: Okay, let's read and see. *The morning air was warm and bright when the bear stepped out of his den. He stretched and sniffed.* What do you think the bear might have been doing right before this picture? He comes out in the morning, and he's stretching. What might he have been doing before?

Callie: Sleeping.

Molly: Why do you think so? What clues make you think he was sleeping?

Callie: 'Cause he just woke up.

Molly: He just woke up? And what do you do sometimes when you wake up?

Callie: Stretch.

Molly: Yup. *The scent of ripe berries drifted toward him and led to a wonderful discovery.* Look at this picture of a truck, and in the back are some of those berries. What do you think the discovery might be? What clues do you see in the picture that might make you think the bear discovered something?

Callie: Umm . . .

Molly: All those berries. *After a berry feast, the bear curled up in the sunlight and listened to the buzzing of the bees. Before long, he was asleep. By the time the bear had opened his eyes, the buzzing had become a rumbling.* The author is giving us clues about buzzing and rumbling sounds. What might those sounds be?

Callie: Cars.

Molly: Cars? What makes you think that?

Callie: 'Cause sometimes cars make buzzing and rumbling sounds.

Molly: And what does this picture show?

Callie: Cars and boats.

continued . . .

. . . from previous

Molly: What does this look like, do you think?

Callie: A city and cars.

Molly: A city, so there might be lots of cars in that city. *He was being quickly swept along like a leaf and a great river. The forest disappeared in the distance and the high cliffs rose up around him.* Where might the bear be now? Is he still in the forest?

Callie: Mm-mm [shakes head].

Molly: Where do you think he is?

Callie: In the city.

Molly: In the city. How? What's your clue? There he is in the back of the truck. What pictures help you make that guess?

Callie: This and, umm, I see the bear and the car and the truck driving to the city.

Molly: Driving to all those tall buildings that might be in the city? *Once the rumbling stopped, the bear found himself in a new forest. It was like nothing he'd ever seen before.* What are the pictures, and what is the author telling us about this new forest? Is it really forest?

Callie: No, it's really the city.

Molly: What do you see in it? There's the bear looking all around.

Callie: There's no berries, and he's like "hmm."

Molly: "Hmm, where am I?" This forest looks a little bit different, huh?

Callie: Mm-hm.

Molly: *This forest had many great climbing spots. The trees were itchy here. There was good bark for scratching*—there, he's scratching—*and the mud squished nicely under his feet.* What's going on? Are these really trees?

Callie: Mm-mm [shakes head].

Molly: What are they?

Callie: A lamp pole.

Molly: Lamp poles and telephone poles. And is this mud you think under his feet that's squishing so nicely?

Callie: No, it's wa- . . . like water.

Molly: Look, see this. Have you ever seen somebody pouring cement for new sidewalks?

Callie: No.

Molly: That's what this man is doing. *There were many interesting smells in this forest, but some of the tastiest ones had already been found. Leafy green smells led the bear to new fun.* Look at this picture. Where do you think the bear is now?

Callie: The playground.

Molly: Why do you say that?

Callie: 'Cause . . .

Molly: There he is on the slide and the swings and seesaws. Look at him! He fell right over on that seesaw because he's probably too big for it. That is when he saw it. What do you think he saw? Make an inference; make a guess.

Callie: I don't know.

Molly: You want to read and find out? *There it was, your beautiful and delicious sandwich all alone. He waited to make sure no one saw him, not even the sandwich, before he made his new move.* What do you think he's gonna do?

Callie: [Makes an eating noise.]

Molly: *It was such a great sandwich the bear loved it. But just as he was almost finished, he heard "sniffle, snuffle, slobber, snort!" behind him.* What do you think sniffling and snuffling and slobbering and snorting . . . ?

Callie: Dog!

Molly: You think? Why do you think that? What clues do you have?

Callie: The picture.

Molly: The picture is showing you what? You're making a prediction?

Callie: Yeah.

Molly: All right, let's see. *He had been seen!* Look at all those dogs, you were right. *The bear was so surprised that he ran out of the park and down the street until he spotted a very tall tree. From the top of the tree, the bear could see the forest. It was time to go home. The waves rocked the bear and he began to doze.* So the pictures give us hints about how the bear got home. How do you think the bear got home?

Callie: By boat.

Molly: By boat. There he is on the boat, and the waves are on the boat. *When he opened his eyes, he heard the breeze and familiar branches and the birds and the bugs' evening song. Well, the bear made it home just fine. So that's what happened to your sandwich. The bear ate it. I saw*

continued . . .

. . . from previous

it all. I tried to save your sandwich. I was able to save this little bit of lettuce here. The bear dropped it as he ran off, but I couldn't save the rest. I'm sorry to have to tell you about your sandwich this way, but now you know. So what clues does this page give us about who really ate the sandwich?

Callie: The bear.

Molly: Do you think the bear ate the sandwich? Who's that?

Callie: A dog.

Molly: And what do you think the dog might have done? Who do you think really ate the sandwich?

Callie: Umm, the bear.

Molly: Why?

Callie: 'Cause in the picture it showed the bear.

Molly: In the picture it showed the bear? Let's look at the last page. *Ruff, ruff, ruff.* Who do you think ate the sandwich now?

Callie: The bear.

Molly: The bear, not the dog?

Callie: The bear.

Molly: Why? What makes you think that?

Callie: I don't know, just the bear.

Molly: I sort of think the dog is trying to blame the bear. He made up this whole crazy story about the bear. We'll have to read again and see.

Let's begin with what I did well. I believe that I effectively elicit language with open-ended prompts. Callie tends to answer with short responses, and I give open-ended responses to elicit more. I hold her accountable for basing her responses in the text and in the pictures. I aim to make this an interactive read aloud, with an exchange of talk around the book. At the start of the read aloud, I make the book personally relevant to Callie by relating it to her dog. Finally, even with a very young reader, I introduce the sophisticated language of reading comprehension—words like *inference* and *prediction*.

In hindsight, this think aloud is largely ineffective because I do not truly model my insights and reading processes. The humor of this book is based on a hugely important inference—it was not really the bear who ate the sandwich, but rather a dog who was framing the bear! Callie misses this point entirely, and her failure to "get the book" is due to my ineffective read aloud. There are simply too many times that I ask her "What do you think?" rather than giving her a model of what I actually think. For these reasons, I'd be hard-pressed to call this an actual think aloud, since there are few moments where I show Callie the skills and strategies I use to make the necessary inferences for this book. In other words, I elicit her opinions many times but don't showcase the processes I am using to understand this picture book.

Now, take a look at a few think aloud scripts from teachers. In the right column, I added my feedback on their efforts. I can't emphasize enough that there is no absolutely "right" or "wrong" stopping point or think aloud wording, but I hope my feedback to these teachers provides some helpful pointers to you as you develop your own.

A Teacher's Think Aloud and My Feedback

The Giver by Lois Lowry, presented to fifth graders

What the Text Says	What I Say	The Comprehension Strategy I Model	The Feedback I'd Give to This Teacher
Cover of book	*The cover and title remind me of The Giving Tree by Shel Silverstein. The image of the old man juxtaposed with the forest leads me to believe that the book gets its namesake from this character, who spends his time in rural territory. I know Lois Lowry also wrote Number the Stars, a historical fiction novel set during the Holocaust. Perhaps this book will also contain elements of historical fiction.*	**Connection to previously discovered literature. Question about the trajectory of the narrative.**	*Simplify. For students who haven't read* The Giving Tree, *might this allusion confuse them? Is it the clearest thing to say? Your second sentence is long and hard to "get." Watch words like* namesake *and* juxtapose, *which are a stretch for most kids.*
It was almost December and Jonas was beginning to be frightened. No. Wrong word, Jonas thought. Frightened meant that deep, sickening feeling of something terrible about to happen. Frightened was the way he had felt a year ago when an unidentified aircraft had overflown the community twice. He had seen it both times. Squinting toward the sky, he had seen the sleek jet, almost a blur at its high speed, go past, and a second later heard the blast of sounds that followed. Then one more time, a moment later, from the opposite direction, the same plane. (p. 1)	*The more closely I regard this opening passage, the less likely I believe the novel will evolve as a work of historical fiction. What is this alleged "community" that harbors the protagonist Jonas and his friends, family, and acquaintances? Why would an aircraft elicit feelings of fear? I might return to this passage once I absorb more of the chapter.*	**Clarification about my initial impression based on the novel's title and cover. Questions about the opening passage's nuances. Possibility of rereading the varying events that the reader encounters in this brief passage.**	*Try to revise so your language is more like simple fleeting thoughts readers have. Maybe "The author uses* frightened *three times. Wow. Why would an aircraft be so terrible? What is this community he and his family are in?" This passage also evokes questions for me—where is this taking place? Is this during a war?*
Then all the citizens had been ordered to go into the nearest building and stay there. IMMEDIATELY, the rasping voice through the speakers had said. LEAVE YOUR BICYCLES WHERE THEY ARE. (p. 2)	*I picture this community more closely resembling a concentration camp or a prison than a quaint village. There are no inviting characteristics about raspy loudspeakers or barked orders. Immediately, the narrative takes an unnerving turn.*	**Visualization of the scene. Clarification of previously posed questions.**	*I appreciate how you try to clarify since that's one of the strategies with which we often struggle. I see this point as a valuable time to make an inference. The author doesn't come right out to tell us, but I'm getting the sense that Jonas and his community are in danger.*

What the Text Says	What I Say	The Comprehension Strategy I Model	The Feedback I'd Give to This Teacher
NEEDLESS TO SAY, HE WILL BE RELEASED, the voice had said, followed by silence. There was an ironic tone to the final message, as if the Speaker found it amusing; and Jonas had smiled a little, though he knew what a grim statement it had been. For a contributing citizen to be released from the community was a final decision, a terrible punishment, an overwhelming statement of failure.	*Despite the questionable conditions and evident restrictions bestowed upon the citizens of the community, they allegedly avoid displacement considering its disarming connotations. Nobody wants to leave, even if they sacrifice freedom. Maybe the outside world is a dangerous place.*	? **Asking questions.**	*Let's continue to simplify your language so that it's more student-friendly. Let's also let your voice shine through—by using those "I" statement sentence starters. How about "I'm wondering who the citizen was. What did he contribute? Why was he released, and why would being released be seen as a punishment?"*

The Kissing Hand by Audrey Penn, presented to first graders

What the Text Says	What I Say	The Comprehension Strategy I Model	The Feedback I'd Give to This Teacher
"Sometimes we all have to do things we don't want to do," she told him gently. "Even if they seem strange and scary at first. But you will love school once you start. You'll make new friends. And play with new toys. Read new books. And swing on new swings. Besides," she added. "I know a wonderful secret that will make your nights at school seem as warm and cozy as your days at home."	*I am curious to find out what her secret might be to make Chester feel better while they are apart during school.*	**Clarifying that Chester's mom has a secret to make him feel better and that will make him want to go to school.**	*Because you're not really addressing how you're fixing any confusion, this isn't really clarifying. You're really asking a question here, but it might be more fruitful to synthesize. How about "I'm really getting the sense that Chester's mom is trying to reassure him about how much he will like school"?*
Chester wiped away his tears and looked interested. "A secret? What kind of secret?" "A very old secret," said Mrs. Raccoon. "I learned it from my mother, and she learned it from hers. It's called the Kissing Hand."	*This made me happy and made me smile. It reminded me of when I am sad and I think of how my mom used to make me feel better when I felt sad. Thinking of my mom's tight hugs always makes me feel better.*	**Making a connection between my own experiences and the text.**	*Because the Common Core State Standards place less emphasis on making connections and more focus on close reading, I'd use this spot as a time to clarify. Young readers*

continued...

. . . from previous

What the Text Says	What I Say	The Comprehension Strategy I Model	The Feedback I'd Give to This Teacher
"The Kissing Hand?" asked Chester." "What's that?" "I'll show you." Mrs. Raccoon took Chester's left hand and spread open his tiny fingers into a fan. Leaning forward, she kissed Chester right in the middle of his palm. Chester felt his mother's kiss rush from his hand, up his arm, and into his heart.			*might be confused by this last sentence and its figurative language, so I might say, "At first I thought that Chester really felt the kiss moving up his body, but when I reread it, I realized that the author just means that the kiss made him feel safe and loved."*
Mrs. Raccoon took Chester's hand and carefully wrapped his fingers around the kiss. "Now, do be careful not to lose it," she teased him. "But, don't worry. When you open your hand and wash your food, I promise the kiss will stick." Chester loved his Kissing Hand. Now he knew his mother's love would go with him wherever he went. Even to school. That night, Chester stood in front of his school and looked thoughtful. Suddenly, he turned to his mother and grinned. "Give me your hand," he told her. Chester took his mother's hand in his own and unfolded her large, familiar fingers into a fan. Next, he leaned forward and kissed the center of her hand. "Now you have a Kissing Hand too," he told her. And with a gentle "Good-Bye" and "I love you," Chester turned and danced away.	*Chester seems happy to be going to school now. His mom's secret Kissing Hand really did make him feel much better.*	**Making a comment about how the Kissing Hand impacted the character to reach a happy conclusion.**	*While you give an accurate summary and make an inference about how Chester is feeling, this would be more powerful if it were delivered in "I" statements. How about "I'm getting the sense that the Kissing Hand reassures Chester"? Better yet, I see this as a chance to understand the author's purpose. I might say, "I like how the author has Chester use the Kissing Hand to reassure his mom. This makes me think that the author is telling me that moms miss their kids, just like kids miss their parents."*

Example of a Successful Think Aloud

Note: The italicized portions reflect the text directly.

***Miss Bindergarten Stays Home From Kindergarten* by Joseph Slate, presented to kindergartners**

Molly: *Miss Bindergarten Stays Home From Kindergarten*. Does anyone know Miss Bindergarten? Has anyone seen this character before? I chose this book because I know a teacher of yours who had to stay home this week. Is that true?

Kids: Yeah.

Molly: Who missed a couple days of school? Tell me.

Kids: Mrs. Rosado.

Molly: Mrs. Rosado? You made a connection between you and Mrs. Rosado.

Kid 1: Miss . . .

Molly: Oh my gosh! All these teachers who miss school. This is about a teacher who misses school. It's called *Miss Bindergarten Stays Home From Kindergarten*. And not only are you guys lucky to have Mrs. Rosado as your teacher, but you are lucky because in kindergarten you learn to read. And one of the things we know readers do is think while they're reading. So, when I read this book to you, I'm going to show you some of the thinking that I'm doing in my head. When you see me pointing to my head, that means I'm thinking about something that's going on in the book. When you see my finger tapping my head [Molly taps her head], it means my brain is going and that I'm thinking all sorts of things. *Miss Bindergarten Stays Home* From Kindergarten. *On Sunday morning, sad but true, Miss Bindergarten got the flu. "I'm aching and shaking right down to the bone. Tomorrow I fear I shall have to stay home."* I am thinking [Molly taps her head] the basic idea here is Miss Bindergarten is too sick. Even teachers have to miss school just like Miss Bindergarten. *On Monday—Miss Bindergarten stays home from kindergarten.* But she is in bed [Molly points to Miss Bindergarten], and her parrot is making her soup to help her feel better [Molly points to the parrot]. And bringing it to her in bed! *But at school—Adam hangs his jacket. Brenda stores her doll. Christopher asks, "Where is Miss B? I don't see her at all."* Hmm. I have a question [Molly taps her head]. Who might be the substitute for Miss Bindergarten, who is sick? We will find out. *"Good morning, kindergarten. I'm sorry to have to say, Miss Bindergarten called in sick and won't be here today." "I will be her substitute. My name is Mr. Tusky. I hope you'll help me through the day—I'm just a wee bit rusty."* I am wondering [Molly taps her head] what he means by

continued . . .

rusty. He is not covered in rust [Molly points to Mr. Tusky]. Maybe he means that he hasn't taught in a while so he's going to need the kids to help out. *Danny says, "I'll take you round!" Emily shows off Lizzy. After lunch, Franny moans, "My tummy hurts. I'm dizzy."* Hmm [Molly taps her head]. I am thinking that maybe Franny [Molly points to Franny] is getting the flu too. *On Tuesday, Miss Bindergarten and Franny stay home from kindergarten.* Hmm [Molly taps her head]. At first I thought they were both sick in the same house. But then when I looked at the pictures [Molly points to the pictures], I saw that, oh, this is one house—this is Miss Bindergarten's house. And then this is Franny's house. Here she is with her mom, sick in bed. *But at school Gwen fills in the calendar. Henry names who's who.* There he is helping Mr. Tusky and saying who's at school [Molly points to Henry]. *Ian cries, "Without Miss B, I don't know what we'll do."* I'm getting the sense that the class and Ian really miss their teacher [Molly taps her head]. *"I know you may be feeling sad, but there's not a thing to fear. Miss Bindergarten sent lesson plans. I have them all right here." "We'll sing a song, we'll read a book—oh, here's what we will do. Franny and Miss Bindergarten would love a card from you."* Have you guys made a card for someone who got sick? Anyone ever do that? It might be a nice thing to do. *Jessie paints a get-well card. Lenny's card says, "I feel hot, but I hope you're feeling better."* Hmm, I'm getting some new evidence [Molly taps her head]. I'm getting the idea that Lenny might be getting sick too. He says "I feel hot." I'm thinking maybe he might be getting the flu too [Molly points to the pictures]. On Wednesday—*Miss Bindergarten, Franny, and Lenny stay home from kindergarten.* I was right. Looks like Lenny's got the flu too [Molly points to the pictures]. *But at school—Matty snacks on crackers. Ophelia shares her celery, carrot sticks, and dip. Patricia says, "It's sharing time." Quentin does a trick. Raffie's yo-yo twirls and whirls. "Uh-oh," he says. "I'm sick."* I think [Molly taps her head] the author is telling me that the flu is contagious. The word *contagious* means that you could catch it from somebody. The teacher got sick, and now it looks like there are three kids who are sick. *On Thursday—Miss Bindergarten, Franny, Lenny, and Raffie stay home from kindergarten.* Sounds like a lot of that class is gone. *But at school—Mr. Tusky strums and sings. Sara drums along. Tommy claps and Ursula taps to Mr. Tusky's song. That afternoon—"It's time to go," says Mr. T. "I hate to say good-bye. But tomorrow, I'm advised, you'll have a big surprise."* Big surprise [Molly taps her head]. Please turn to a neighbor and say what you think the surprise might be.

[The students discuss their ideas in pairs. They raise their hands to share their thoughts.]

Molly: I see some of you are ready to share your ideas. Let's hear. Tell me more. Make that into a whole sentence.

Kid 1: Miss Bindergarten is coming back.

Molly: The surprise might be Miss Bindergarten is coming back? Thumbs up if that was your surprise. Did anyone have another idea? Let me hear some more ideas.

Kid 2: Everyone is going to be back.

Molly: Everyone is going to be back. Not just Miss Bindergarten but all the sick kids? That might be an idea. Let's hear more.

Kid 3: Someone is going to come over and do something.

Molly: Wow. We will have to read on and see. *Vicky pulls her parka on. She's the first in line. "Mr. Tusky," Wanda says, "we've had a real nice time."* And just like you, I am wondering what the surprise will be. *On Friday—surprise! Franny, Lenny, Raffie, and Miss Bindergarten are back in kindergarten.* Was that what you said [points to the students]? Good prediction. Good thinking. Readers are always thinking. *Xavier says, "We missed you!" Ulanda shouts, "Hurray!" "Mr. T. was fun," says Zack. "But I'm glad you're back today." "Thank you, kindergarten. I'm feeling so much better. I know we're all excited to be once again together. I never will forget your lovely cards and wishes. They made me feel that you were near, blowing get-well kisses. And I'm oh-so-very proud, as proud as I can be, that you worked like little troupers for our dear sub, Mr. T."* Hmm. In a nutshell, the big idea here is that everyone is glad to be back to the same old routine. *On Saturday and Sunday, everybody stays home from kindergarten . . . especially Mr. Tusky.* Take a look and see Mr. Tusky [Molly shows the book to the students]. How do you think Mr. Tusky is feeling now?

Kid 4: Sick!

Molly: How do you think he got sick? What do you think?

Kid 5: 'Cause everyone had the flu.

Molly: Yes! Remember that the flu is contagious and all the kids got sick? Maybe he got it, too. So, I am thinking [Molly taps her head] that it could be that Mr. Tusky caught the flu. That the germs were in the classroom.

Kid 5: Maybe because it was a little bit dirty everybody got sick.

Molly: That's why we always wash our hands in class. You guys are such good readers and thinkers, and I am hoping to come back to your class more this year and do some more reading. What do you think?

© Rick Harrington Photography

Reality check with a colleague! Think aloud your think alouds and get feedback from another teacher. Here I confab with Deborah Rosado, a kindergarten teacher.

As you can see from all these examples, reflecting on think alouds requires us to put our ego aside and embrace our mistakes as opportunities for improvement. This takes time and patience. If you are not quite ready to be critical of your own teaching, I have provided an additional transcript of a think aloud in Appendix F. This think aloud comes from my daughter's kindergarten classroom, where I read aloud Chris Van Dusen's *The Circus Ship* (2009).

Final Thoughts

Finally, I encourage you to work collaboratively with your colleagues to build your think aloud skills. Invite each other into your classrooms and ask your colleagues to watch you think aloud. As I watch teachers think aloud, I like to not only record the think aloud but also use an open-ended feedback form such as the one provided on the facing page. This form encourages both positive and constructive feedback, but also allots space for general comments and questions.

The opportunities for ongoing professional development in thinking aloud are plentiful. Work in your school and district communities to create and share a repository of think aloud videos; your school could create a private YouTube channel where teachers could upload videos to share and critique. Log into preexisting online outlets to watch and evaluate videos of think alouds—my favorite are YouTube, TeacherTube, and the Teaching Channel. Follow the steps of my research team and commit to constant improvement of your think alouds.

FEEDBACK FORM FOR THINK ALOUD REFLECTIONS

Jot down what worked in the think aloud you observed.	Jot down what was less effective in the think aloud you observed.
Jot down any questions you had about what you observed.	Jot down any additional comments, thoughts, or feedback.

online resources

Available for download at **resources.corwin.com/ness-thinkalouds**

Big Possibilities

Here are some ideas for incorporating technology into your think alouds.

- With teachers in your community, create a modified version of a book club. Your texts could be transcripts of think alouds to evaluate, tweak, critique, and revise.
- Visit NowComment.com. The purpose of this free website is to facilitate conversations. It allows users to create an account and upload documents, video clips, or audio segments. Upload videos or transcripts of yourself to your account, and then specify who should view them. Viewers can then watch and comment at exact points. Imagine the possibilities! Novice teachers can record themselves thinking aloud and share the video with their mentors. The mentors can watch the video, comment at exact points, and share their reflections—all from the comfort of their couch! Upper-grade readers may even be ready to use NowComment.com to watch videos of their teachers thinking aloud.

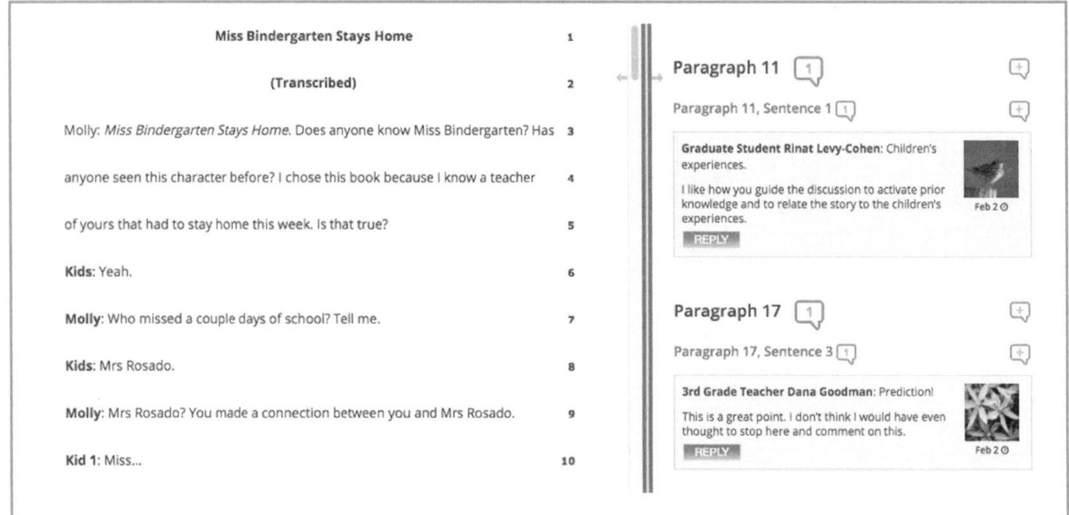

A screenshot from NowComment.com.

- Many elementary classrooms use tablets or computers to have students watch and listen to audiobooks on headphones; many teachers use these as their fluency centers. Modify this time to model think alouds so students get a dose of fluency instruction and comprehension! Work with teachers in your school to create a private YouTube channel of your think alouds involving favorite classroom literature. As students watch your videos, they get the benefit of seeing you think aloud—on a previously recorded video!

Ready for a Trial Run?

Have you had the opportunity to watch or listen to yourself while teaching? Let's follow the recommendations of Linda Kucan (2007), who recommends that teachers select a manageable chunk of time—like fifteen minutes—and write down every word that they say and that students say:

> Transcript analysis allows teachers to capture what cannot be captured in any other way—the talking and thinking that transpires in classrooms on a daily basis. Transcript analysis also allows teachers to see what happens when they are more thoughtful about the kinds of texts they ask students to think about and to become more aware of the kinds of questions they ask and the kinds of responses they make to students. (p. 236)

Take one of the think aloud scripts you've generated so far and record yourself while thinking aloud in front of students. Make the video- or audiotaping a simple process—use your smartphone or tablet. As you watch yourself teach, transcribe your lesson so that you can examine how closely you followed your originally planned script and evaluate the appropriateness of your think alouds. Reflect on the following questions:

- What was the think aloud process like for you? What about thinking aloud worked for you? What about thinking aloud didn't work?
- What about thinking aloud was easy for you? What about thinking aloud was hard for you?
- How closely did you follow your original script? Where did you deviate from your original plans? As you changed your plans, did it make your think aloud more or less effective?

CHAPTER 7

Students Do

Tips and Tools for Helping Your Readers Think Aloud on Their Own

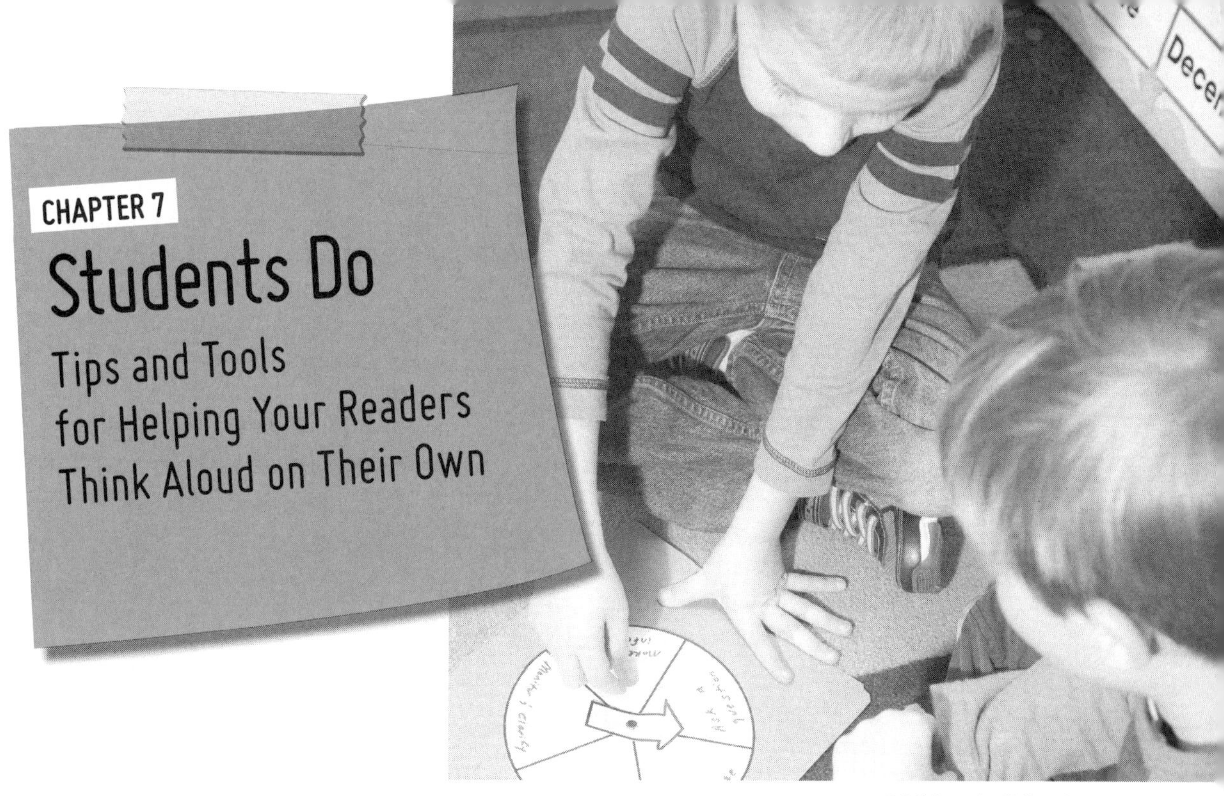

© Rick Harrington Photography

By this point in the book, I've shown you exactly how to approach a text, how to choose your stopping points, and how to generate a think aloud. As you become adept at thinking aloud, you'll be more and more ready to hand over the reins to students so their reading brains do the complex work that leads to skilled reading. As Jeffrey Wilhelm (2001) wrote, "think-alouds are a means to an end—and that end is engaged and reflective reading" (p. 16). But how do we get there? How do we transfer thinking aloud to our students, who in time morph the "aloud" aspect so it's a good, old, strong reading process?

In this chapter, we move out of the pure "I Do" phase of teacher as sole generator of think alouds and into the "We Do" and "You Do" phases of the *gradual release of responsibility* model (Pearson & Gallagher, 1983a) that I introduced in Chapter 1. This "I Do, We Do, You Do" movement will help facilitate students' independent use of comprehension strategies in their everyday reading.

Using Gradual Release of Responsibility to Scaffold Think Alouds

This long-standing instructional model shifts the cognitive load from the teacher to students, no matter the endeavor. The steps are purposeful and deliberate, moving from teacher/expert centered to student/novice centered. Gradual release of responsibility begins with the "I Do" phase, in which the teacher (the "I") provides direction instruction, which is often referred to as modeling or demonstrating. Next is the "We Do" phase—often called guided instruction or guided practice—which can take different forms, including partner work, small group work, fishbowl, and so on. This phase is guided by the teacher or another expert, but the students should be doing the lion's share of the work. The third phase is independent practice, or the "You Do" phase (with the "You" being students). As I explain each phase in further detail below, I focus on how it might look with think alouds. The gradual release of responsibility can actually be a recursive process, rather than linear (for example, you could jump in with "We Do" and then move to "I Do"), but for the sake of explanation of think alouds, I will walk through the model in a linear manner.

The "I Do" Phase

By far the most teacher-dominated step, the focused instruction phase aims to establish the purpose of the lesson/learning endeavor. The aim here is for teachers to be explicit in their explanation and modeling of the whys and hows of a skill. The explicitness of teacher description is essential here. In the "I Do" phase of reading comprehension instruction, a teacher should model and define the strategy. Duke and Pearson (2002) provide the following example to illustrate the "I Do" phase:

> Predicting is making guesses about what will come next in the text you are reading. You should make predictions a lot when you read. I am going to make predictions while I read this book. I will start with just the cover here. Hmm . . . I see a picture of an owl . . . I predict that this is going to be a make-believe story. (p. 209)

The majority of this book focuses on the "I Do" phase, walking you through the steps necessary for the explicit modeling of thinking aloud. Much like the example above, the "I Do" phase begins when the teacher defines and sets a purpose for his or her think aloud—I've provided student-friendly definitions of this book's five focal strategies to jump-start your explicit definitions (see Chapter 2). In the "I Do" phase, you use the scripts you've written (with this book's three-column chart and sentence starters) and a visual cue (as explained in Chapter 5) to explicitly model your think aloud.

Encouraging Students' Noticing and Noting

As students become accustomed to watching their teachers think aloud, I like to get them more actively involved in the process. I do this through a checklist I call the "Think Aloud Catcher: Put a Check ✓ When You Hear a Strategy." Typically, this is more appropriate for students in Grades 3 and up, with the idea being that students monitor how many strategies a teacher incorporated. I give each student a checklist—as shown on the next page—on which they simply note the strategy I'm using. Remember that I use a visual cue to signify that I'm thinking aloud, so this action alerts my students that it's time to determine which strategy I'm using. I might direct them as follows:

> As I think aloud, I want you to use your observation sheet to determine which strategy I'm using. Listen for the sentence starters you've heard before. You'll see me tap my head to show you I'm thinking aloud, and then it's your turn to put a check mark next to the strategy I've used. Sometimes I'll ask you to turn and talk to a neighbor to check in about which strategy I've used.

To modify this idea for younger children, I might give each child a ring of five index cards; on each card is the name of a strategy and the strategy symbol. As I read and think aloud, I might direct my students to wave the appropriate strategy symbol from their ring in the air and say:

> As I think aloud, I want you to show me on your ring of cards which strategy I'm using. Listen for the sentence starters you've seen before. You'll see me tap my head to show you I'm thinking aloud, and then it's your turn to hold up a card. So if you hear me say, "I wonder," you'll put the card with the question mark in the air.

Build in plenty of opportunities for students to turn and talk in the midst of your think aloud. The brain that does the work is the brain that learns!

Quickly scanning the room and seeing which cards are in the air gives me a snapshot of which students are grasping my think aloud and which ones need additional support.

THINK ALOUD CATCHER
Put a ✓ When You Hear a Strategy

Your teacher will be thinking aloud to show you what readers do when they read. Tally up how many times you hear your teacher use the following strategies.

Strategy	Number of Times You Heard It (put a ✓ for each time!)
Asking questions	
Making inferences	
Synthesizing	
Understanding the author's purpose	
Monitoring and clarifying	

Available for download at **resources.corwin.com/ness-thinkalouds**

Either variation—using an observation sheet for older readers or a ring of strategy symbols for younger readers—begins to hold students accountable for noticing and identifying which comprehension strategies I include in a think aloud.

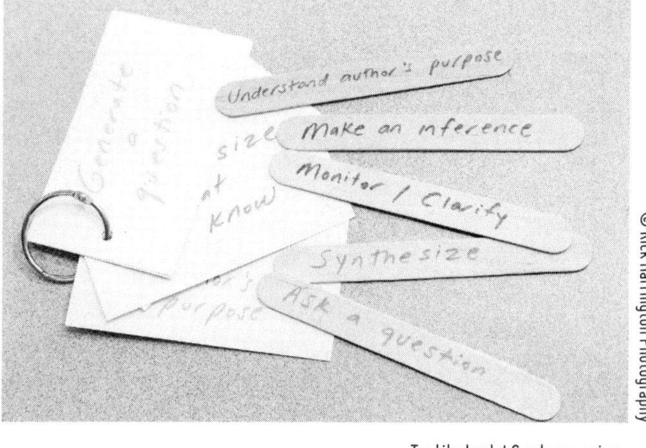

Tactile tools! Cards on a ring and Popsicle sticks are two crowd pleasers with readers of any age.

The "We Do" Phase: Introducing the Think Along

As the name implies, in this second phase of the gradual release of responsibility, the teacher shares the instructional responsibility with students as they approach the task collaboratively. This is often referred to as guided instruction or guided practice. Students no longer merely watch a teacher as he or she provides instruction; they join in to complete the process alongside their classmates and teacher. Following the example from Duke and Pearson (2002), a teacher in the "We Do" phase might say:

> I have made some good predictions so far in the book. From this part on, I want you to make predictions with me. Each of us should stop and think about what might happen next. . . . Okay, now let's hear what you think and why. . . . After every few pages, I will ask each of you to stop and make a prediction. We will talk about your predictions and then read on to see if they come true.

The teacher here is still an integral player, jumping in to provide feedback, lend additional support, and clarify confusion.

I'd like to borrow a term from Wilhelm (2001) and introduce the idea of a *think along* as a key step in the "We Do" phase of thinking aloud. In a think along, a teacher completes *some* of the initial steps of thinking aloud, leaving others purposefully incomplete to which students contribute.

My adaptation of a think along has two important elements: (1) preselected stopping points and (2) a logical reading comprehension strategy that corresponds to each of the stopping points. To introduce a think along, I preselect the stopping points in a particular text. Knowing when to stop is often one of the most difficult elements for students; without this complicated process, students have ample energy to focus on comprehension. Not only do I choose the stopping points, but I also provide a logical comprehension strategy to apply to each stopping point. In other words, my sticky note marks where I want readers to stop and what I want them to do at each stopping point. Students then choose from one of the relevant sentence starters to complete the think along.

"We Do" Chart

Where You Should Stop	The Comprehension Strategy You'd Use	What You Might Say

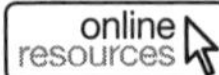

Available for download at **resources.corwin.com/ness-thinkalouds**

Let's try it out with the classic storybook *A Bad Case of Stripes* by David Shannon (1998). This engaging book tells the story of Camilla Cream, a young girl. When Camilla turns into a rainbow of colors, the only cure is for her to be true to herself. The book helps young readers explore the risks of trying to be like everyone else. To involve students in a think along, I might use a modified version of the three-column chart. As you will see, this think aloud chart looks a bit different—I've identified the stopping point and the comprehension strategy that is a logical fit. The only missing element is the script—this is where students jump in. In the "We Do" phase, students revisit the sentence starters (introduced in Chapter 2 and provided in Appendix D) to jump-start their thinking.

The third column is not meant to be done as independent seatwork or homework. Why? Because we are still in the second of three steps of the gradual release of responsibility, where teacher and students share the task. Completing the "What You Might Say" task should be collaborative work; a teacher might do this as a whole group activity, for example by having students turn and talk with small groups to work on the third column together. Overall, students really need and benefit from this guided support.

That said, even within the "We Do" phase, there are levels of scaffolding that we can remove to increase students' responsibility. In the most supportive approach, the teacher identifies the stopping point and the comprehension strategy that makes sense for it. The opportunities for differentiation here are numerous. Some struggling students might need the additional support of the best-fit sentence starter provided for them so that they essentially fill in the remainder of the sentence. More advanced students might need only the stopping point identified; they may be ready to make the leap to the best-fit comprehension strategy and what they would say. Some students might not be ready to write out their think alouds and might merely say them, with the teacher or an aide acting as their scribe. Older students might be ready to complete the third column as a sort of writing log.

The "We Do" Phase for *A Bad Case of Stripes* by David Shannon

Where You Should Stop	The Comprehension Strategy You'd Use	What You Might Say
Camilla Cream loved lima beans. But she never ate them.	? **Asking questions**	
All of her friends hated lima beans, and she wanted to fit in. Camilla was always worried about what other people thought of her.	**Making inferences**	
Today she was fretting even more than usual. It was the first day of school, and she couldn't decide what to wear. There were so many people to impress! She tried on forty-two outfits, but none seemed quite right. She put on a pretty red dress and looked in the mirror. Then she screamed.	? **Asking questions**	
Her mother ran into the room, and she screamed, too. "Oh my heavens!" she cried. "You're completely covered with stripes!"	? **Asking questions**	
This was certainly true. Camilla was striped from head to toe. She looked like a rainbow. Mrs. Cream felt Camilla's forehead. "Do you feel all right?" she asked. "I feel fine," Camilla answered, "but just look at me!" "You get back in bed this instant," her mother ordered. "You're not going to school today." Camilla was relieved. She didn't want to miss the first day of school, but she was afraid of what the other kids would say. And she had no idea what to wear with those crazy stripes.	**Synthesizing**	
That afternoon, Dr. Bumble came to examine Camilla. "Most extraordinary!" he exclaimed. "I've never seen anything like it. Are you having any coughing, sneezing, runny nose, aches, pains, chills, hot flashes, dizziness, drowsiness, shortness of breath, or uncontrollable twitching?"	A **Understanding the author's purpose**	

Where You Should Stop	The Comprehension Strategy You'd Use	What You Might Say
"No," Camilla told him. "I feel fine." "Well then," Dr. Bumble said, turning to Mrs. Cream. "I don't see any reason why she shouldn't go to school tomorrow. Here's some ointment that should help clear up those stripes in a few days. If it doesn't, you know where to reach me." And off he went.	**Synthesizing**	
The next day was a disaster. Everyone at school laughed at Camilla. They called her "Camilla Crayon" and "Night of the Living Lollipop." She tried her best to act as if everything were normal, but when the class said the Pledge of Allegiance, her stripes turned red, white, and blue, and she broke out in stars!	? **Asking questions**	
The other kids thought this was great. One yelled out, "Let's see some purple polka dots!" Sure enough, Camilla turned all purple polka-dotty. Someone else shouted, "Checkerboard!" and a pattern of squares covered her skin. Soon everyone was calling out different shapes and colors, and poor Camilla was changing faster than you can change channels on a T.V.	**Making inferences**	
That night, Mr. Harms, the school principal, called. "I'm sorry, Mrs. Cream," he said. "I'm going to have to ask you to keep Camilla home from school. She's just too much of a distraction, and I've been getting calls from the other parents. They're afraid those stripes may be contagious."	**Monitoring and clarifying**	
Camilla was so embarrassed. She couldn't believe that two days ago everyone liked her.	**Monitoring and clarifying**	
Now, nobody wanted to be in the same room with her.	**Monitoring and clarifying**	

continued...

. . . from previous

Where You Should Stop	The Comprehension Strategy You'd Use	What You Might Say
Her father tried to make her feel better. "Is there anything I can get you, sweetheart?" he asked. "No, thank you," sighed Camilla. What she really wanted was a nice plate of lima beans, but she had been laughed at enough for one day.	? **Asking questions**	
"Hmmmm, well, yes, I see," Dr. Bumble mumbled when Mr. Cream phoned the next day. "I think I'd better bring in the Specialists. We'll be right over." About an hour later, Dr. Bumble arrived with four people in long white coats. He introduced them to the Creams. "This is Dr. Grop, Dr. Sponge, Dr. Cricket, and Dr. Young." Then the Specialists went to work on Camilla. They squeezed and jabbed, tapped and tested. It was very uncomfortable. "Well, it's not the mumps," concluded Dr. Grop. "Or the measles," said Dr. Sponge. "Definitely not chicken pox," put in Dr. Cricket. "Or sunburn," said Dr. Young. "Try these," said the Specialists. They each handed her a bottle filled with different colored pills. "Take one of each before bed," said Dr. Grop. Then they filed out the front door, followed by Dr. Bumble.	A **Understanding the author's purpose**	
That night, Camilla took her medicine. It was awful. When she woke up the next morning, she did feel different, but when she got dressed, her clothes didn't fit right. She looked in the mirror, and there, staring back at her, was a giant, multi-colored pill with her face on it.	III **Making inferences**	
Dr. Bumble rushed over as soon as Mrs. Cream called. But this time, instead of the Specialists, he brought the Experts.	? **Asking questions**	

Where You Should Stop	The Comprehension Strategy You'd Use	What You Might Say
Dr. Gourd and Mr. Mellon were the finest scientific minds in the land. Once again, Camilla was poked and prodded, looked at and listened to. The Experts wrote down lots of numbers. Then they huddled together and whispered. Dr. Gourd finally spoke. "It might be a virus," he announced with authority. Suddenly, fuzzy little virus balls appeared all over Camilla. "Or possibly some form of bacteria," said Mr. Mellon. Out popped squiggly little bacteria tails. "Or it could be a fungus," added Dr. Gourd. Instantly, Camilla was covered with different colored fungus blotches.	A **Understanding the author's purpose**	
The Experts looked at Camilla, then back at each other. "We need to go over these numbers again back at the lab," Dr. Gourd explained. "We'll call you when we know something." But the Experts didn't have a clue, much less a cure.	**Synthesizing**	
By now, the T.V. news had found out about Camilla. Reporters from every channel were outside her house, telling the story of "The Bizarre Case of the Incredible Changing Kid."	**Making inferences**	
The Creams were swamped with all kinds of remedies from psychologists, allergists, herbalists, nutritionists, psychics, an old medicine man, a guru, and even a veterinarian.	**Monitoring and clarifying** A **Understanding the author's purpose**	
Each so-called cure only added to poor Camilla's strange appearance until it was hard to even recognize her. She sprouted roots and berries and crystals and feathers and a long furry tail. But nothing worked.	? **Asking questions**	

continued...

. . . from previous

Where You Should Stop	The Comprehension Strategy You'd Use	What You Might Say
One day, a woman who called herself an Environmental Therapist claimed she could cure Camilla. "Close your eyes," she said. "Breathe deeply, become one with your room." "I wish you hadn't said that," Camilla groaned. Slowly, she started to melt into the walls of her room. Her bed became her mouth, her nose was a dresser, and two paintings were her eyes. The therapist screamed and ran from the house. "What are we going to do?" cried Mrs. Cream. "It just keeps getting worse and worse!" She began to sob.	**Synthesizing**	
At that moment, Mr. Cream heard a quiet knock at the front door. He opened it, and there stood an old woman who was just as plump and sweet as a strawberry. "Excuse me," she said brightly. "But I think I can help."	? **Asking questions**	
She went into Camilla's room and looked around. "My goodness," she said with a shake of her head. "What we have here is a *bad* case of stripes. One of the worst I've ever seen!" She pulled a container of small green beans from her bag. "Here," she said. "These might do the trick."	? **Asking questions**	
"Are those magic beans?" asked Mrs. Cream. "Oh my, no," replied the kind old woman. "There's no such thing. These are just plain old lima beans. I'll bet you'd like some, wouldn't you?" she asked Camilla.	A **Understanding the author's purpose**	

Where You Should Stop	The Comprehension Strategy You'd Use	What You Might Say
Camilla wanted a big, heaping plateful of lima beans more than just about anything, but she was still afraid to admit it. "Yuck!" she said. "No one likes lima beans, especially me!" "Oh, dear," the old woman said sadly. "I guess I was wrong about you." She put the beans back in her bag and started toward the door.	**Monitoring and clarifying**	
Camilla watched the old woman walk away. Those beans would taste *so* good. And being laughed at for eating them was nothing, compared to what she'd been going through. She finally couldn't stand it. "Wait!" she cried. "The truth is . . . I really love lima beans." "I thought so," the old woman said with a smile. She took a handful of beans and popped them into Camilla's mouth. "Mmmmm," said Camilla.	**Making inferences**	
Suddenly the branches, feathers, and squiggly tails began to disappear. Then the whole room swirled around. When it stopped, there stood Camilla, and everything was back to normal. "I'm cured!" she shouted. "Yes," said the old woman. "I knew the real you was in there somewhere." She patted Camilla on the head. Then she went outside and vanished into the crowd.	**Synthesizing**	
Afterward, Camilla wasn't quite the same. Some of the kids at school said she was weird, but she didn't care a bit. She ate all the lima beans she wanted, and she never had even a touch of stripes again.	A **Understanding the author's purpose**	

In Appendix G, you'll find my script of the think aloud for *A Bad Case of Stripes*. It's not important that your think aloud matches exactly the one I've provided; after all, different readers approach the text differently.

Some students may prefer think alongs that go in the other direction; rather than the teacher providing the comprehension strategy and having students generate the script, they may benefit from determining the comprehension strategy based on a script written by the teacher. The following think along is an example of this; I've used the historical fiction picture book *Mighty Jackie: The Strike-Out Queen* (Moss, 2004) and generated the think aloud. In the "We Do" phase, students would work to identify the comprehension strategy behind each thought. To make this a more challenging process, I would not use the exact language of the sentence starters; otherwise students could merely scan for key phrases, rather than doing the thinking process behind the task. The example below shows how I've included alternate types of language for this task. Some prompts rely on multiple strategies, so it is acceptable for students to identify more than one strategy.

A Think Along for *Mighty Jackie: The Strike-Out Queen* by Marissa Moss

What the Text Says	What I Say	The Comprehension Strategy I Model
It was April 2, 1931, and something amazing was about to happen. In Chattanooga, Tennessee, two teams were about to play an exhibition game of baseball.	*I wonder what exhibition means. I'm thinking about the root word exhibit—a display or a show of something. I'm thinking that an exhibition game doesn't really count, but it's just for show.*	
One was the New York Yankees, a legendary team with famous players—Babe Ruth, Lou Gehrig, and Tony Lazzeri. The other was the Chattanooga Lookouts, a small team, a nothing team, except for the pitcher, Jackie Mitchell.	*It sounds like the Chattanooga Lookouts don't matter so much as a team, but the word except is an important signal. The author is using this word to tell me that Jackie Mitchell is somehow important. I wonder why this pitcher is so important.*	
Jackie was young, only seventeen years old, but that's not what made people sit up and take notice. Jackie was a girl, and everyone knew that girls didn't play major-league baseball.	*I've got all sorts of questions. Is it the rule that girls can't play—or is it just that they don't play? How did Jackie get to be on a major-league team, as a girl?*	

What the Text Says	What I Say	The Comprehension Strategy I Model
The *New York Daily News* sneered that she would swing "a mean lipstick" instead of a bat. A reporter wrote that you might as well have "a trained seal behind the plate" as have a woman standing there. But Jackie was no trained seal. She was a pitcher, a mighty good one. The question was, was she good enough to play against the New York Yankees?	*I'm really getting the sense that people doubt Jackie's skills.*	
As long as she could remember, Jackie had played ball with her father. She knew girls weren't supposed to. All the kids at school, all the boys in her neighborhood told her that. When one boy yelled at another one, "You throw like a girl!" it was an insult—everyone knew girls couldn't throw a ball. Or that's what they thought.	*Again, the author is giving me a hint—by telling me "Or that's what they thought." I think I may find out that girls can throw a ball.*	
Day after day, in the neighborhood sandlot, Jackie's father told her differently. He said she could throw balls, and she did. She ran bases, she swung the bat. By the time she was eight years old, Dazzy Vance, the stat pitcher for the Brooklyn Dodgers, had taught her how to pitch. A real pitcher talking to a little girl was all Jackie needed to start dreaming of playing in the World Series. Her father saw her talent and so did Dazzy. He told her she could be good at whatever she wanted, as long as she worked at it. And Jackie worked at baseball. She worked hard. She practiced pitching till it was too cold and dark to stay outside. She threw balls until her shoulder ached and her fingers were callused. She pitched until her eyes blurred over and she couldn't see where she was throwing. But it didn't matter, her arm knew.	*The author is giving me lots of clues about how hard Jackie works at baseball. I wonder if she practices so much because she wants to make her dad proud or if it's something she really loves. My guess is that she's so determined because she likes hard work and she wants to prove her skill to everyone who doubts her.*	

continued . . .

...from previous

What the Text Says	What I Say	The Comprehension Strategy I Model
And now she was finally going to have her chance to play on a real baseball team, to pitch to real players. The stands were packed. A crowd of four thousand had come to see the strange sight of a woman on the pitcher's mound.	*I'm wondering whether those 4,000 fans are going to support Jackie, or whether they might boo her. The author has already told me that newspapers poked fun of Jackie. This story also takes place in the 1930s, when women didn't have as many rights and as many jobs as they do now. The word strange also makes me think that people aren't there to support her, but maybe that they will make fun of her.*	
She stood tall on the field and looked back at the crowd in the bleachers. They were waiting for her to make a mistake, and she knew it. They were waiting for her to prove that baseball was a man's game, not her game. "It is my game," she muttered to herself and bit her lip. The Yankees were up, top of the first, and the batter was walking up to the plate. Jackie was ready for him, the ball tight in her left hand. Except the batter was Babe Ruth—Babe Ruth, the "Home Run King," a big mountain of a man—and Babe didn't like the idea of a woman pitcher at all. He thought woman were "too delicate" for baseball. "They'll never make good," he said. "It would kill them to play ball every day." He walked to the plate and tipped his cap at Jackie. But if she thought he was going to go easy on her, she could forget it! He gripped the bat and got ready to slam the ball out of the ballpark.	*The author is building a lot of suspense here—a definite conflict between Jackie and Babe Ruth, who doubts the abilities of women.*	
Jackie held that ball like it was part of her arm, and when she threw it, she knew exactly where it would go. Right over the plate, right where the Babe wasn't expecting it, right where he watched it speed by and thwunk into the catcher's mitt. "Strike One!" Babe Ruth gaped—he couldn't believe it! The crowd roared. Jackie tried to block them out, to see only the ball, to feel only the ball.	*I can visualize Jackie standing on the mound, staring down Babe Ruth—now there are two balls and one strike and she's feeling nervous. It's loud because so many people are there to watch her, but I predict that Jackie is going to strike out Babe Ruth and show them all—just like she's saying to herself.*	

What the Text Says	What I Say	The Comprehension Strategy I Model
But Babe Ruth was facing her down now, determined not to let a girl make a fool out of him. She flinched right before the next pitch, and the umpire called a ball. "Hmmmph," the Babe snorted. "You can do it!" Jackie told herself. "Girls can throw—show them!" But the next pitch was another ball. Jackie closed her eyes. She felt her fingers tingling around the ball, she felt it heft in her palm, she felt the force of her shoulder muscles as she wound up for the pitch. She remembered what her father had told her: "Go out there and pitch just like you pitch to anybody else."		
"Strike Two!" This was serious. The Babe was striking out and the pitcher was a girl! Jackie wasn't mad, but she wasn't scared either. She was pitching, really pitching, and it felt like something was happening the way it had always been meant to. She knew the batter would expect the same pitch, close and high, even if the batter was Babe Ruth.	*The author is giving me all sorts of hints about Jackie's personality. I get the sense that she's hardworking and determined—from all that practice. She's confident in her abilities and unfazed by the crowd or by the fame of Babe Ruth. But the author is also telling me that she's smart—she's thinking through the best pitch to throw. All of these clues make me think that the author is rooting for Jackie.*	
So this time she threw the ball straight down the middle with all the speed she could put on it. "Strike Three!" Babe Ruth glared at the umpire and threw the bat down in disgust. He told reporters that that would be the last time he'd bat against a woman! The crowd was stunned. A girl had struck out the "Sultan of Swat!" It couldn't be! It was a mistake, a fluke! But wait, here came Lou Gehrig, the "Iron Horse," up to the plate. He'd show her. She couldn't strike him out too.	*I predict that Jackie will strike out Lou Gehrig—I'm still thinking that the author is rooting for Jackie!*	
Lou Gehrig swung with a mighty grunt, but his bat hit nothing but air. "Strike One!" He looked stunned, then dug in his heels and glared at Jackie. "Strike Two!"	*I'm also getting the sense that Jackie is calm and can't be intimidated. Earlier, Babe Ruth threw his bat down. Now Lou Gehrig is glaring at her. The crowd is yelling. She doesn't seem to be nervous, though!*	

continued . . .

. . . from previous

What the Text Says	What I Say	The Comprehension Strategy I Model
Jackie grinned. She was doing what she'd worked so hard and long to do, and nothing could stop her. She pitched the ball the way she knew best, a lefty pitch with a low dip in it. No one could touch a ball like that when it was thrown right. "Strike Three!" The crowd, so ready to boo her before, rose with a roar, clapping and cheering like crazy.	*I wonder why the crowd now supports her. Are they starting to think that she's a good pitcher, when before they just figured that girls couldn't pitch?*	
Back to back, Jackie had struck out two of baseball's best batters, Babe Ruth and Lou Gehrig. She'd proven herself and now the fans loved her for it. But Jackie didn't hear them. She was too proud and too happy. She'd done what she'd always known she could do. She's shown the world how a girl could throw—as hard and as fast and as far as she wanted.	*I've always heard "throwing like a girl" be used in a negative connotation—sort of like a pejorative thing. But this author is telling me that throwing like a girl—like Jackie Mitchell—is a good thing!*	

Think alongs provide a supportive way for students to begin the process of thinking aloud. Students are no longer passive receivers of teacher-generated think alouds. They get their feet wet as they take on some of the responsibility for thinking aloud. They rely on safety nets—the predetermined stopping points, the clearly identified comprehension strategies, and the sentence starters—to build the skills to get them one step closer toward independence.

The "You Do" Phase

In the final step, the teacher removes her- or himself from instruction and allows students to take over. The last phase—independent practice—gives students the opportunity to practice their newly learned skill in a new situation. While students work, the teacher circulates to observe, leap in when needed, assess, and provide corrective feedback. A teacher might give directions as follows:

> It is time for silent reading. As you read today . . . be sure to make predictions every two or three pages. Check as you read to see whether your prediction came true. (Duke & Pearson, 2002, pp. 208–210)

Our ultimate goal in the "You Do" phase is that the think alouds we have modeled are so internalized that our students engage in strategic reading. There is no secret recipe to know when your students are ready for this last phase. In my previous work with struggling readers at a university reading clinic, I provided at least five think alouds in the "I Do" phase to ensure students had solid models of my approach. I was sure to think aloud across various genres, as I've done in previous chapters of this book. I would then allow students about two weeks of the "We Do" phase, where we did think alongs with various levels of support.

Monitoring Student Progress During the "You Do" Phase

Stepping back as a teacher often evokes feelings of uncertainty and anxiety. We've removed the training wheels from students' bicycles, held them as they try to balance, protected them with helmets and pads—and now it feels like they are taking off by themselves, speeding down a steep hill. With regard to think alouds and independent reading, teachers often wonder, "How do we know our students are 'getting it'? How do we gauge how well they are applying the skills and strategies we taught?"

In the initial parts of the "You Do" phase, I build in checks to ensure that students are focused and productive. Think alouds transform boring reading logs into highly personal reading reflection. Most children are assigned independent reading as either classwork or homework; writing a summary of that day's reading is a frequently assigned task. This assignment becomes highly personal and relevant with a slight modification to the prompt. Instead of a summary, there are endless possibilities for students to respond to the following prompt: *Tell me what you were thinking as you read today. What were you wondering, learning, questioning, and inferring?*

When writing an entire entry is too cumbersome, students might use sticky notes to record quick thoughts. I visited a fourth-grade classroom where students independently read Andrew Clements's *Frindle* (1996). During their assigned reading time, students were required to produce a predetermined number of think alouds:

> As you finish Chapter 5 in *Frindle*, use three sticky notes to jot down your thinking at any three points in the chapter. Write exactly what you'd say, but don't identify a reading comprehension strategy.

Students then shared their sticky notes with a partner, who was responsible for identifying the reading comprehension strategy associated with each think aloud. Finally, students placed their sticky notes on large sheets of butcher paper, titled with the various reading comprehension strategies.

In a whole group conversation, the teacher led a discussion about which strategies the class had favored and the various ways that individuals had approached the same strategy.

Encouraging Self-Evaluation With Think Alouds

In my work with teachers, I am frequently asked about tying assessment to think alouds. Teachers naturally want to know how to evaluate students' independent abilities to think aloud. This question is not a simple one to answer; we cannot ever truly know what is going on inside the minds of our readers. Because of their highly personal and qualitative nature, I have a difficult time grading think alouds with a letter or a number equivalent. Because a primary goal of thinking aloud is to encourage students to be metacognitive, I encourage the use of self-evaluations. Walker (2005) explains that passive readers often have difficulty getting excited or recognizing the positive strategies that they have used; thus, self-evaluations are a meaningful way to encourage engagement, build metacognition, and reward readers. The chart on the next page (and in Appendix H) shows a version of a think aloud self-evaluation, modified from the work of Wilhelm (2001).

Applying Think Alouds Across Content Areas

During my yearlong study, I observed that the majority of participants relied on narrative text for their think alouds. As much as I encouraged them to think aloud using a variety of texts, participants naturally gravitated toward narratives. Evidence from multiple researchers shows that reading comprehension improves when students are taught to think aloud using informational text (Coiro, 2011; Lapp, Fisher, & Grant, 2008; Ortlieb & Norris, 2012). Considering the weight that informational text carries in the Common Core State Standards (CCSS Initiative, 2010), it is especially important that teachers have ample opportunities to think aloud across content areas and text genres.

Think alouds are not only the purview of English language arts or reading teachers. They should not be relegated to literacy blocks. We have the opportunity to think aloud many times a day across many instructional purposes. Any time I have the opportunity to read a text aloud to my students, I can model my thinking. Not every think aloud should be isolated to what I think of as traditional read aloud environments. By this, I mean that not every think aloud should occur using a picture book, with students sitting on the rug in front of you.

Effective teachers think aloud while they tackle content-heavy passages in science and social studies. I have watched teachers think aloud

SELF-EVALUATION CHART FOR READERS

How often did I . . . ?

	Not much	Sometimes	Often
Ask questions			
Make inferences			
Synthesize			
Understand the author's purpose			
Monitor and clarify			

The strategy I used the most is ____

____.

The best example of exactly what I thought while I used that strategy is ____________________

____.

One strategy that I did not use at all or enough is ________________________________

____.

An example of how I could use that strategy in this text is ____________________________

____.

Available for download at **resources.corwin.com/ness-thinkalouds**

using a page from a social studies book or a short paragraph during guided reading instruction. I even saw a teacher think aloud during math to demonstrate the skills needed to tackle a word problem. Many of the teachers in my study reported applying this think aloud approach to the passages that they encountered with high-stakes test materials and preparation. Let me showcase some examples below. During a fourth-grade math lesson, I watched a teacher synthesize using the following word problem.

> Jazmin had 1,209 dolls, and Geraldine had 2,186 dolls. If they put their dolls together, how many would they have? [The teacher points to her head to indicate a think aloud.] Hmm . . . let me scan for important words that will give me hints about solving this problem. I'm getting the sense that "if they put their dolls together" is essential. If I am trying to answer "how many would they have," I'm thinking I need to add the dolls from both girls. So in a nutshell, I need to add up these two numbers to find out how many dolls they had total.

In a third-grade social studies lesson, I witnessed a teacher do the following think aloud using a portion of a 2003 article in *Time for Kids*.

"Hard at Work" by Ritu Upadhyay

What the Text Said	What the Teacher Said
Ten-year-old Wilbur Carreno is less than four feet tall and weighs only 50 pounds. He is small for his age. That's exactly what makes him good at his job.	*I'm wondering what kind of job Wilbur has that it would be useful to be so small.*
Wilbur spends his afternoons climbing banana trees four times his height. He expertly ties the heavy stalks of bananas so the trees won't droop from the weight of the fruit. "I've been working since I was 8," he said. "I finish school at noon and then go to the field." In Wilbur's poor country of Ecuador, one in every four children is working.	*In a nutshell, I'm learning that kids work in Ecuador because it is such a poor country.*
An estimated 69,000 kids toil away on the vast banana plantations along the country's coast. Ecuador is the world's largest banana exporter. Kids working in the industry are exposed to harmful chemicals, pull loads twice their weight and use sharp, heavy knives.	*This last line makes me think about what the author is really trying to tell me in this article. The author is telling me about how hard and dangerous this job is.*

Let's look at a think aloud that I observed during a second-grade science lesson. The teacher used an original work to think aloud, as shown below.

The Food Chain	
What the Text Said	**What the Teacher Said**
All living things need food. Most plants make food.	*How do plants make food?*
Some animals eat plants. Other animals eat those animals. This is called the food chain. Food chains start with the Sun. Plants use energy from the Sun to make food. Animals get energy from the food they eat.	*The big picture here is that the food chain helps all the different types of animals find food.*
All food chains have predators and prey. A predator is an animal that catches and eats other animals. Prey is an animal that is caught and eaten.	*The author really wants to inform me about how the Sun begins the food chain and how predators and prey contribute to the food chain.*

Thinking Aloud With Visuals

There's a lot more to a book than simply the words. Publishing houses pay top dollar to include visuals—diagrams, timelines, graphs, illustrations, tables, photos. I'll admit it: when I was a kid, I used to look at those visuals as a "freebie," meaning a page that I didn't need to read. Don't tell my statistics instructor, but I used the same approach there! Suddenly, the thirty-seven pages of assigned reading was reduced to twenty-nine! In hindsight, I lost a lot of important and engaging content with this approach. It's no wonder I still struggle with interpreting data tables in quantitative research articles!

Our students need to see that visuals are not merely placeholders, but that they convey information that either enhances the text or introduces new material. For instance, it would be difficult in a geography lesson to teach the idea of a peninsula without an illustrative visual of land almost surrounded by water. And how—in a science lesson—would we teach the layout of the solar system without a diagram depicting the position of each planet in relation to the Sun?

My point here is that we also need to think aloud with visuals so that we clarify how to navigate through these text features. Let's try it out with the classic visual on the next page—depicting the water cycle.

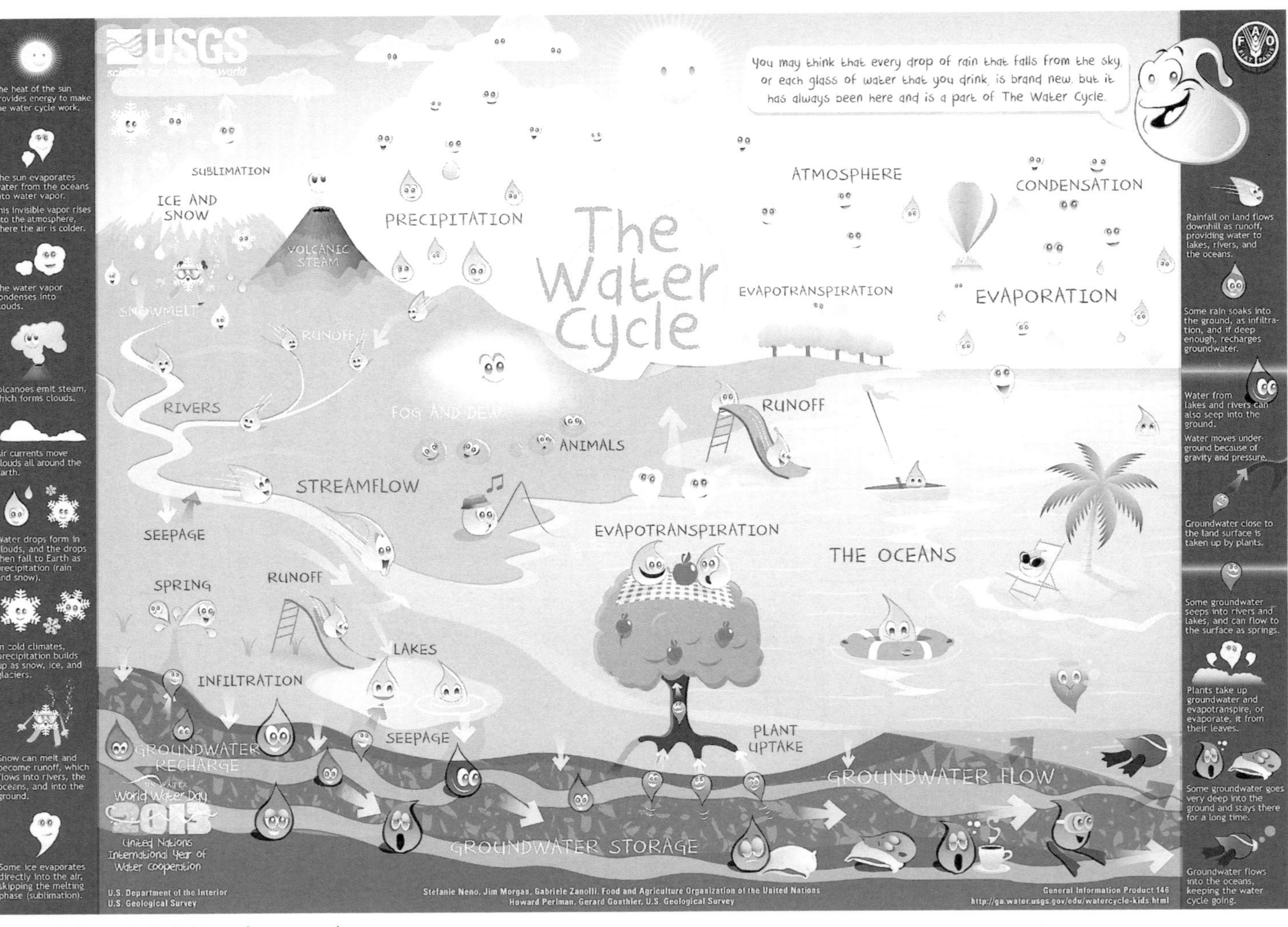

Source: United States Geological Survey (www.usgs.gov).

Watch how I think aloud:

I'm getting the sense that this image shows me the entire process of the water cycle, so I need to slow down to read all of the information it conveys. The first thing I notice is the label "The Water Cycle" and the arrows that form a circle around it. This suggests a process—I'm going to start at "evaporation." Right below the word *evaporation*, I see arrows pointing up from the ocean. These images are telling me that water evaporates from the ocean in this step. If I follow the arrows, I see how evaporated water forms clouds in the *condensation* stage. As I continue following the cycle, I see arrows pointing down and raindrops falling—that's showing me *precipitation*, which I know is a fancy name for rain. The most important part of this visual is the arrows, which represent the order of evaporation to condensation to precipitation to groundwater that flows back to the oceans. Just as the name *cycle* implies, I can see that this is a process that keeps on going and going.

Big Possibilities to Encourage Thinking Aloud During Independent Practice

- Create a game spinner with a brad or paper clip. Write a different reading comprehension strategy on each section of the spinner. Assign students a text, and prior to reading, have them spin to see which strategy they are responsible for. After reading, have students share their stopping point and the script for their strategy. This same idea can be modified by making dice for reading comprehension strategies. (Spinner and die templates are provided in Chapter 5, pages 82–83.)
- Have a think aloud tea party. Buy a packet of colored Popsicle sticks at a craft store or teacher supply store. Assign one reading comprehension strategy per color so the green sticks are for asking questions, the red sticks are for making inferences, and so on. Prior to reading, have students randomly select a Popsicle stick. Read a short text aloud, or have students read silently. After reading, have students write down a think aloud corresponding to the strategy on their Popsicle stick. For a tea party, have students mingle with each other. They must find two other students with different colors than their own. While mingling, students share their stopping point, think aloud script, and strategy.

continued . . .

. . . from previous

- Use the clip art provided for each reading comprehension strategy; print out and laminate cards for each student. Using double-sided Scotch tape, tape cards to each student's desk. Prior to independent practice, place a coin or chip on a particular strategy on each student's card to signal to students that they should focus on that particular strategy while reading independently.
- Play Sage and Scribe. This activity allows one student to play the role of the sage, while the other plays the role of the attentive scribe. The sage is responsible for explaining a skill, and the scribe works on building his or her listening and note-taking skills. Put students in pairs. Give each pair a portion of a text to use for thinking aloud. The sage stops at certain times during the reading to think aloud, while the scribe records what the sage says; then they switch roles.
- Play Detective. Give partners a portion of text and have them write down three think aloud scripts. Their job is to read their script to their partner, not telling them where the stopping point was. The detective tries to figure out the best stopping point for that think aloud and which strategy the thinker was using.

Final Thoughts

In this final chapter, I've given you a lot to think about. I've asked you to shift your teacher-led think alouds to student-generated think alouds. I've asked you to use think alongs and observational checklists to transfer responsibility to students. I've given you tools to encourage students to reflect on their own think alouds. I've encouraged you to see every read aloud opportunity—across all content areas—as an opportunity to think aloud. I've modeled how to think aloud using the visuals and text features that are omnipresent in children's books today.

As you try the process I've outlined in this book, I encourage you to build your confidence with the think aloud strategy slowly. When you are ready, have a colleague you trust watch you present a think aloud to students and get his or her feedback. To start, select texts that you especially love and are super comfortable with. Read your students' expressions, and ask them questions after a think aloud about what they noticed, what they liked, and what they found helpful. If you have questions or successes to share, I'd love to hear from you. You can find my contact information at www.drmollyness.com.

Ready for a Trial Run?

I'd like you to challenge yourself to think aloud across content areas and to get out of your comfort zone with your text choice. Below, you will find texts (mostly pulled from the Common Core text exemplars) that span the content areas of science, social studies, and math. As you use these texts to think aloud (or supplement them with text from your content-area textbooks), reflect on the following questions:

- Were there any strategies you favored when thinking aloud using content-area text? Were there any strategies you struggled to incorporate?
- What challenged you in thinking aloud using content-area text? What came naturally to you while thinking aloud using content-area text?
- Reflect on how often you think aloud during your science, social studies, and math instruction. Are you satisfied with how frequently you think aloud in these areas?

Thinking Aloud in Science

Starfish by Edith Thatcher Hurd (2000)

> "Starfish live in the sea. Starfish live deep down in the sea. Starfish live in pools by the sea. Some starfish are purple. Some starfish are pink. This is the sunflower starfish. It is the biggest of all. Starfish have many arms. The arms are called rays. Starfish have arms, but no legs. Starfish have feet, but no toes. They glide and slide on tiny tube feet. They move as slowly as a snail. The basket star looks like a starfish, but it is a little different. It doesn't have tube feet. It moves with its rays. It has rays that go up and rays that go down. Tiny brittle stars are like the basket star. They hide under rocks in pools by the sea. The mud star hides in the mud. It is a starfish. It has tiny tube feet. A starfish has no eyes. A starfish has no ears or nose. Its tiny mouth is on its underside. When a starfish is hungry, it slides and it glides on its tiny tube feet. It hunts for mussels and oysters and clams. It feels for the mussels. It feels for the oysters. It feels for the clams. It feels for something to eat."

Thinking Aloud in Social Studies

From "The Mysterious Mr. Lincoln" by Russell Freedman (1987)

"Abraham Lincoln wasn't the sort of man who could lose himself in a crowd. After all, he stood six feet four inches tall. And to top it off, he wore a high silk hat. His height was mostly in his long bony legs. When he sat in a chair, he seemed no taller than anyone else. It was only when he stood up that he towered over other men. At first glance, most people thought he was homely. Lincoln thought so too, once referring to his 'poor, lean, lank face.' As a young man he was sensitive about his gawky looks, but in time, he learned to laugh at himself. When a rival called him 'two-faced' during a political debate, Lincoln replied: 'I leave it to my audience. If I had another face, do you think I'd wear this one?' According to those who knew him, Lincoln was a man of many faces. In repose, he often seemed sad and gloomy. But when he began to speak, his expression changed. 'The dull, listless features dropped like a mask,' said a Chicago newspaperman. 'The eyes began to sparkle, the mouth to smile, the whole countenance was wreathed in animation, so that a stranger would have said, "Why, this man, so angular and solemn a moment ago, is really handsome."' Lincoln was the most photographed man of his time, but his friends insisted that no photo ever did him justice. It's no wonder. Back then cameras required long exposures. The person being photographed had to 'freeze' as the seconds ticked by. If he blinked an eye, the picture would be blurred. That's why Lincoln looks so stiff and formal in his photos. We never see him laughing or joking."

Thinking Aloud in Math

From "Trek 7: The Fractal Pond Race" by Ivars Peterson and Nancy Henderson (2000)

"From the meanderings of a pond's edge to the branching of trees and the intricate forms of snowflakes, shapes in nature are often more complicated than geometrical shapes such as circles, spheres, angles, cones, rectangles, and cubes. . . . Swedish mathematician Helge von Koch created an intriguing but puzzling curve. It zigzags in such an odd pattern that it seems impossible to start at one point and follow the curve to reach another point. Like many figures now known to be fractals, Koch's curve is easy to generate by starting with a simple figure and turning it into an increasingly crinkly form."

Appendix A

Sample Think Aloud

One morning as I stood drinking my cup of coffee, I came across a newspaper article titled "Spider-Hunting Nudist Ends With Ring of Fire." With a catchy title like that, how could I not read it? To demonstrate how think alouds can be readily applied to all kinds of texts at all different levels, I've written out a transcript of the think aloud that I, as a proficient reader, might do with this article.

"Spider-Hunting Nudist Ends With Ring of Fire" From *Zee News*

What the Text Says	What I Say
"Spider-Hunting	*Why would someone go spider hunting? When I see spiders, I run the other way—I don't seek them out!*
Nudist	*Nudist? I know that the titles of articles have to be short and the author can only include the most important parts, so it must be important that this person was naked.*
Ends With Ring of Fire"	*I wonder what is meant by ring of fire. I've heard it be used when I've learned about volcanoes. I also know a Johnny Cash song about a ring of fire. Or maybe a ring of fire is a bull's-eye pattern like in a tick bite.* *This is a really intriguing article that lends itself to predictions! I predict this article will be about a naked person who gets a bad spider bite.*
A red-faced Australian nudist	*This phrase red-faced intrigues me because it could mean so many different things. Is this person red-faced because he is sunburned? I know that lots of Australia has beaches and deserts, so maybe this person had too much sun. Or maybe the person has been drinking, because I know alcohol can make some people's skin flush.*

continued...

. . . from previous

What the Text Says	What I Say
	Or maybe this person is red-faced because he's embarrassed and blushing. I think the author is giving me an important clue here, but I need more information to find out why this person is red-faced or why the author included this detail.
who tried to set fire to what he thought was a deadly funnel web spider's nest	*What is a funnel web spider? The author is telling me it's deadly, so it must be poisonous. Maybe after I finish reading, I'll do an Internet search for this kind of spider.*
ended up with badly burned buttocks, emergency officials said on Monday.	*The author is telling me exactly where this man's burns are. That's an important detail, and I wonder why the author specifically includes it. Maybe the author thinks it's silly that of all places to get burned, it was this man's buttocks.*
The 56-year-old man was at a nudist colony near Bowral, about 60 miles southwest of Sydney, Sunday when he spotted what he believed to be a funnel web spider hole. Ambulance workers, including a helicopter crew, were called to the scene after the man poured petrol	*I already know that petrol is another word for gasoline—when I went to England, we filled our car with petrol. My hunch must be right because I also know that gas is highly flammable.*
down the hole and then lit a match in an attempt to kill the offending arachnid.	*Clearly the man was scared of this spider. But why didn't he just walk away and leave it alone?*
"The exploding gasoline fumes left the man with burns to 18 percent of his body, on the upper leg and buttocks," the NRMA Careflight	*This is a term I don't know, but the author is giving me clues to help figure it out. I've got ambulance workers and an emergency helicopter as clues, so I'm guessing that NRMA Careflight is the equivalent to EMS in the United States.*
helicopter rescue service said in a statement.	*I'm trying to visualize exactly what happened here. In my mind's eye, I can see this man standing naked over this spider hole and pouring gas down it. What I can't visualize is how the flames got to his upper leg and buttocks. Wouldn't the flames burn his face and chest if he were looking down this spider hole? Maybe he was running away, and that explains how he got burned where he did.*

What the Text Says	What I Say
It said the man's lack of clothing probably contributed to the extent of his burns.	*This statement confuses me. The phrase "contributed to the extent" is ambiguous to me. Is the author telling me that being nude helped or hurt him? It's obviously a big part of this story that the man is naked, so if I had to guess, I'd say that not wearing clothes made it so he was burned less—because he didn't have any clothes to catch on fire.*
"The fate of the bunkered spider was unknown, although other guests at the resort thought it was probably a harmless trapdoor spider and not a deadly funnel web," the statement said.	*If the other guests could wager a guess, does that mean they got a look at the spider, too? Had anyone seen the spider before this man—and maybe just walked away?*
NRMA Careflight said it was called to a property in the same area in January when another man kicked a spider that was crawling up the wall of a friend's cabin.	*The author is telling me about another time someone in this same place hurt himself by trying to get rid of a spider. I wonder why the author included this detail.*
The man broke his leg in two places, it said.	*The author is even more descriptive here about these injuries—I'm sensing that the author thinks it's a bit ridiculous that these people do these crazy things to get rid of spiders rather than just leaving them be. Could the author's purpose in this article be to send a message, like "Leave scary wildlife alone"? Or maybe the author is trying to entertain us with these comical antics.* *One of my purposes for reading this article was to figure out why this person was originally described as red-faced. While I can't be sure (because the author didn't explain it), I'm making the inference that this man was red-faced because he was embarrassed that his actions resulted in an emergency helicopter rescue, his burns, and everyone knowing what he did.*

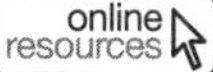

Available for download at **resources.corwin.com/ness-thinkalouds**

Appendix B

Sample Texts

The texts below are to be used with the "Ready for a Trial Run?" activities in Chapters 3, 4, and 5. Chapter 3 asks you to identify juicy stopping points. Chapter 4 asks you to narrow down your selections to the ones that you will actually use. Chapter 5 asks you to create a three-column chart to write the actual think aloud scripts you'll use.

"The Owl and the Pussy-Cat" by Edward Lear

Overview and Rationale

This classic poem tells the story of an unlikely romance between an owl and a cat. They go on a boating adventure, traveling to gather things for a wedding ceremony. Rich with imagery, engaging rhyme, and unique vocabulary, this poem is a bedtime classic.

Lexile Framework: 230

Grade-Level Equivalent: 2.5

Guided Reading Level: L

I

The Owl and the Pussy-cat went to sea
In a beautiful pea-green boat,
They took some honey, and plenty of money,
Wrapped up in a five-pound note.
The Owl looked up to the stars above,
And sang to a small guitar,
"O lovely Pussy! O Pussy, my love,
What a beautiful Pussy you are,
You are,
You are!
What a beautiful Pussy you are!"

II

Pussy said to the Owl, "You elegant fowl!
How charmingly sweet you sing!
O let us be married! too long we have tarried:
But what shall we do for a ring?"
They sailed away, for a year and a day,
To the land where the Bong-Tree grows
And there in a wood a Piggy-wig stood
With a ring at the end of his nose,
His nose,
His nose,
With a ring at the end of his nose.

III

"Dear Pig, are you willing to sell for one shilling
Your ring?" Said the Piggy, "I will."
So they took it away, and were married next day
By the Turkey who lives on the hill.
They dined on mince, and slices of quince,
Which they ate with a runcible spoon;
And hand in hand, on the edge of the sand,
They danced by the light of the moon,
The moon,
The moon,
They danced by the light of the moon.

The Sandwich Swap by Her Majesty Queen Rania Al-Abdullah and Kelly DiPucchio

Overview and Rationale

This sweet story tells of two best friends, Salma and Lily. These girls do everything together, but can't see eye to eye on their lunch choices. At the end of the story, the girls come together to learn that their friendship matters more than their differences. Salma and Lily lead their classmates in joining together in a message of tolerance and acceptance.

Lexile Framework: 630

Grade-Level Equivalent: 2.5

Guided Reading Level: L

It all began with a peanut butter and jelly sandwich . . . and it ended with a hummus sandwich.

Salma and Lily were best friends at school. They drew pictures together. They played on the swings together. They jumped rope together. And they ate their lunches together.

But just *what* they ate was a little different. Lily ate a peanut butter and jelly sandwich every day for lunch. Salma ate a hummus and pita sandwich every day for lunch. And although Lily never said it out loud, she thought Salma's sandwich looked weird and yucky. She felt terrible that her friend had to eat that icky chickpea paste every day. Ew. Yuck.

And although Salma never said it out loud, *she* thought *Lily's* sandwich looked strange and gross. She felt just awful that her friend had to eat that gooey peanut paste every day. Ew. Gross.

Then one day, Lily just couldn't hold back those pesky thoughts any longer. "Your sandwich looks kind of yucky," she blurted out.

"What did you say?" Salma asked, thinking she must have misunderstood her friend. "I said, your sandwich looks yucky." Salma frowned.

She looked down at the thin, soft break, and she thought of her beautiful, smiling mother as she carefully cut Salma's sandwich into two neat halves that morning.

Her hurt feelings turned mad. "Yeah, well your sandwich looks gross, and it smells bad too!" Salma snapped back.

Lily looked surprised. She sniffed the thick, squishy bread, and she thought of her dad in his silly apron, whistling as he cut Lily's sandwich into two perfect triangles that morning

Lily scowled. "It does not smell bad!"

"Does, too!"

"Ewww . . . YUCK!"

"Ewww . . . GROSS!"

That afternoon the friends did not draw pictures together. They did not swing together, and they did not jump rope together either. The next day, Salma ate her lunch at one table and Lily ate her lunch at another.

Meanwhile, the peanut butter vs. hummus story had spread, and everyone began choosing sides. Each side had something not so nice to say to the other. Pretty soon the rude insults had nothing at all to do with peanut butter or hummus. You're weird! You're stupid! You look funny! You dress dumb!

And then it happened. Somebody yelled, "FOOD FIGHT!" Peanut butter and hummus sandwiches and other lunch favorites began flying back and forth between both sides of the lunchroom. They stuck to the walls. They stuck to the ceiling. They stuck to the lunch lady.

When the sandwiches were all gone, pudding cups and applesauce and carrot sticks took flight. Salma and Lily looked at one another from across the rowdy, splattered room. They both felt ashamed by what they saw.

They both felt really ashamed when the principal called them into her office—after they had helped clean up the mess.

The following day, Salma set her lunch down across from Lily's. The two girls nibbled on their sandwiches in silence.

Finally, Lily got up the courage to speak. "Would you like to try a bite of my peanut butter and jelly?"

Salma grinned. "Sure. Why not? Would you like to try my hummus and pita?"

Lily laughed. "I'd like that."

"On the count of three?"

"Okay. On the count of three! 1 . . . 2 . . . 3!"

"Hey, this is delicious!"

"And this is heavenly!"

The girls giggled. And hugged. And traded sandwiches. After lunch, Salma and Lily met with the principal again. This time they were there to suggest a very special event for the whole school.

And *that's* how it all began with a peanut butter and jelly sandwich . . . and ended with a hummus and pita sandwich.

The William Hoy Story: How a Deaf Baseball Player Changed the Game by Nancy Churnin

Overview and Rationale

William Hoy, a deaf baseball player, forever changed the sport in the 1880s. All he wanted to do was play baseball. In addition to the prejudice Hoy faced, he could not hear the umpires' calls. One day he asked the umpire to use hand signals: strike, ball, out. The results were the hand signals still used in baseball today.

This biography tells his story, with inspiring messages of perseverance and a "can do" attitude.

Lexile Framework: 620

Grade-Level Equivalent: 3

William scooped dust to dry the sweat off his slick rubber ball. He stared at the small X he'd chalked on the barn wall. He closed his eyes. He opened them and threw. Bam! He hit the mark. He stepped back so he could try again.

His mother waved her arms. She was applauding him.

She touched her fingers to her mouth to signal eating. He read her lips as she said, "Dinner."

William pulled out his pad and pencil. He scribbled: "Just a few more? I want to be perfect for tryouts."

His mother nodded.

His family was passing the mashed potatoes around the table when William pushed open the door. He read his father's lips telling him to wash up for dinner. He also read what his father's lips mouthed to his mother.

"Baseball," his father said. "It will never last."

Still, William couldn't wait to try out at his school, the Ohio State School for the Deaf. At tryouts, he threw the ball. He caught it. He batted. He waited.

"Too small," the team captain said.

William never got much taller than five-foot-five. He couldn't do anything about that.

But maybe they'd give him another chance if he aimed better and ran faster.

So every day, after homework and chores, he practiced.

One day William was standing outside the cobbler shop where he fixed shoes, wistfully watching men play baseball in a far-off field. A foul ball crashed by his feet. With his strong, sure arm, he threw the ball straight into an amazed player's waiting hand.

"Hey, kid," the player called. "Want to join us?"

But William couldn't read the player's lips from where he was. So he turned back to work.

The man ran to William and tapped his back to get his attention. William whirled around, and this time, when the man repeated the question, he understood. He scrambled happily to the outfield.

William threw the ball smack into his teammates' hands. When he was up at bat, he sent it soaring where no one would catch it.

"What's your name?" asked one of the players.

William Hoy, William wrote.

The man looked at the piece of paper a long time. He seemed to be thinking. "Do you want to try out for our team?" he asked William at last.

William grinned. He sure did!

William soon learned life in the hearing world wasn't easy. Unlike his parents, few people used sign language in the 1880s, and certainly not in baseball. He won a spot on the first team he tried out for, but the manager smirked when he offered William less money than he paid the others.

"I quit," William told him with his notebook. He quickly found another team.

But even on his new team, some players talked behind his back so he wouldn't know what they were saying. Others hid their mouths so he couldn't read their lips.

One day a pitcher played the meanest trick of all. William let three pitches go by because he thought they were balls. He was too far to read the umpire's lips and didn't know they were actually strikes.

He stood, gripping his bat, waiting for the next pitch. But the next pitch never came. William was confused.

Suddenly the pitcher burst out laughing. He pointed to the fans in the stands laughing too.

William's face grew hot. He walked off quickly. He wasn't going to cry. Not about baseball, he told himself.

He jammed his hands in his pockets. Paper crunched against his fist. He pulled out a letter from his mother. He read again how much she missed him.

William missed his family too. He remembered how his mom would raise her arms to applaud him.

That's it! William pulled out his pad and drew pictures. He scribbled words next to the pictures. He wrote. He wrote. He WROTE! He ran to find the umpire.

The umpire read William's notes.

"Yes, that could work," he said.

The next time William was at bat, the umpire raised his right hand for a strike and his left for a ball.

He used American Sign Language symbols for safe and out. This time William got on base. He stole bases. He scored! . . .

With his strong, sure arm, he became the first player to throw three base runners out at the plate in one game—from the outfield!

William taught his teammates signs so they could discuss plays. . . .

The fans enjoyed learning signs too. In those days, before speakers and giant screens, hearing the umpire's calls from the back of the bleachers was hard to do!

Now, even the farthest member of the crowd could see the signals.

Carefully watching the signals, he led the American League in walks in 1901. He was called the king of center field because for ten years he was ranked among the top five outfielders to get hitters out by catching hard-to-reach fly balls. . . .

Then, one day, when he ran out onto the field, fans waved their arms from the stands just as his mother did when he was a boy. They waved hats too.

William said he'd never cry about baseball. But he did cry at the sight of deaf applause.

All he'd wanted to do since he was a boy was find a way to play his favorite game. He never dreamed he'd change how the game was played. But he did, and we still cheer him today.

Available for download at **resources.corwin.com/ness-thinkalouds**

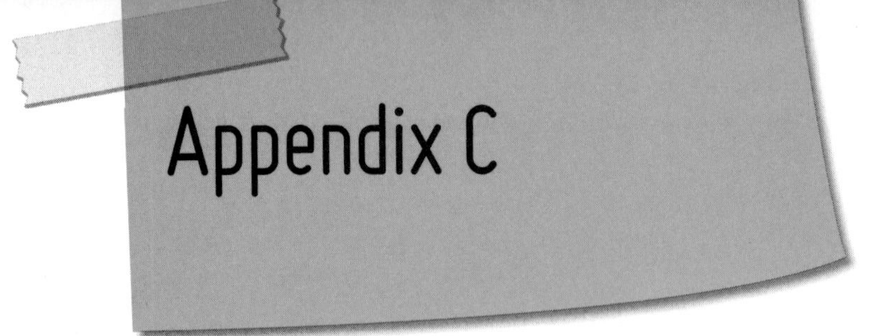

Appendix C

Think Alouds for Sample Texts

Think Aloud for "The Owl and the Pussy-Cat" by Edward Lear

What the Text Says	What I Say	The Comprehension Strategy I Model
The Owl and the Pussy-cat went to sea In a beautiful pea-green boat, They took some honey, and plenty of money, Wrapped up in a five-pound note.	*I'm wondering what the relationship between the Owl and the Pussy-cat is. I wonder where they might be going. I'd also like to know what the money is for.*	? **Asking questions**
The Owl looked up to the stars above, And sang to a small guitar, "O lovely Pussy! O Pussy, my love, What a beautiful Pussy you are, You are, You are! What a beautiful Pussy you are!"	*One of the questions I had was about the relationship between the Owl and the Pussy-cat. As I kept reading, I found out that the Owl calls the Pussy-cat "my love" and sings about how beautiful she is. This lets me know that the Owl and the Pussy-cat are in love.*	**Monitoring and clarifying**
Pussy said to the Owl, "You elegant fowl! How charmingly sweet you sing! O let us be married! too long we have tarried: But what shall we do for a ring?"	*The key information here is that the Owl and the Pussy-cat want to get married, but they aren't sure what to use for a wedding ring.*	**Synthesizing**
They sailed away, for a year and a day, To the land where the Bong-Tree grows And there in a wood a Piggy-wig stood With a ring at the end of his nose, His nose, His nose, With a ring at the end of his nose.	*What is a piggy-wig? Is that just another name for a pig? Are the Owl and the Pussy-cat going to take this ring and use it as a wedding ring?*	? **Asking questions**
"Dear Pig, are you willing to sell for one shilling Your ring?" Said the Piggy, "I will."	*I learned that the pig sells them the ring.*	**Synthesizing**

What the Text Says	What I Say	The Comprehension Strategy I Model
So they took it away, and were married next day By the Turkey who lives on the hill. They dined on mince, and slices of quince, Which they ate with a runcible spoon;	*I think the author is entertaining me with a made-up story. He makes this poem imaginative with his fantasy characters. I've never see an owl and cat getting married or a turkey marrying anyone!*	A **Understanding the author's purpose**
And hand in hand, on the edge of the sand, They danced by the light of the moon, The moon, The moon, They danced by the light of the moon.	*This poem is about an owl and a cat who fall in love and get married, and are so happy that they dance under the moon.*	6 **Synthesizing**

Think Aloud for *The Sandwich Swap* by Her Majesty Queen Rania Al-Abdullah and Kelly DiPucchio

What the Text Says	What I Say	The Comprehension Strategy I Model
It all began with a peanut butter and jelly sandwich . . . and it ended with a hummus sandwich.	*I wonder what the "it" here is. I wonder what began here. What is a hummus sandwich?*	? **Asking questions**
Salma and Lily were best friends at school. They drew pictures together. They played on the swings together. They jumped rope together. And they ate their lunches together.	*The key information here is that Salma and Lily are friends who have a lot in common.*	6 **Synthesizing**
But just *what* they ate was a little different. Lily ate a peanut butter and jelly sandwich every day for lunch. Salma ate a hummus and pita sandwich every day for lunch. And although Lily never said it out loud, she thought Salma's sandwich looked weird and yucky. She felt terrible that her friend had to eat that icky chickpea paste every day. Ew. Yuck. And although Salma never said it out loud, *she* thought *Lily's* sandwich looked strange and gross. She felt just awful that her friend had to eat that gooey peanut paste every day. Ew. Gross.	*I'm noticing these two parts—about what Salma ate and thought and what Lily ate and thought—are written in the exact same way. I wonder if the author did this to show me that even though the girls have so much in common, they also have things that are different.*	A **Understanding the author's purpose**

continued . . .

. . . from previous

What the Text Says	What I Say	The Comprehension Strategy I Model
Then one day, Lily just couldn't hold back those pesky thoughts any longer. "Your sandwich looks kind of yucky," she blurted out.	*I'm noticing some words that don't always mean nice things—pesky, yucky, blurted. These words make me think that Lily was acting unkindly.*	**Making inferences**
"What did you say?" Salma asked, thinking she must have misunderstood her friend. "I said, your sandwich looks yucky." Salma frowned.	*At first I wasn't sure why Salma asked, "What did you say?" I thought maybe she hadn't heard Lily. But when I kept reading, I understood Salma said that because she was surprised her best friend had said something so unkind.*	**Monitoring and clarifying**
She looked down at the thin, soft break, and she thought of her beautiful, smiling mother as she carefully cut Salma's sandwich into two neat halves that morning.	*From the text clues, I get the sense that the hummus sandwich reminds Salma of home and of how much her mother loves her.*	**Making inferences**
Her hurt feelings turned mad. "Yeah, well your sandwich looks gross, and it smells bad too!" Salma snapped back.	*I wonder how Lily will react. What will she say? Did Salma say something equally unkind just to make Lily feel bad—like she is now feeling?*	**Asking questions**
Lily looked surprised. She sniffed the thick, squishy bread, and she thought of her dad in his silly apron, whistling as he cut Lily's sandwich into two perfect triangles that morning	*I'm noticing that the sandwich reminds Lily of how much her dad loves her, just like Salma's sandwich.*	**Understanding the author's purpose** **Making inferences**
Lily scowled. "It does not smell bad!" "Does, too!" "Ewww . . . YUCK!" "Ewww . . . GROSS!"	*The most important idea here is that both girls have hurt feelings and both girls said something unkind to their best friend.*	**Synthesizing**
That afternoon the friends did not draw pictures together. They did not swing together, and they did not jump rope together either. The next day, Salma ate her lunch at one table and Lily ate her lunch at another.	*Now I understand that these friends are so hurt that they don't spend time together—like they normally do.*	**Synthesizing**
Meanwhile, the peanut butter vs. hummus story had spread, and everyone began choosing sides. Each side had something not so nice to say to the other. Pretty soon the rude insults had nothing at all to do with peanut butter or hummus. You're weird! You're stupid! You look funny! You dress dumb!	*Now I understand that the rest of the class is making this fight even worse, by being rude, saying insults, and taking sides.*	**Synthesizing**

What the Text Says	What I Say	The Comprehension Strategy I Model
And then it happened. Somebody yelled, "FOOD FIGHT!" Peanut butter and hummus sandwiches and other lunch favorites began flying back and forth between both sides of the lunchroom. They stuck to the walls. They stuck to the ceiling. They stuck to the lunch lady.	*I'm wondering why the kids thought that having a food fight was a good idea. Why would having a food fight make things any better?*	? **Asking questions**
When the sandwiches were all gone, pudding cups and applesauce and carrot sticks took flight. Salma and Lily looked at one another from across the rowdy, splattered room. They both felt ashamed by what they saw.	*I'm getting the sense that Lily and Salma feel responsible for the food fight and for the conflict with their classmates.*	III **Making inferences**
They both felt really ashamed when the principal called them into her office—after they had helped clean up the mess.	*I'm wondering how the principal will handle this. Will Lily and Salma get in trouble? What will their punishment be? Did the principal call their parents? Did other kids have to help clean up, too?*	? **Asking questions**
The following day, Salma set her lunch down across from Lily's. The two girls nibbled on their sandwiches in silence. Finally, Lily got up the courage to speak.	*I like how the author is showing me how uncomfortable the girls feel—they can't even talk to each other.*	A **Understanding the author's purpose**
"Would you like to try a bite of my peanut butter and jelly?" Salma grinned. "Sure. Why not? Would you like to try my hummus and pita?" Lily laughed. "I'd like that." "On the count of three?" "Okay. On the count of three! 1 . . . 2 . . . 3!" "Hey, this is delicious!" "And this is heavenly!" The girls giggled. And hugged. And traded sandwiches.	*I'm noticing that the girls didn't apologize to each other. They just tried each other's lunch and realized how much they liked it. I wonder why the author doesn't write about apologies.*	A **Understanding the author's purpose**
After lunch, Salma and Lily met with the principal again. This time they were there to suggest a very special event for the whole school. And *that's* how it all began with a peanut butter and jelly sandwich . . . and ended with a hummus and pita sandwich.	*I can see from the pictures that the entire class has a picnic where they all try different kinds of food and learn about each other's families and cultures. I'm thinking that the author wrote this book to make us realize that friends can have lots of things in common but that differences are not a bad thing.*	A **Understanding the author's purpose**

Think Aloud for *The William Hoy Story: How a Deaf Baseball Player Changed the Game* by Nancy Churnin

What the Text Says	What I Say	The Comprehension Strategy I Model
He stepped back so he could try again. (p. 1)	*Based on the clues of a rubber ball and him aiming at the wall, I'm guessing William is playing a sport. When I look at the subtitle and the pictures, I can tell he's trying to throw a baseball accurately. Maybe he's trying to be a pitcher.*	**Making inferences**
"I want to be perfect for tryouts." His mother nodded. (p. 3)	*I've got some clues that make me think William is deaf. His mother is signaling with her hands, and William is reading lips and writing instead of speaking.*	**Making inferences**
"It will never last." (p. 4)	*It could be that his father doesn't think baseball is a good idea for William—he shakes his head and says, "It will never last." Maybe his dad thinks sports are silly. I wonder if he thinks William is not a very good baseball player.*	**Making inferences** **Asking questions**
So every day, after homework and chores, he practiced. (p. 5)	*In a nutshell, I can tell that William is a hard worker. He's determined. Even though he's deaf and he's short, he still practices hard and is hopeful about making the team. He's optimistic and he won't give up.*	**Synthesizing**
William threw the ball smack into his teammates' hands. (p. 9)	*Now I understand that it's even harder for William to play baseball because he's deaf. Despite what a good player he is, William can't hear the other players.*	**Synthesizing**
William grinned. He sure did! (p. 11)	*I'm curious about why the man seems to look at the paper for such a long time. Was he debating whether or not to invite William on the team? Could it be that the man thinks he won't be a very good player because he's deaf?*	**Asking questions**
"I quit," William told him with his notebook. (p. 12)	*I'm getting the sense that people treat William unfairly just because he's deaf, but that William won't tolerate this. The manager tries to pay him less, and his reaction is to quit. This also makes me think that William is true to himself and believes in his own value.*	**Synthesizing** **Making inferences**
Others hid their mouths so he couldn't read their lips. (p. 13)	*This evidence is confirming what I was thinking. Not only are coaches unfair to him, but players treat him differently too.*	**Synthesizing**

What the Text Says	What I Say	The Comprehension Strategy I Model
He pointed to the fans in the stands laughing too. William's face grew hot. He walked off quickly. He wasn't going to cry. Not about baseball, he told himself. (p. 15)	*The author doesn't come right out and say it, but I'm getting the sense that William is proud, and that pride makes it so he won't cry in front of the crowd who is laughing at him.*	**Making inferences**
He remembered how his mom would raise her arms to applaud him. (p. 16)	*From these bits of evidence—his mother's letter, her applause for him, her watching him practice—the author is hinting that William and his mother are very close. She's very supportive of him.*	**Making inferences**
The umpire read William's notes. "Yes, that could work," he said. (p. 19)	*I'm really curious about what words he wrote. What did he write that the umpire thinks could work? What was his idea?*	? **Asking questions**
With his strong, sure arm, he became the first player to throw three base runners out at the plate in one game—from the outfield! (p. 21)	*Now I understand that his idea was for the umpire and coaches to use hand symbols to help him. Those hand symbols improved his baseball career!*	**Synthesizing**
Now, even the farthest member of the crowd could see the signals. (p. 23)	*The big idea here is that hand symbols were useful for the players, the umpires, and the fans!*	**Synthesizing**
He was called the king of center field because for ten years he was ranked among the top five outfielders to get hitters out by catching hard-to-reach fly balls. (p. 25)	*I learned that William was not only popular, but skilled. Teams wanted him, and he was highly ranked!*	**Synthesizing**
They waved hats too. (p. 27)	*From the picture and the reminder about "just how his mother did when he was a boy," I'm guessing that the fans were waving their hands and hats as a way to applaud him.*	**Making inferences**
But he did, and we still cheer him today. (p. 27)	*I think the author's purpose in writing this was to show how important William Hoy was to baseball. The author is telling me that William overcame the challenge of being deaf to achieve his dreams. The author is also telling me that William made an important contribution to baseball—the hand signals that we still see in games today.*	A **Understanding the author's purpose**

Available for download at **resources.corwin.com/ness-thinkalouds**

Appendix D

Think Aloud Sentence Starters

Comprehension Strategy	Sentence Starters
Asking Questions Purposeful readers are naturally curious. They ask questions about what happens in the text. Sometimes the answers to their questions are found in the text, and sometimes they are not.	• I wonder . . . • I would like to ask the author . . . • Who . . . ? • What . . . ? • When . . . ? • Where . . . ? • Why . . . ? • How . . . ? • This makes me wonder about . . . • How is this different? • How does this part here add to . . . ?
Making Inferences Purposeful readers make inferences. An inference is something that is probably true. The author doesn't tell us exactly, but good readers take clues from the text and combine them with what they already know. An inference is made when a reader says, "This is probably true."	• From the text clues, I can conclude that . . . • Based on what the text says and what I know, I think . . . • This information makes me think . . . • This evidence suggests . . . • That is probably why . . . • Although the author does not come right out and say it, I can figure out that . . . • It could be that . . . • Maybe/perhaps . . . • This could mean . . . • Based on what I know about these characters, I bet he/she is going to . . . • With what just happened, I imagine this character is feeling . . .

Comprehension Strategy	Sentence Starters
Synthesizing Purposeful readers constantly change their minds as they read. They use the unfolding information or events in the book to adapt thoughts, opinions, and conclusions. In fiction, readers often synthesize to refine their understanding of characters and themes; in nonfiction, readers synthesize in order to get the most important points about parts of a text. Readers may also synthesize to draw a conclusion about what the author's perspective of a topic is, and what their own perspective is, based on the text.	• Before I read, I thought . . . , but now I think . . . • My schema before I read was . . . , and now I understand . . . • This part gives me an idea . . . • When I put all these parts together, it seems the author is focusing on this big idea . . . • My synthesis is . . . • Mostly, . . . • I learned . . . • Now I understand . . . • Now I think . . . • The author keeps using these similar terms, so I think this whole section is really about this aspect of . . . • Some of the most important ideas are . . . • The text is mainly about . . . • The text, pictures, and boxes all seem to point at informing me that . . . • The author's most important ideas were . . . • The details I need to include are . . . • Some important concepts are . . . • The most important evidence was . . . • The basic gist is . . . • The key information is . . . • In a nutshell, this says that . . . • If I asked the author to just tell me in one sentence what the big idea is, this is what he/she would say . . .
A Understanding the Author's Purpose Purposeful readers try to figure out the reason that the author wrote a text. They want to know the purpose of the text. If a text gives a clear opinion or tries to convince the reader of something, the author's purpose is to persuade. If a text gives facts or tells a reader how to do something, the author's purpose is to inform. If the text is enjoyable, tells a story, or uses a story to teach a lesson, the author's purpose is to entertain.	• The author wants me to learn about . . . [specific to nonfiction] • The author's purpose in writing this story was . . . • I wonder why the author . . . • I think the author's purpose is . . . because . . . • The main character learns . . . in the end, so I wonder if the author wants me to reflect on . . . • This story is set in history during [a famous event], so I think the author's purpose is to . . . • I predict that the author's purpose is to inform/entertain/persuade because . . . • After reading the selection, I believe the author's purpose is . . . because . . . • The author's purpose is . . . based on . . . • I am curious why the author . . . • A golden line for me is . . . • I like how the author uses . . . to show . . . • This word/phrase stands out for me because . . .

continued . . .

. . . from previous

Comprehension Strategy	Sentence Starters
Monitoring and Clarifying Purposeful readers know when they stop understanding what they are reading. Just as when the train is going too fast the conductor applies the brake, a reader slows down and takes steps to get back on track. A reader uses one or more "fix it" strategies for repairing his or her comprehension.	• I had to slow down when . . . • It really surprised me, so I had to go back and reread because . . . • I wonder what . . . means. • Is this a different point in time? • Is this a flashback? • I wonder if this is a different narrator speaking, because . . . • What is the author doing differently with the text here because I keep losing track . . . ? • I need to know more about . . . • This last part is about . . . • I was confused by . . . • I still don't understand . . . • I had difficulty with . . . • I used [name strategy] to help me understand this part. • I can't really understand . . . • I wonder what the author means by . . . • I got lost here because . . . • I need to reread the part where . . .

online resources

Available for download at **resources.corwin.com/ness-thinkalouds**

Appendix E

Three-Column Think Aloud Chart

What the Text Says	What I Say	The Comprehension Strategy I Model
(Write out the last five words of the sentence before you think aloud.)	**(Write exactly what you will say in first-person narrative.)**	**(Write the name of the comprehension strategy you are employing in this think aloud.)**

online resources

Available for download at **resources.corwin.com/ness-thinkalouds**

Appendix F

Think Aloud Script for *The Circus Ship* by Chris Van Dusen

*Note: The italicized portions reflect the text directly.

Molly: Good readers think when they read. So this is what you're going to see me do. When I'm holding the book in my hands up here, for you to see [Molly holds the book up], I'm going to be reading the book. Sometimes I'm going to put the book flat on my lap [Molly lays the book flat on her lap]. That's when I'm going to be thinking in my head. Okay? So when I'm holding it [Molly holds the book up], I'm reading, and if it's flat [Molly lays the book flat on her lap], I'm thinking. *Five miles off the coast of Maine and slightly overdue, a circus ship was steaming south in fog as thick as stew.* [Molly lays the book flat on her lap.] So I'm thinking that the fog is going to make it hard to see. Have you ever been out when it's foggy and hard to see? The boat might have a hard time steering. [Molly picks up the book.] *On board were fifteen animals who traveled to and fro. The next day, it was to Boston for another circus show.* [Molly lays the book flat on her lap.] So I've seen all of these animals in this boat because they are traveling to go to different towns to be in a circus. You can't take animals in a car. [Molly picks up the book and points to an illustration.] Could you put a giraffe in a car and drive it?

Students: No.

Molly: No. So they have to go in this.

Student 1: The elephant is too big.

Molly: Yes, the elephant is way too big for a car. [Molly picks up the book.] *The captain, Mr. Carrington, was honest and sincere. He thought they should drop the hook and wait for things to clear.* [Molly points to an illustration.] It looks like this is a picture of Mr. Carrington. [Molly lays the book flat on her lap.] It sounds like the captain thinks it's too foggy to keep going on the boat. He wants to put the anchor down and stay for the night. [Molly holds the book up and points to a character.] But, let's find out who this man is. *But Mr. Paine, the circus boss, was terribly demanding. He stomped up* [Molly stomps her feet] *to the helm, where Captain Carrington was standing, and screamed, "Don't stop! Keep going! I've got a show to do! Just get me down to Boston town tomorrow, sir, by two!"* [Molly lays the book flat on her lap.] So the author is giving us some hints. [Molly holds up the book and points to Mr. Paine.] This character is stumped. His face is red. He's yelling. How do you think he might feel?

Student 2: Angry.

Molly: Angry! Look at how angry he is. Maybe he is angry because the boat is slow because it's so foggy. Let's read more and find out. [Molly holds the book up.] *Then came a CRASH! An awful BASH! Things flew into the air! The ship had smashed into a ledge that no one knew was there.* [Molly points to the rocks in an illustration.] Can you see under here? What did they crash into?

Student 3: Rock.

Molly: Rock. *Ledge* is another word for rock. It's so foggy that they couldn't see where they were going and—crash!—they went into the rock and everything flew up into the air.

Student 4: And him.

Molly: And him. Yes, there's the boss, an ostrich, a cheetah, and a giraffe.

Student 5: Alligator.

Molly: Yes, all those animals.

Student 6: The alligator does not have to worry.

Molly: You're right the alligator might not have to worry, but what about the other animals?

Student 6: They're worried.

Molly: [Molly holds the book up.] *The shattered ship began to tip, then sank without a sound. The splashing, thrashing animals swam round and round.* [Molly puts the book flat on her lap.] So this page is going to make me ask some questions, because we know good readers ask questions. So, I wonder, are they far from shore? Are they going to have to swim a long time?

continued . . .

. . . from previous

Students: Yeah.

Molly: What do you think? Can all these animals swim? You were right that the alligator could maybe swim pretty easily. [Molly points to other animals in the illustration.] What about this zebra? What about this giraffe? How are they going to be able to swim? I'm thinking they will get rescued. We will find out.

Students: Yes, they will get rescued.

Molly: You think? You are making a prediction. You are making a guess about what's going to happen. Let's see if another boat comes to rescue the animals or maybe an airplane.

Student 4: Or a jet.

Molly: Or a jet. Could be. [Molly holds the book up to continue reading.] *The captain said to Mr. Paine, "Pray tell—what shall we do? We can't just leave them here to drown—we've got to save them too!" "The animals?" yelled Mr. Paine. "Why, sir, what are you DAFT?" Daft* means silly. "Are you crazy?" he's saying. *It's me that you should rescue! Pull me up into the raft. "Now ferry me to safety, sir, before I die of cold. Don't question me!" barked Mr. Paine. "Just do as you are told."* [Molly points to the illustration of the captain.] So there's the captain who said they shouldn't go any further because it's too foggy. And there is that angry circus boss who said they should keep going. It sounds like he should have listened to the captain's advice. [Molly points to the captain.] And he wants to go and save all the animals, and the circus boss says to forget them and get him into the boat instead. [Molly holds the book up to continue reading.] *Through chilly water, all night long, the animals swam on, until they reached an island beach, just before the dawn. They pulled themselves up on the shore—bedraggled, cold, and beat—then staggered to the village on weary, wobbly feet.* Take a look. How do you think the animals are feeling?

Student 1: Wet.

Molly: Well, they are wet. They might be feeling tired.

Student 2: Sad.

Molly: They might be feeling sad. They might be feeling exhausted.

Student 3: They all have their tongues out.

Molly: Yeah. Have you ever seen a dog who has played a lot and is panting? Maybe your dog sticks his tongue out, too. The animals are also tired because they stayed awake all night. [Molly holds the book up to continue reading.] *The people* *in the neighborhood had just begun to rise, and when they saw those animals, they had to rub their eyes.* [Molly rubs her eyes.] Imagine if you just woke up and looked out of your window and just saw that. What? You'd be like, "That's crazy!" *They thought they saw an elephant—but wait, how could that be? And what's that little monkey doing in the cherry tree?* [Molly points to every scene as she reads the following lines.] *Soon the animals were everywhere, and into everything. "There's an ostrich in the outhouse!" "There's a hippo in the spring!" "There's a tiger in the tulips!" "There's a lion on the lawn!" "There's a python in the pantry!" It went on and on and on.*

Student 1: What is a python?

Molly: *Python* is another word for a snake. I know Callie does not like snakes. Right, Callie?

Student 2: I like snakes.

Student 3: I love tigers and cheetahs.

Molly: Well, we'll see some pictures of tigers and cheetahs later. [Molly holds the book up to continue reading.] *Mr. Hood was stacking wood and nearly jumped a mile when he found the alligator sleeping on his pile! And Mrs. Dottie Dailey, who grew daisies by the bunch, discovered that the zebra had been eating them for lunch!* I'm going to make a connection. I know you guys have read *Mercy Watson*, right?

Student 1: Yeah.

Molly: This part is just like when Mercy Watson ate the flowers and Eugenia and baby Lincoln were not so happy. [Molly holds the book up to continue reading.] *And Miss Fannie Feeney found—according to the rumors—the silly little circus monkey swinging in her bloomers! Bloomers* is an old word for underwear. Look at the monkey swinging in his underwear on the clothesline. [Students start laughing.] *But everything changed quickly, like the turning of the tide, the night the Abbotts' shed caught fire with Emma Rose inside!* Look. There's a tiger up on the hill and you see the fire down below. *From high above the Abbotts' farm, the tiger saw the shed. The sight of smoke and fire triggered something in his head. He'd jumped through flames a thousand times back in his circus days, so he ran past all the people and he leapt into the blaze!* [Molly puts the book flat on her lap.] Let's make a prediction. A predication is a guess. What do you think the tiger is going to do?

continued...

. . . from previous

Student 1: Jump into the fire.

Student 2: Rescue her.

Molly: Rescue her? That's a good guess.

Student 3: Or jump through the fire.

Student 4: Take out the fire.

Molly: Take out the fire? Let read more and see because that's what we do with predictions. We see if we are right. *Then everybody panicked—"Help! Help! What can we do?"—when from the raging fire, something big burst into view. It was the most amazing sight, and everybody froze when they saw the tiger saving little Emma Rose!* [Molly points to Emma Rose.] How is Emma Rose feeling on the top of the tiger?

Student 1: Happy.

Molly: Does she look scared?

Student 2: No.

Students: Happy.

Molly: She doesn't look scared. She looks happy. "Look at me! The tiger saved me!" [Students start laughing.] *The tiger's risky rescue changed everybody's mind—the animals weren't bothersome—the animals were kind.* I know you guys know that word. *Kind.* Because this class is kind. *And so they lived together; side by side they got along. It didn't seem like anything could possibly go wrong.* [Molly puts the book flat on her lap.] So with the words and the pictures here, the author is telling me that the town people don't mind that the animals are there. They're having fun with them. Look. The students are using the elephant like a water slide. They're riding the camel. The bear is dragging them in a wagon. [Molly points to the pictures as she speaks.]

Student 1: The tiger is with them.

Molly: It seems like everybody's getting along.

Student 2: The tiger is a pillow.

Molly: The tiger is a pillow. We sometimes use our dog as a pillow. *Then little Red, the messenger, came running with the word. Apparently a circus ship had sunk, from what he'd heard. "The animals are from that boat. They swam in from the bay. The greedy owner wants them back. He'll be here any day!"* Remember that angry circus boss? This boy is saying

[Molly points to an illustration] he's coming back. So make a guess. If he's coming, what do you think the town people might want to do? What do you think, Juan Carlos?

Juan Carlos: I think hide.

Molly: Maybe they'll hide the animals. What do you think?

Student 2: Maybe they'll help them.

Molly: Maybe. We'll have to see. Let's read more. What do you think?

Student 3: Disguise.

Molly: *Disguise*. It's a fancy word for what Juan Carlos said—hide. *So the people called a meeting, and they quickly hatched a plan: No animal that came ashore would sail off with that man.* So you're right. Sounds like they are going to hide them or disguise them. Because no animal is going to go back with the angry circus boss. *The next day at the crack of dawn a ship was at the pier, and up the lane marched Mr. Paine, whose voice was loud and clear: "I am the circus owner. My ship sank in the murk. I've come to find my animals and put them back to work."*

Student 1: Nope.

Molly: You don't think so?

Student 1: I don't think that's going to happen.

Molly: No. This is my favorite page.

Student 2: What?

Molly: I'll read it, and then I want you to look very carefully at the pictures. *He hiked until he came into the center of the town. His face was red. He scratched his head.* [Molly scratches her head.] *He stood there with a frown.* Look at how the artist used color and space in the picture. I notice that Mr. Paine's coat color is very red and bold. The artist has also planted him right in the middle with everyone giving him nervous, sideways glances. He looks almost menacing. *Mr. Paine looked high and low, but still he couldn't see the fifteen circus animals of his menagerie.* So the author is telling us that there are fifteen animals hidden in the town.

Students: I can see. I can see all of them.

Molly: Okay, Juliana, come point out one. Tell me what you see.

Juliana: [walking up and pointing to the elephant] There's the elephant.

continued . . .

. . . from previous

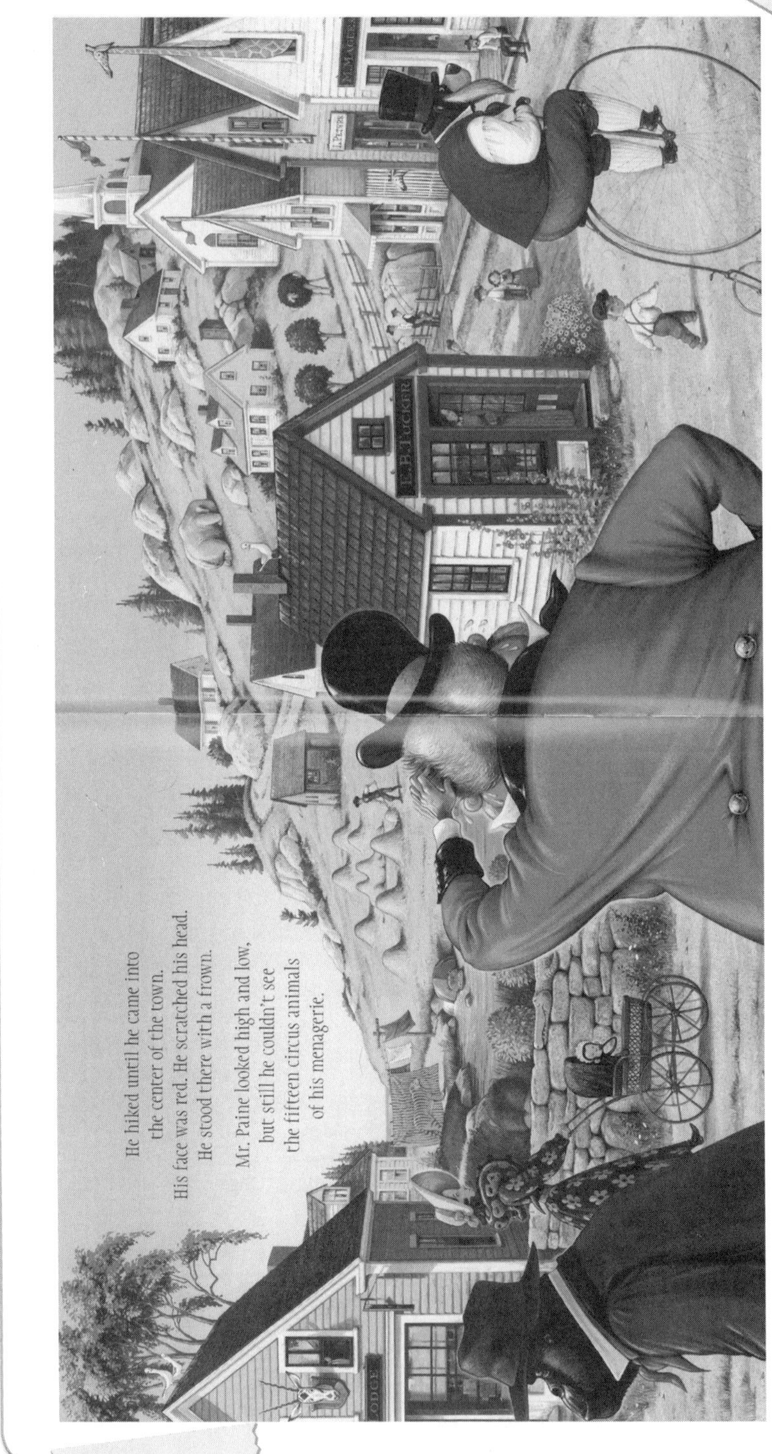
He hiked until he came into
the center of the town.
His face was red. He scratched his head.
He stood there with a frown.
Mr. Paine looked high and low,
but still he couldn't see
the fifteen circus animals
of his menagerie.
E.B. TUCKER

Can you find all fifteen animals hidden in Chris Van Dusen's clever illustration?

Molly: Juliana found an elephant. It looks just like a rock. [Molly points to the elephant.] What did you find? Come show us.

Molly: [Student 1 points to the gorilla.] You found this man? That's not a man. That's a gorilla. [Molly points to the gorilla.] Okay, we found two. All right. James, come find one for me. [James points to the bear.] Is that a person riding those bikes? No. It's a bear. We found three. Charlotte, come up and find one for me. [Charlotte points to the giraffe.] That's not a flagpole. That's a giraffe. Maisy, come find one. [Maisy points to the ostrich.] Oh my gosh. That's not a tree. That's an ostrich. Grace, come find one. [Grace points to the tiger.] Oh, this is a really tricky one. Look at that laundry on the line. A tiger's camouflaged. Callie, since it's your birthday today, would you like to find the last one that we'll look for? And then, I'll point them all out. I know you found some other ones. What did you find, Callie? [Callie points to the camel.] Oh my gosh. Those are not lumps of sand. That's a camel. [All the students are raising their hands and waiting to be called on.]

Student 1: I see one.

Student 2: I see two.

Student 3: I see more.

Molly: I'll know you're ready when you're sitting back down. I'll show them all to you. And I know some of you already found them. One. Two. Look, she is not wearing a scarf—she is wearing a python. Three. Four. Five. That's not a baby in the carriage—it's a monkey. Six. Look at that hippo. Seven. Eight. Let's see. Nine. Ten. Eleven. Twelve. Oh my gosh, I need three more. Thirteen.

Student 1: There's the tiger.

Molly: We've got the tiger.

Student 2: What about the giraffe?

Molly: We got the giraffe.

Student 3: But not the elephant.

Molly: Oh. We didn't get the elephant? Fourteen.

Student 4: No, we did.

Molly: [The children are calling out, trying to help Molly find more animals.] Later, I'll come around and let you find them all. Did you find the last one? We are looking for fifteen. It's a pretty tricky picture.

Student 6: I don't see it.

continued...

. . . from previous

Student 7: Oh, I know. [She walks up and looks for the fifteenth animal, but can't find it.]

Molly: All right. We'll find them all later. We found fourteen. What, James? Last chance. [James points to a seagull.] I don't think a seagull is a circus animal. All right. So remember Mr. Paine is looking for them and, just like you guys, he can't find them all. *He ran around the alleyways. He searched the village square. He even checked a chicken coop—his animals weren't there. Then Mr. Paine was tuckered out.* Look at his face. [Molly points to Mr. Paine.] He's red and sweating. *His heavy chest was heaving. Then Little Red stepped out and said: "I think your boat is leaving."* Let's make another prediction. What do you think Mr. Paine will do?

Students: Leave!

Molly: Let's find out if you're right. *He ran off in a fit of rage. His ship was leaving sight, so he jumped into a rowboat and he rowed with all his might. And from that day they like to say their lives were free of "Paine." It was a happy, peaceful place upon that isle in Maine.*

Available for download at **resources.corwin.com/ness-thinkalouds**

Appendix G

Think Aloud Script for *A Bad Case of Stripes* by David Shannon

What the Text Says	What I Say	The Comprehension Strategy I Model
But she never ate them. (p. 1)	*Why—if this girl loves lima beans—does she not eat them?*	? **Asking questions**
Camilla was always worried about what other people thought of her. (p. 1)	*From these clues, I can tell that Camilla is self-conscious and is just trying to fit in. Maybe she's afraid other kids will think it's weird that she likes lima beans, when they don't.*	**Making inferences**
Then she screamed. (p. 1)	*Why did she scream? Who is she trying to impress? What was wrong with the forty-two outfits she tried on?*	? **Asking questions**
"You're completely covered with stripes!" (p. 2)	*How did she get stripes all over? Is she sick? What will they do about the stripes?*	? **Asking questions**
And she had no idea what to wear with those crazy stripes. (p. 2)	*Now I understand that Camilla isn't faking! At first I thought she had drawn on herself with marker to get out of school—she was so worried about the first day. But now I see that she really did want to go to school.*	**Synthesizing**
"I've never seen anything like it. Are you having any coughing, sneezing, runny nose, aches, pains, chills, hot flashes, dizziness, drowsiness, shortness of breath, or uncontrollable twitching?" (p. 4)	*A golden line for me is "I've never seen anything like it." I can really tell this doctor is baffled and has no idea what is wrong with Camilla!*	A **Understanding the author's purpose**
And off he went. (p. 4)	*This part is mostly about how Camilla is perfectly fine, except for being different colors!*	**Synthesizing**

continued . . .

. . . from previous

What the Text Says	What I Say	The Comprehension Strategy I Model
. . . and she broke out in stars! (p. 6)	*I wonder why she begins to look like the flag. Why does she change from stripes to red, white, and blue?*	? **Asking questions**
. . . poor Camilla was changing faster than you can change channels on a T.V. (p. 8)	*The author isn't telling me why Camilla keeps changing, but I got an important clue earlier about how Camilla worries about what others think about her. Maybe the other kids are the ones who are making her change so many colors!*	**Making inferences**
"I'm going to have to ask you to keep Camilla home from school. She's just too much of a distraction, and I've been getting calls from the other parents. They're afraid those stripes may be contagious." (p. 10)	*At first, I wasn't sure about the meaning of the word contagious. I don't get many clues about what distraction means, but I do know that it's not a good thing. She's such a distraction that she's not supposed to come to school. Maybe the principal is worried that the kids won't learn with her there.*	**Monitoring and clarifying**
She couldn't believe that two days ago everyone liked her. (p. 10)	*I don't understand why she thinks the kids don't like her. Just because the principal thinks she's a distraction does not mean they dislike her.*	**Monitoring and clarifying**
Now, nobody wanted to be in the same room with her. (p. 10)	*Now I see—they are afraid they will catch what she has. That's what they mean with the word contagious.*	**Monitoring and clarifying**
. . . but she had been laughed at enough for one day. (p. 10)	*Why wouldn't she eat lima beans now? There are no kids around to laugh at her!*	? **Asking questions**
Then they filed out the front door, followed by Dr. Bumble. (p. 12)	*The author really wants to show that these doctors are stumped. They have no idea what is wrong with Camilla!*	A **Understanding the author's purpose**
. . . was a giant, multi-colored pill with her face on it. (p. 14)	*I'm getting some clues that might help me figure out what is wrong with Camilla. When the kids at school yelled for her to turn purple, she did. When the doctors gave her medicine, she turned into medicine. Maybe her illness has something to do with how other people want her to look.*	**Making inferences**
. . . he brought the Experts. (p. 16)	*How are the Experts different from the Specialists?*	? **Asking questions**

What the Text Says	What I Say	The Comprehension Strategy I Model
Instantly, Camilla was covered with different colored fungus blotches. (p. 16)	*The author really wants me to see how quickly Camilla is changing for these Experts. He uses the words suddenly and instantly to show how fast this takes place.*	A **Understanding the author's purpose**
But the Experts didn't have a clue, much less a cure. (p. 16)	*At first, I thought the Experts would have an answer, but now I see they are just as stumped as the other doctors and Specialists.*	**Synthesizing**
. . . telling the story of "The Bizarre Case of the Incredible Changing Kid." (p. 18)	*I'm guessing that Camilla is totally embarrassed now. She worries so much about other people's opinions, and now she's on the news! She must feel terrible.*	**Making inferences**
. . . an old medicine man, a guru, and even a veterinarian. (p. 21)	*Wow—that's a really long list of people whose jobs I don't really understand. I don't know what a guru or an herbalist is. I wonder if the author will explain more to me, or if this is just supposed to be a long list to show me how many people are trying to cure Camilla.*	**Monitoring and clarifying** A **Understanding the author's purpose**
But nothing worked. (p. 21)	*At this point, I'm wondering if Camilla will be like this forever. What will cure her?*	? **Asking questions**
She began to sob. (p. 22)	*Earlier I had the idea that Camilla was becoming what other people wanted her to become, and I get more evidence of that here—she becomes her room, just like this therapist suggests.*	**Synthesizing**
"But I think I can help." (p. 24)	*Who is this woman? How can she help?*	? **Asking questions**
"Here," she said. "These might do the trick." (p. 26)	*What is a bad case of stripes? And how will green beans help them?*	? **Asking questions**
"There's no such thing. These are just plain old lima beans. I'll bet you'd like some, wouldn't you?" she asked Camilla. (p. 26)	*I remember from the first line of the book that lima beans are one of Camilla's favorite foods—and here the lima beans are coming back. They must have a really important role in this story.*	A **Understanding the author's purpose**
"Oh, dear," the old woman said sadly. "I guess I was wrong about you." She put the beans back in her bag and started toward the door. (p. 26)	*I don't understand what the woman means by "I guess I was wrong about you." The author hasn't told me what she thought, so how does she know she was wrong? Maybe if I read on, I will find out.*	**Monitoring and clarifying**

continued . . .

. . . from previous

What the Text Says	What I Say	The Comprehension Strategy I Model
"Mmmmm," said Camilla. (p. 26)	*I'm guessing that Camilla is starting to make her own decisions and not care what other people think.*	**Making inferences**
"I knew the real you was in there somewhere." She patted Camilla on the head. Then she went outside and vanished into the crowd. (p. 28)	*The key information here is the line "I knew the real you was in there somewhere." It seems like the cure to a bad case of stripes was for Camilla to make up her own mind on what she likes.*	**Synthesizing**
. . . and she never had even a touch of stripes again. (p. 30)	*So what was the author's message here? I don't think he wrote the book just to tell us to eat lima beans—there's a bigger message than that. I think the message comes from the lady at the end of the story, who reminds us that the real Camilla was there somewhere, and the parts where Camilla doesn't care what other kids think. I think the author is telling me that it's okay to be my own person and to be a bit different from everyone else.*	A **Understanding the author's purpose**

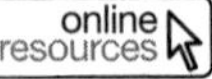

Available for download at **resources.corwin.com/ness-thinkalouds**

Appendix H

Think Aloud Self-Evaluation

How often did I . . . ?

	Not much	Sometimes	Often
Ask questions			
Make inferences			
Synthesize			
Understand the author's purpose			
Monitor and clarify			

The strategy I used the most is ____

____.

The best example of exactly what I thought while I used that strategy is ______________

____.

One strategy that I did not use at all or enough is ______________________________

____.

An example of how I could use that strategy in this text is __________________________

____.

online resources

Available for download at **resources.corwin.com/ness-thinkalouds**

Appendix I

Think Aloud Scripts

The final portion of this book contains the think aloud transcripts where I model the five comprehension strategies using authentic text. For each of the five comprehension strategies, I include at least two transcripts: one appropriate for K–2 readers and one appropriate for readers in Grades 3–5. I've made deliberate efforts to select high-quality children's books that are inclusive of gender, race, ethnicity, and social issues. Among the titles are award-winning books, some familiar and some less so. With each book, I provide an overview, my rationale for selecting the book, and its approximate reading level. You should feel free to use the transcript verbatim as I've provided it so that you are literally borrowing my words as you think aloud. You should also feel free to modify the transcripts for your readers and your teaching style. In other words, these transcripts are ready for immediate classroom use verbatim, but they are also flexible springboards from which you can jump-start your own think alouds. The following chart will help you keep track of which texts are aligned to which grade area and which comprehension strategy. When you are ready for transcripts that don't teach strategies in isolation, but rather interweave multiple strategies, check out Appendix J.

Strategy	Grade Level	Format	Title	Author
Asking Questions	K–2	Picture Book	*Smoky Night*	Eve Bunting
	3–5	Biography	*Who Was Anne Frank?*	Ann Abramson
Making Inferences	K–2	Narrative Picture Book	*Miss Nelson Is Missing!*	Harry Allard
	3–5	Narrative Picture Book	*The Stranger*	Chris Van Allsburg
Synthesizing	K–2	Picture Book	*My Lucky Day*	Keiko Kasza
	3–5	Historical Fiction	*The Story of Ruby Bridges*	Robert Coles
Understanding the Author's Purpose	K–2	Informational Text	*Lizards*	Laura Marsh
	K–2	Entertainment	*Private I. Guana: The Case of the Missing Chameleon*	Nina Laden
	K–2	Persuasive Text	*I Wanna Iguana*	Karen Orloff
	3–5	Entertainment, Informational Text	*Balloons Over Broadway: The True Story of the Puppeteer of Macy's Parade*	Melissa Sweet
Monitoring and Clarifying	K–2	Historical Fiction	*My Name Is Sangoel*	Karen Lynn Williams and Khadra Mohammed
	3–5	Informational Text	*Simple Machines: Wheels, Levers, and Pulleys*	David Adler

THINKING ALOUD WITH ASKING QUESTIONS

Good readers are naturally curious. They ask questions about what happens in the text. Sometimes the answers to their questions are found in the text, and sometimes they are not.

Teaching Asking Questions in Grades K–2 *Smoky Night* by Eve Bunting

Overview and Rationale

Inspired by the Los Angeles riots of the early 1990s, this book tells the story of one burning apartment building one night. Although they're neighbors, Daniel's cat and Mrs. Kim's cat don't get along. Nor do Daniel and his mother shop at Mrs. Kim's market. When Daniel's apartment building goes up in flames, all of the neighbors (including the cats) come together in spite of their differences. This visually appealing picture book presents opportunities for rich conversations about race, urban violence, and bridging differences.

This book was the recipient of the 1995 Caldecott Medal and earned a Parents' Choice Award; it is also an American Library Association Notable Children's Book and a School Library Journal Best Book of the Year.

Lexile Framework: 360L
Grade-Level Equivalent: 2.5
Guided Reading Level: P

What the Text Says	What I Say
We don't have our lights on though it's almost dark. (p. 1)	*Who is the "I" in this story? Where does this story take place? Why are the lights not on?*
People are rioting in the streets below. (p. 1)	*I know that people riot when they are angry, so this makes me wonder why they are rioting. What are they upset about? How do Mama and the narrator feel watching people riot? I guess they might be a bit scared, since they are watching and trying to hide in their home with no lights on.*
". . . They don't care anymore what's right and what's wrong." (p. 3)	*I wonder what would make people so angry that they would want to smash and destroy.*
". . . But they look happy, too," I whisper. (p. 3)	*Why would people look happy while rioting?*
"Are they stealing it?" I ask. Mama nods. (p. 3)	*I want to know where the police might be. Why are they not stopping the rioting and stealing?*
I've never heard anybody laugh the way they laugh. (p. 5)	*I wonder why they are laughing while breaking into a store. Is it because they think this is a game?*
. . . the distant flicker of flames. (p. 5)	*The clues of smoke and flames make me understand there is a fire somewhere. Is the fire a part of the rioting? Are people also starting fires?*
. . . go in Mrs. Kim's market even though it's close. (p. 7)	*I wonder why the narrator and Mama don't go into this store if it's so close.*
. . . it's better if we buy from our own people. (p. 7)	*I think this is an important line, but I wonder what this line means. What does "our own people" mean? Who are the other people?*
They pay no attention. (p. 7)	*What are the words the narrator can't understand? Are they in another language? Are people mad at Mrs. Kim? Or are they just rioters who are destroying anything in their way?*
". . . They're moving on." (p. 9)	*Finally I know who the narrator is—a boy named Daniel. I'm getting clues that Daniel feels scared—he's hiding behind his Mama and asking if the rioters will come there. I wonder who these rioters are.*

What the Text Says	What I Say
The plastic bags are still over them. (p. 9)	*The author is giving me clues about the setting of this story—I know there are different kinds of stores here, and Daniel is looking down at the street—maybe from an apartment building. I'm guessing that this story takes place in a city. This makes me wonder if this story really happened. Is the author's purpose to tell about real riots that actually happened?*
"We'll sleep together tonight," Mama tells me. (p. 11)	*Are there other characters in Daniel's family? Is there anyone besides him and Mama?*
Mama is shaking me. (p. 13)	*Why is she shaking him? Is it morning and time to wake up?*
"Quick, Daniel! Get up!" (p. 13)	*I've got a clue that it's not morning—Mama sounds anxious, so I wonder if she's waking Daniel up because something bad is happening.*
"Fire! Fire!" (p. 13)	*Here's an answer to my question. I think Mama is waking Daniel up in the middle of the night because they need to get away from the fire as fast as they can.*
"Put on your shoes. Hurry!" (p. 13)	*I wonder if Jasmine is really gone or if Mama just told Daniel that to get him to hurry up.*
The smoke makes me cough. (p. 13)	*I think I can answer my question about where this takes place—there are stairs and other people, which confirms my guess that this story takes place in an apartment building.*
"Hooligans!" (p. 13)	*I'm not exactly sure what hooligans are, but I think it's not a nice way to describe someone. Mr. Ramirez must be angry about the fire, and so he's upset with the hooligans who are rioting.*
Loco's squawking something awful. (p. 13)	*The author is showing me here how everyone is scared—babies are crying, adults are shouting, and animals are squawking. I wonder where everyone will go to be safer.*
The fire hasn't reached it yet. (p. 15)	*I want to know if the fire fighters will be able to stop the fire before it reaches their window.*
". . . She'll be long gone." (p. 15)	*What does the fireman mean by "long gone"? Does that mean the cat has died, or does it mean she went somewhere safe to escape the fire?*
"Everyone follow me." (p. 17)	*Who is this lady, and how does she know about the shelter? Is she there to help, or is she one of the neighbors escaping the fire?*
There are empty cartons everywhere. (p. 17)	*Who is the "we"? How many people follow the lady, besides Mama and Daniel? Is the glass from smashed windows? Why are there empty cartons? Are they things stolen from stores?*

continued . . .

. . . from previous

What the Text Says	What I Say
"We're almost at the shelter," the lady tells her. (p. 17)	*Is Mrs. Kim going to the shelter? I'm still wondering who this lady is. I'm getting the sense that she's not a rioter, since she seems ready to help. Is she from "our own people" like Mama described before?*
We see people from our building. (p. 19)	*Does Daniel go to this church? Who set up this shelter? How long will people stay at the shelter? Do they have to pay to stay at the shelter?*
What will happen to us? (p. 19)	*This question that Daniel asks seems really important, so it makes me ask more questions. Will Daniel and Mama be able to move back to their home? Who started the fire? Will they find Jasmine? How will they clean up from the riots?*
But I don't. (p. 19)	*It seems important that Daniel doesn't add his thoughts about her cat being mean. I wonder why he stays quiet. Is the author trying to show me that Daniel is trying to be kind to Mrs. Kim, because it's a sad sad night?*
She's always making me lie down. (p. 19)	*Now I'm wondering how old Daniel is. Is he a teenager? Is he younger than that? I'm thinking he's a bit younger, if his Mama is always wanting him to rest.*
I hide under my blanket. (p. 19)	*Are all these people Daniel's neighbors? Are they all leaving their homes because of the fire?*
". . . Thank you for finding her!" (p. 21)	*Where did the fire fighter find Jasmine? Will the cats be allowed to stay in the shelter too?*
I grin. "No, they weren't!" (p. 23)	*I think the author is telling me something important here. I know these cats didn't used to get along, sort of like Daniel and Mrs. Kim didn't really get along. But now, on this sad sad night, they are sticking together. It seems like an important event in the story. It's also the first time I've seen Daniel happy in this story.*
". . . You'll be able to go back in a day or two." (p. 23)	*How badly did the fire damage the building? Will they be able to go back to live forever, or just to collect their things and find a new place to live?*
"I thought those two didn't like each other." (p. 25)	*I'm just noticing that the author doesn't tell us the name of Mrs. Kim's cat. Is there a reason we don't know its name? Why did the author not give it a name?*
I whisper to Mama. (p. 25)	*I want to know more about people's reactions to what Daniel says. Why does everyone look at him and get so quiet?*

What the Text Says	What I Say
. . . the way she does when she's nervous. (p. 25)	*Why might Mama feel nervous in this instance?*
I think that's pretty funny, but nobody laughs. (p. 25)	*It's clear that this is the first time Mama introduces herself, but it seems like they've lived in this area for a while. I wonder why they haven't gotten to know each other as neighbors before this.*
Maybe she's not going to say anything. (p. 27)	*What is Mrs. Kim thinking? How will she react to this invitation?*
I reach out and stroke Mrs. Kim's big old orange cat, too. (p. 27)	*I'm noticing that Daniel doesn't say "big fat mean cat." Is Daniel changing his mind about the cat after he found out that it stayed with Jasmine in the fire?*
"He's purring!" (p. 27)	*At first I wasn't sure which cat was purring, but then I remembered that Jasmine is a girl and Daniel says "he's purring." I know cats purr when they feel safe or happy, so I think the author is telling me something important here. Maybe the cats are getting along for the first time, just like these neighbors are learning to meet each other. Is the author trying to tell me about one happy instance on an otherwise sad night?*
	After reading this book, I have more unanswered questions. How does the neighborhood recover from the riot? Do Daniel, Mama, and Mrs. Kim have a better relationship after this sad sad night?

Teaching Asking Questions in Grades 3–5
Who Was Anne Frank? by Ann Abramson

Overview and Rationale

The popular Penguin series *Who Was* is a collection of nonfiction books that introduce kids to important historical and popular figures. This biography examines Anne Frank's life before the secret annex, what life was like in hiding from the Nazis, and the legacy of her diary. Text features include maps, diagrams, and historical references to help young readers understand the time period during which Anne lived and died. Because of its unfamiliar content, new vocabulary, and technical text features, this nonfiction text presents ample opportunities for students to generate their own questions.

Lexile Framework: 660L

Grade-Level Equivalent: 3.8

What the Text Says	What I Say
Who Was Anne Frank? Anne Frank's life was short.	*I wonder why the author tells us right from the start that Anne Frank's life was short.*
She was only fifteen years old when she died in 1945.	*How did she die? What was life like in 1945?*
She was born in Germany, where her father's family had lived a very long time. Her father was very proud of being German. He expected his children to live in Germany, and their children after them.	*Why was Germany so important to her father?*
But that did not happen. The Franks' lives were turned upside down. They had to flee from their country. They had to go into hiding.	*Why did they have to flee? Who were they hiding from?*
They lost everything that was dear to them . . . all because they were Jewish and a man named Adolf Hitler was in power.	*This sentence is making me think that Adolf Hitler did not like people who were Jewish, and I wonder why.*
Hitler hated Jewish people. All Jewish people.	*Why did Hitler have such hatred for Jewish people?*
By the time Hitler was defeated, Anne's mother was dead. So were Anne and her sister. The only person in the family who survived was Anne's beloved father, Otto.	*Who defeated Hitler? Who fought against him? How was Anne's family killed? How did Otto survive?*
But something else survived, too. Anne's diary. Anne kept a diary for two years.	*I wonder why she kept a diary for so long. I wonder what she wrote in it. Did she write in it every day? How did her diary survive?*
During that time, her family was in hiding. They were hiding from Hitler's soldiers.	*Where did they hide? What might have happened if Hitler's soldiers had found them?*
Anne understood the dangers that her family faced. Yet in her diary she remained hopeful about the world even though terrible things were happening. She drew comfort from the beauty of nature even though she couldn't step outside for a single breath of fresh air.	*I'm getting the sense that she hid inside for two years, since she never breathed fresh air. How is it possible never to go outside for two whole years? How does she remain hopeful? Wouldn't she get discouraged?*
After her death, her diary was turned into a book.	*How did her diary become a book? Who found it and decided her story was important enough to make into a book?*
Today, more than sixty years after Anne's last diary entry, she remains a symbol of hope. Her diary has been translated into more than sixty-five languages. It has sold more than thirty million copies. There have been plays and movies about her. A short life—even a very short life—can be full of meaning.	*Why is she so important that there are plays and movies about her? Why do so many people want to read her book? What meaning was there in Anne's short life?*
Chapter I—A Happy Home Anne Frank was born on June 12, 1929, in the city of Frankfurt, Germany. Twelve days later, little baby Anne and her mother, Edith, came home from the hospital.	*Where on the world map is Germany? Why did they stay twelve days in the hospital? Was she sick as a baby?*

What the Text Says	What I Say
The Franks were like many other families of the time. Anne's father, Otto, was a businessman. Her mother stayed at home caring for Anne and Anne's older sister, Margot. The Franks led a comfortable life. There was a nanny to help Mrs. Frank. The family had nice clothes and good food. Anne had her own little sandbox to play in. Their apartment in Frankfurt was full of books.	*How do we know—so many years later—these details of Anne's life, like that she had a sandbox? Do we have pictures that show us these things?*
Otto Frank was many years older than his wife. In many ways they were opposites. Otto was tall and thin; Edith was plump. Otto loved being around people. He was high-spirited and outgoing. Edith was shy and quiet.	*Who was Anne more like—Otto or Edith? I wonder if she was closer to her mother or her father.*
Otto loved to read to his daughters. He also made up wonderful stories at bedtime. Some were about two sisters named Paula. One of the Paulas was very well behaved and polite, like Margot. The other Paula was always getting into lots of trouble.	*Does this mean that the other Paula was supposed to be like Anne? Did Anne get into trouble?*
That Paula was more like Anne, who was full of mischief.	*I answered my own question, but I want to know more about the kinds of mischief Anne got into. Did she get punished?*
Both girls adored their father. Their nickname for him was Pim.	*How did they come up with that nickname? Does it mean something special?*
Besides telling stories, Pim loved to play games. He was also a very good photographer. He took many pictures of his girls and kept a photo album for Anne.	*Did these photos survive? Are they some of the reasons we know so much about Anne?*
Anne was also very close to her grandmother, who was called Oma.	*Is Oma German for grandmother? Did her grandmother live with the family?*
Oma loved spoiling Anne. Once, when Anne was on a bus with Oma, Anne looked around and said, "Won't someone offer a seat to this old lady?" Anne was only four and a half at the time! But that was Anne. She was always outspoken.	*Did her family see her outspokenness as a good quality, or was it one of the reasons for her mischief?*
Her father understood her. He and Anne were very much alike. Anne did not get along nearly as well with her mother. They often had fights.	*What did Anne and her mother fight about?*
Anne was jealous because she felt that her sister was her mother's pet. While Margot was serious and mild-mannered, Anne was moody and had a temper. But she was also lively and full of fun. Both sisters had dark shining hair, large eyes, and lovely smiles.	*I'm getting a sense of how Anne got along with her parents, but I wonder if she got along with her sister.*
The Frank family was Jewish. They followed certain customs and went to pray at their synagogue on important days.	*I'm not really familiar with the word synagogue, but this sentence is telling me that it is a place the Jewish people went to pray. Maybe it's like a church.*

continued . . .

. . . from previous

What the Text Says	What I Say
They celebrated some Jewish holidays but not all of them. There were Jewish practices that they chose not to follow.	*I wonder why there were some holidays they didn't celebrate. I wonder why they didn't follow all of the Jewish practices.*
Many of Anne and Margot's friends in the neighborhood were not Jewish. They sometimes came to the Franks' house to celebrate Jewish holidays such as Hanukkah.	*I know that Hanukkah is a winter holiday, close to the time of Christmas. I wonder if it is a sad holiday or a happy one. Why is it important?*
Like all small children, Anne was not really aware of the bigger world around her. She knew her home, her family, her friends. That was her world. She did not know that Germany was going through many changes—many frightening changes.	*What were these changes, and why were they so frightening?*
World War I had ended in 1918 with Germany's defeat.	*The name World War I makes me think that the whole world was at war. Is that true? Who was fighting? Who defeated Germany?*
Unlike Otto Frank, many Germans were out of work until after the war's end. And prices for everything—even milk and bread—were sky high.	*Why were people unemployed during the war? Why did things cost so much?*
A new leader came to power in 1933: Adolf Hitler. He was head of the National Socialist, or Nazi, party.	*Was Hitler elected the head, like we elect our president? Or was he born into a family of leaders, like the queen and king in England?*
Hitler made the Germans feel better about themselves. He said German people were smarter and better than any other people on earth. "Pure" Germans, that is. Not Jews. In loud speeches before huge crowds, Hitler blamed Jewish people for all of Germany's problems.	*Did people believe Hitler? Why was Hitler so opposed to the Jews?*
Anti-Semitism is a word that means "hatred of the Jews."	*Did Hitler make up this word? Did people hate Jews before Hitler came to power?*
There was anti-Semitism long before Adolf Hitler in many places besides Germany. Throughout the world, at different times in history, Jewish people had to live in special neighborhoods. They couldn't go to schools with Christians or hold certain kinds of jobs.	*I know this is a big question, but throughout history, why did people see Jews as any different from themselves?*
But Adolf Hitler went much further. His plan was to get rid of the Jews.	*How did he plan to get rid of them? Was he going to make them live somewhere besides Germany? Can a leader really do that?*
Of course, he did not say that out loud. Not at first. But as soon as he came to power he started making life harder for German Jews like the Franks. Hitler was dangerous. Otto Frank saw that. He decided that his family would be safer if they left Germany.	*Where did Otto Frank plan to take his family to be safer?*

What the Text Says	What I Say
It must have been a hard decision for Anne's father to leave home. He loved his country. He had fought for Germany in World War I. In 1933, there were more than five hundred thousand German Jews. In the next six years, more than half of them fled the country.	*Where did the ones who fled go? What happened to those who stayed in Germany?*
For a short time, the family lived with one of Anne's grandmothers in Switzerland. Then, in the fall of 1933, Otto Frank moved to Amsterdam. By January 1934, the rest of the family had moved there, too. Amsterdam is the largest city in the Netherlands, a small country to the west of Germany.	*Was life better for Jews in Amsterdam?*
Why did the Franks pick this country? It was close by, for one thing. And Otto already knew how to speak Dutch, the language of the Netherlands. But even more important, the people were known for getting along with everyone—including Jews. In Amsterdam, Otto started a new company. It made pectin. Pectin is a powder used to make jam. The Franks moved into an apartment in a block of new houses. The girls started school. They made new friends. They learned to speak Dutch right away. Only Edith Frank had trouble with the new language. She stuck to German, which made her feel out of place in the Netherlands.	*How long were they planning to stay in Amsterdam?*
Still, Otto thought that his family was now safe from Hitler. But he was wrong.	*How could Hitler make them unsafe if they lived in a different country?*

THINKING ALOUD WITH MAKING INFERENCES

Good readers make inferences. An inference is something that is probably true. The author doesn't tell us exactly, but good readers take clues from the text and combine them with what they already know. An inference is made when a reader says, "This is probably true."

Teaching Making Inferences in Grades K–2
Miss Nelson Is Missing! by Harry Allard

Overview and Rationale

In my opinion, there is no better text to model making inferences than Harry Allard's *Miss Nelson Is Missing!* This back-to-school classic tells about a classroom full of misbehaving students, who blatantly disregard their good-natured teacher Miss Nelson. When a witch substitute Miss Viola Swamp appears, the children begin to regret their behavior. A savvy reader is able to use multiple clues from the text to infer that Miss Nelson and Miss Viola Swamp are the same person. The coincidental timing of Miss Nelson's disappearance and the appearance of Miss Swamp, a sighting of Miss Swamp by Miss Nelson's house, and a black dress hanging in Miss Nelson's closet lead to this inference. The humor of this book lies in its inferences. Without this important inference, the humor of the story and the message of appreciating the people we value are lost on young readers.

Lexile Framework: 340L

Grade-Level Equivalent: 3.1

Guided Reading Level: L

What the Text Says	What I Say
"Now settle down," said Miss Nelson in a sweet voice. (p. 4)	*Spit balls, paper airplanes—the author is giving me details to show me the kids are misbehaving. I can picture it! Hmmm, "sweet voice." Based on this detail, I wonder if Miss Nelson is too gentle to get this class to listen to her. Maybe her plea to "settle down" won't work!*
They were even rude during story hour. (p. 6)	*The author is giving me a clue with the word even. It suggests that story time is their favorite part of the day, but even during that, the kids will not listen!*
And they always refused to do their lessons. (p. 7)	*I wonder why these students are misbehaving. I'll keep reading to see if the author tells me why.*
"Something will have to be done," said Miss Nelson. (p. 7)	*Wow. I bet Miss Nelson is cooking up a plan. I know when a character says something, the author wants me to pay attention. I'm getting clues that Miss Nelson is planning something.*
Miss Nelson did not come to school. (p. 8)	*Maybe Miss Nelson is taking a day off because she's sick of dealing with a disruptive class. Perhaps she's staying home.*
A woman in an ugly black dress stood before them. (p. 10)	*The ugly dress, this person hissing, and her unpleasant voice make me think that somebody mean and strict is not going to tolerate these students misbehaving. Maybe this is the principal of the school. Maybe this is a substitute teacher.*
Miss Nelson's kids did as they were told. (p. 10)	*Wow! She rapped the desk and hissed. That behavior is a lot different from Miss Nelson's sweet approach. And the kids did what they were told. That's different too! I'm going to conclude that these kids are scared of Miss Swamp.*
"We'll have no story hour today," said Miss Swamp. (p. 14)	*Earlier I guessed that the kids really liked story time, and here I'm getting proof that my thinking was right. Maybe Miss Swamp knows how much they love story hour, and she takes it away as a punishment.*

What the Text Says	What I Say
The kids in Room 207 had never worked so hard. (p. 14)	*Earlier I made an inference that the kids were scared of Miss Swamp. I'm getting more evidence here to support that inference. The author suggests to me that they are working really hard so that Miss Swamp won't punish them more.*
The kids missed Miss Nelson! (p. 15)	*I'm getting the sense that the kids are starting to realize how good they had it with Miss Nelson.*
"Hmmmm. I think Miss Nelson is missing." (p. 17)	*The words and actions of Detective McSmogg make me think that he's not the smartest detective. I'm getting the sense that the kids are on their own to find Miss Nelson.*
. . . and no one answered the door. (p. 18)	*I'm getting clues that Miss Nelson is hiding and does not want to be found!*
But that was the least likely of all. (p. 24)	*The author is giving me more hints to make me think about how much the kids miss Miss Nelson. They are coming up with all sorts of possibilities for where she could be, and that makes me think that they are curious about where she went or that they are concerned about her.*
It was Miss Nelson! (p. 28)	*I'm making the inference here that the kids must be very excited about Miss Nelson's return. Just when they're thinking they'll be stuck with Miss Viola Swamp forever, they hear Miss Nelson's sweet voice. The author also uses an exclamation point to show that something exciting or important is happening.*
. . . during story hour no one was rude or silly. (p. 28)	*It could be that the kids are on their best behavior because they are so excited Miss Nelson has returned. Perhaps they've realized their behavior for Miss Nelson before was bad.*
"That's *our* little secret," said the kids. (p. 28)	*Miss Nelson won't tell her secret of where she was, and the kids won't tell their secret about the change in their behavior. The author also used italics on the word our to show that the kids are in on the secret.*
"I'll never tell," she said to herself with a smile. (p. 30)	*Throughout the end of the story, the author has given me some important clues. I'm going to add up those clues to make an inference about the identity of Miss Viola Swamp. I know that Miss Nelson disappeared at the same time Miss Swamp appeared. I know the kids saw Miss Swamp right by Miss Nelson's house. Now I know that Miss Nelson has a black dress in her closet and a secret she won't tell. All of this evidence makes me think that Miss Nelson and Miss Swamp are the same person. I'm making an inference that Miss Nelson dressed up in a disguise to teach her kids a lesson about their behavior.*

continued . . .

What the Text Says	What I Say
He is now looking for Miss Viola Swamp. (p. 32)	*Earlier I inferred that Detective McSmogg wasn't that bright, and I've got even more evidence of that here. I was able to make the inference that Miss Nelson and Miss Swamp were the same person—but Detective McSmogg couldn't figure that out. This makes me think he won't be successful looking for Miss Swamp!*

Teaching Making Inferences in Grades 3–5 *The Stranger* by Chris Van Allsburg

Overview and Rationale

Chris Van Allsburg is a master of making inferences. He creates mystery by leaking a story slowly and carefully onto the page through both his words and his illustrations. The clues that he embeds are clear enough to provoke thinking and guessing, but not so blunt as to remove the sense of mystery and wonder.

I've chosen to model making inferences to upper-elementary students with *The Stranger*. Late one summer, Farmer Bailey has an accident. Driving along in his truck, he hits a man dressed in an unusual suit of leather. The farmer brings the stunned and confused (but otherwise unharmed) fellow back with him to his home. Farmer Bailey's wife and daughter welcome the stranger. The doctor comes and tells the Baileys that the man has temporarily lost his memory but will probably be fine in a few days. The man stays on and becomes a part of the family in spite of his odd ways. At the conclusion of the story, students are left to make their own inferences about the stranger's identity. Even though I'm using this mentor text to model making inferences, there are logical stopping points where I also ask questions.

Lexile Framework: 640L

Grade-Level Equivalent: 3.5

Guided Reading Level: P

What the Text Says	What I Say
"Oh no!" he thought. "I've hit a deer." (p. 1)	*I'm making the inference that Farmer Bailey is upset about hitting a deer because of the damage it might do to his truck. Or maybe he's upset because he is an animal lover and is worried about the deer.*
. . . the farmer took his arm and helped him to the truck. (p. 3)	*I wonder why the man tries to run off. Maybe he's scared. Maybe he's hurt.*

What the Text Says	What I Say
"I don't think," whispered Mrs. Bailey, "he knows how to talk." (p. 5)	*The author is giving me clues about this stranger. This man doesn't talk and is dressed in weird clothes. These clues are making me ask some questions. I wonder what the Baileys will do next with this stranger. Will they call the cops? Will they take him to a doctor or a hospital? How is Katy feeling—scared of this stranger or curious? What makes Mr. Bailey think this man is a hermit—just his clothes and his not talking? It seems really important to figure out who this stranger is.*
". . . the mercury is stuck at the bottom." (p. 7)	*I know that old-fashioned thermometers show that as something gets hotter, the mercury rises. Here the doctor says that the mercury is stuck at the bottom, so I can make an inference that when he took the stranger's temperature, he was very cold.*
The fellow seemed confused about buttonholes and buttons. (p. 9)	*Never seen buttons? This clue is more proof that the stranger lives by himself in a place far away from people and stores and modern conveniences.*
"Brr," she said. "There's a draft in here tonight." (p. 9)	*The author is giving me some clues about temperature playing an important role. First we had the incident with the thermometer. Here we've got the stranger staring at hot soup and the cold air that Mrs. Bailey feels. I also remember that the author set this story at the start of fall, with a cool breeze blowing. Maybe this book has something to do with temperatures and the change of seasons.*
. . . then stopped and looked back, as if they expected the stranger to follow. (p. 11)	*The rabbits hopped toward him? I think the author gave me that important detail for a reason—maybe to show me that the stranger has special powers, or that he's lived in nature so long that wild animals are not afraid of him.*
He didn't even sweat. (p. 13)	*I'm thinking that the fact that the stranger didn't sweat is an important clue about his identity.*
He stared at them like a man who'd been hypnotized. (p. 15)	*This information seems to confirm my earlier thought about nature being important to the stranger. He can't stop looking at the migrating geese.*
The leaves on the trees were as green as they'd been three weeks before. (p. 19)	*Based on these clues, I can conclude that the appearance of the stranger might have something to do with the weather being so different than usual.*
It would be much better, he thought, if all trees could be red and orange. (p. 21)	*I'm thinking that the stranger wants the autumn to come to the Baileys' farm. He sees the green trees as ugly and wishes the fall colors for the Baileys. I'm wondering if he can do anything about this.*

continued . . .

...from previous

What the Text Says	What I Say
... without thinking, blew on it with all of his might. (p. 23)	*I remember earlier how Mrs. Bailey got cold when the stranger blew on her soup. Using that clue plus my knowledge that the stranger wants the trees to change colors, I can make an inference that blowing on the leaf will bring cold air to help the trees change to their autumn colors.*
... the Baileys could tell that their friend had decided to leave. (p. 25)	*I wonder where he is going. I wonder why he's decided that it's time to leave.*
... words that say simply, "See you next fall." (p. 27)	*The author has finished this book without telling me who the stranger is, but I have some clues to make an inference about him. I know that this stranger was cold—the author gave me clues about the thermometer, the draught of cold air, and staring at the steam from the hot soup. I know that this stranger was involved with nature, like the wild animals. I know that this stranger wanted the leaves to change color—like when he blew on the green leaf.*
	And in this last bit of the book, I know that the leaves change every fall—and words are etched on the window. I'm getting clues to make me think that this stranger is Jack Frost. Jack Frost is an imaginary person who brings snow, frost, ice, and cold weather. He colors the trees in the fall and leaves patterns on cold windows in the winter.

THINKING ALOUD WITH SYNTHESIZING

Good readers change their thinking as they read more and add more information from the text.

Teaching Synthesizing in Grades K–2
My Lucky Day by Keiko Kasza

Overview and Rationale

When a delicious-looking piglet knocks on Mr. Fox's door "accidentally," the fox can hardly believe his good fortune. It's not every day that dinner just shows up on your doorstep. It must be his lucky day! Or is it? Before Mr. Fox can say grace, the piglet has manipulated him into giving him a fabulously tasty meal, the full spa treatment (with bath and massage), and . . . freedom.

Lexile Framework: 270
Grade-Level Equivalent: 1.5
Guided Reading Level: J

What the Text Says	What I Say
As he polished his claws, he was startled by a knock at the door. (p. 1)	*The important idea here is that it's dinnertime for this fox.*
If there were any rabbits in here, I'd have eaten them for breakfast. (p. 2)	*I was thinking that someone was looking for the fox, but now I'm thinking that someone is knocking on the wrong door. I'm wondering who is at the door.*
He grabbed the piglet and hauled him inside. (p. 5)	*My schema is that foxes eat other animals, so this part makes me think that the fox grabbed the piglet and is going to eat him since I already know he's hungry.*
". . . Now get into this roasting pan." (p. 7)	*I'm thinking the fox feels lucky because dinner came straight to his door, without him having to do any hunting.*
"You're a terrific scrubber," said the piglet. (p. 11)	*Now I'm wondering if the piglet is trying to trick the fox. It seems odd that the piglet isn't trying to escape when the fox is off starting the fire.*
"I will. But . . ." (p. 13)	*The word* but *gives me more reason to think that the pig is plotting something. Maybe he's going to ask for something else besides a bath.*
"He is on the small side." (p. 13)	*Now I'm wondering if the fox is going to get the pig something to eat—to fatten him up.*
"You're a terrific cook," said the piglet. (pp. 14–15)	*At first, the fox thought he had it so easy—dinner came knocking on his door! But now, he's had to give this pig a bath and cook him dinner. It seems like this fox is working awfully hard.*
"I will. But . . ." (p. 17)	*There's that word* but *again. I think the pig is going to ask for something else. What could it be this time?*
"I do prefer tender meat." (p. 17)	*Now I understand that the pig has some sort of plan to trick the fox. He's asked for a bath, a meal, and now a massage. I'm wondering what he's up to.*
". . . A little to the right, please . . . yes, yes . . . now just a little to the left . . ." (p. 21)	*There's evidence here that the pig is really planning something to trick the fox—he's really demanding that the fox work hard on this massage!*
". . . let alone a roasting pan." (pp. 22–25)	*Now I understand the piglet's plan—to make the fox work so hard he's too tired to cook the pig!*
. . . picked up the rest of his cookies and headed for home. (p. 25)	*At first I thought the pig was doomed—he was about to get eaten! But now I realize the pig outsmarted the fox!*

continued . . .

. . . from previous

What the Text Says	What I Say
"This must be my lucky day!" (p. 26)	*At the beginning of the book, the fox said it was his lucky day—lucky that his dinner knocked on his door without even having to hunt. Now we see the pig saying it was his lucky day.*
"Who shall I visit next?" (p. 29)	*At first, I thought the pig accidentally knocked on the fox's door—that he was lost, and looking for rabbit's home. But now I think that the pig has been using this trick on other animals—in the picture of his address book, I see that the pig crossed out fox and coyote, and he has the addresses for wolf and bear. I'm getting the sense that this pig outsmarts all these animals, and plans to visit the wolf or bear next. What a clever pig to pull off these tricks! And the final page of the book has a picture of the pig knocking on bear's door. I'm going to guess this same trick will work on the bear!*

Teaching Synthesizing in Grades 3–5
The Story of Ruby Bridges by Robert Coles

Overview and Rationale

This powerful story tells of six-year-old Ruby Bridges, who is at the forefront of the school desegregation movement in the 1960s. Every day, Ruby bravely walks through crowds of angry protesters to pursue her education. When white families pull their children from the school, Ruby studies alone with her teacher. The book sends messages about the power of faith, perseverance, and forgiveness.

Lexile Framework: 730L

Grade-Level Equivalent: 5.4

Guided Reading Level: O

What the Text Says	What I Say
". . . I was four, I think." (p. 1)	*The gist here is that Ruby Bridges had a hard childhood. She grew up poor with almost no food. When her dad lost his job, she had to move.*
Ruby's mother went to work scrubbing floors in a bank. (p. 2)	*The text is mostly about how hard Ruby's parents worked.*
"We wanted them to start feeling close to Him from the very start." (p. 2)	*Now I know that religion was also important to Ruby's family.*

What the Text Says	What I Say
And it was against the nation's law. (p. 4)	*The important idea here is that schools were segregated, even though this was against the law.*
Ruby Bridges was sent to first grade in the William Frantz Elementary School. (p. 5)	*The important idea here is that Ruby is about to be the only black girl in a white school.*
We prayed long and we prayed hard. (p. 6)	*At first I thought that Ruby's family would not want her to go to this school, but now I think they saw it as an important opportunity.*
. . . a large crowd of angry white people gathered outside the Frantz Elementary School. (p. 8)	*The most important word here is* angry. *This gives me some hints that things might be difficult for Ruby.*
The city and the state police did not help Ruby. (p. 8)	*The key information here is that Ruby is alone in her struggle; not even the cops seem to protect her.*
The marshals carried guns. (p. 8)	*At first I was nervous for Ruby, but now I'm getting the sense that this is dangerous. The marshals carrying guns shows me that things are violent.*
Ruby experienced that kind of school day. (p. 11)	*Before I thought that the crowds were there just for the first days of Ruby's school, but now I see the violence went on for months.*
Ruby would hurry through the crowd and not say a word. (p. 11)	*At first I thought Ruby might try to sneak into school without people seeing her. But here I learn that Ruby walked proudly to school—slowly, dressed nicely.*
The white people in the neighborhood would not send their children to school. (p. 12)	*I'm getting more evidence of how strongly people reacted—that people kept their white children home from school just because of Ruby.*
. . . she was all alone except for her teacher, Miss Hurley. (p. 12)	*I'm really curious about how Miss Hurley reacts to Ruby. Will she welcome Ruby, or will she be cruel like the others?*
. . . with a big smile on her face, ready to get down to the business of learning. (p. 12)	*Now I'm really seeing how important school is to Ruby and to her family. It doesn't bother her that she's all alone.*
". . . She seemed as normal and relaxed as any child I've ever taught." (p. 12)	*Now I understand that Miss Hurley was a supportive teacher to Ruby, who appreciated her hard work and personality.*
. . . in an empty classroom, an empty building. (p. 12)	*This sentence makes me wonder how long they will keep the school open, if there is only one student in it.*
"Sometimes I'd look at her and wonder how she did it," said Miss Hurley. "How she went by those mobs and sat here all by herself and yet seemed so relaxed and comfortable."	*I'm really getting the idea that Ruby is a strong little girl, who is brave and determined.*

continued . . .

. . . from previous

What the Text Says	What I Say
. . . or even decide that she no longer wanted to go to school. (p. 14)	*I'm seeing the respect that Miss Hurley has for Ruby. She truly cares about how Ruby is doing.*
Then one morning, something happened. (p. 16)	*The way the author wrote this makes me think that it's something bad.*
She seemed to be talking to them. (p. 16)	*At first I thought that someone was going to try to hurt Ruby, but now I'm thinking that Ruby is going to try to calmly talk to the crowd.*
The marshals were frightened. (p. 18)	*Now I understand just how tense this moment is.*
Then Ruby stopped talking and walked into the school. (p. 18)	*I'm really seeing how brave and determined Ruby is, to talk to this crowd. I also really want to know exactly what she said to the crowd and how they reacted!*
Ruby became irritated. (p. 21)	*I'm surprised by Ruby's reaction. Why is she irritated by what Miss Hurley said?*
. . . she was already in the middle of the angry mob. (p. 21)	*Wow. Now I really see how kind Ruby is. All these months, she says prayers and kind words to the people who have treated her with hate and violence. This part also reminds me how important religion is to Ruby, just like I learned at the start of the book.*
Just like You did those folks a long time ago when they said terrible things about You. (p. 22)	*The key idea here is forgiveness. Not only is Ruby brave and determined, but she can forgive the people who hate her. It seems by ending this book with Ruby's prayer, the author sends the message of how important it is to forgive people.*

THINKING ALOUD WITH UNDERSTANDING THE AUTHOR'S PURPOSE

Good readers try to figure out the reason that the author wrote a text. They want to know the purpose of the text. If a text gives a clear opinion or tries to convince the reader of something, the author's purpose is to persuade. If a text gives facts or tells a reader how to do something, the author's purpose is to inform. If the text is enjoyable, tells a story, or uses a story to teach a lesson, the author's purpose is to entertain.

Why was the book written? What was the purpose? Was it to persuade readers? Was it to inform, or give the readers new information? Was it to engage us in an entertaining story? To begin thinking aloud for understanding the author's purpose, I have selected three interrelated texts—all on the same topic. By choosing books on the same topic, young readers can see the different purposes of each author. The scripts with *Lizards*, *I Wanna*

Iguana, and *Private I. Guana: The Case of the Missing Chameleon* will showcase these different purposes.

It is important to note that there are not absolute demarcations between the different categories of an author's purpose. An author does not write a text solely to inform or to persuade; these purposes are not neat and tidy distinctions. Often, texts achieve a couple of purposes. Today's best nonfiction authors can both inform and entertain their readers. For further evidence of this, take a look at the think aloud script of *Balloons Over Broadway: The True Story of the Puppeteer of Macy's Parade*.

Teaching Understanding the Author's Purpose in Grades K–2: Inform *Lizards* by Laura Marsh

Overview and Rationale

Kids are fascinated by the creepy-crawly! This informational text, published through National Geographic Kids, provides fascinating information on all types of lizards—from geckos to iguanas, from Komodo dragons to chameleons. This compact book includes multiple text features, such as a table of contents, detailed glossy photos, and labeled diagrams. Geared toward the early reader, this text clearly demonstrates the author's purpose of informing.

Lexile Framework: 370

Grade-Level Equivalent: 2.6

Guided Reading Level: M

What the Text Says	What I Say
What am I? A lizard! (pp. 4–5)	*I predict that the author's purpose is to inform about all of the different kinds of lizards—some small, some big, some smooth, some bumpy.*
Turtles, snakes, crocodiles, and tortoises are also reptiles. (p. 6)	*Here, the author really wants me to understand what reptiles are, and some of the characteristics of reptiles.*
Lizards live on every continent except Antarctica. (pp. 8–9)	*I think what the author is really telling me is that lizards would rather be warm than be cold. They have to keep themselves warm, and they don't live on the coldest continent, so the purpose here is to show me why lizards are better suited for warm climates.*
Scales keep a lizard from losing water, too. (p. 11)	*The author wants me to learn how important scales are for keeping lizards safe, warm, and hydrated.*

continued...

. . . from previous

What the Text Says	What I Say
It's dinnertime! (pp. 14–15)	*Here, the author is informing me about all of the types of foods a lizard will eat.*
Baby lizards can take care of themselves. (p. 16)	*I'm getting the sense that the author really wants me to see that lizards are unique since the babies don't need their mothers.*
Snakes don't have these. (pp. 18–19)	*The author wants me to be sure that even if they sometimes look alike, lizards and snakes are not the same thing.*
Predators can't see them. (p. 20)	*A golden word for me here is* camouflage. *The author uses it to show me how well lizards can hide.*
And some lizards just try to look big and strong. (pp. 22–23)	*The author doesn't want me to think that lizards only hide—here she informs me of ways that they try to get noticed.*
A new tail will grow back in its place. (pp. 24–25)	*By giving me all of these examples, the author is really making me see how dangerous lizards can be.*
That's about the size of a pushpin. (pp. 26–27)	*The author has written this page to inform me about how different lizards can be—both big and small!*
Let's hear it for the lizards! (p. 28)	*In this last page of the book, I can tell the author wrote this book to inform us about how different and unique lizards are.*

Teaching Understanding the Author's Purpose in Grades K–2: Entertain *Private I. Guana: The Case of the Missing Chameleon* by Nina Laden

Overview and Rationale

This entertaining book opens with Private I. Guana taking a case of a missing chameleon. Noting that chameleons are hard to find with their ever-changing colors, the detective hangs missing posters. His search leads him to the swamp, the forest, and the Lizard Lounge. Inspired by 1940s detective films, this book is replete with wordplay and visual puns.

Grade-Level Equivalent: 2

What the Text Says	What I Say
I guess I'm a sucker for a lizard in distress. (p. 1)	*Right from the start, I think the author is about to tell me a funny clever story. I like how she makes a pun out of the name—*Private *is a nickname for a private investigator, or a detective. I know that an iguana is a kind of lizard, so it's funny to me to think about a lizard as a detective trying to find another lizard. I like how the author says that chameleons are hard to find. That's a pun on how chameleons camouflage, or change colors.*
. . . as she made herself comfortable in my office. (p. 3)	*Another pun! Liz, as in short for* Lizard*!*
"What color was he when you last saw him?" (p. 3)	*The author is taking information about lizards from other books—like crickets changing colors—and making it part of the humor of this book.*
Maybe I'll go talk to some boulders. (p. 5)	*Look how much effort the author is putting into entertaining me—the joke about coloring the posters to show the chameleon, and a bullfrog named Croak who "jumps" to conclusions! All of these little jokes and puns engage me as the reader.*
But maybe I just wasn't looking in the right place. (p. 7)	*Here are some more jokes—usually people say "hit the pavement," but this lizard is "hitting the dirt" instead. His tongue is tied—I know lizards use their tongues a lot.* Tongue-tied *is an expression that means being stumped or confused.*
It was kind of a slimy place, where only the most cold-blooded reptiles hung out. (p. 9)	*I know the author is trying to make me laugh here—we use the word* slimy *as another way to say bad, and that's funny because lizards are slimy. And I learned about how lizards are cold-blooded reptiles, but cold-blooded can also be a way to describe someone who is unkind.*
I scoped out the place, making sure not to ruffle any feathers or step on any tails. (p. 11)	*Let me slow down a bit so I can really notice the author's jokes. There are a couple expressions that are jokes about the creatures in this lounge. "Ruffle feathers" means to not upset anyone. We usually say "step on anyone's feet" to mean not upsetting anyone, but the author changed it to "step on anyone's tails" as a pun.*
"It's probably just a coincidence," I thought to myself. (p. 11)	*I remember Liz saying that Leon's favorite was cricket stew, and it's on the menu tonight at the Lizard Lounge. That seems like an important clue from the author.*
I noticed a sign on the stage that said, *This week: Camille and the Gila Girls.* (p. 13)	*I'm recognizing so many words from the book informing me about lizards—*salamander, amphibian, Gila.
I was hypnotized. (p. 15)	*This is supposed to be a mystery, and I like how the author has really added elements of suspense here. She doesn't come right out and tell me about this "unusual chameleon" but gives me clues about her being familiar and him not being able to concentrate. This really makes me want to find out more about the singer.*

continued . . .

. . . from previous

What the Text Says	What I Say
. . . looking for her dressing room door. (p. 17)	*I'm beginning to wonder how Camille relates to the search for Leon. Why is the author telling me this part of the story?*
. . . I could find from my pocket and handed it to her. (p. 19)	*I like how the author uses his shaking and stammering to show me exactly how nervous Private I. Guana is.*
I was totally confused. (p. 21)	*Camille's reaction and question to the detective stump me—I'm really wondering what is going on, and the suspense that the author has created makes me want to keep reading.*
Camille was Leon, the missing chameleon. (p. 21)	*Wow! The author really surprised me here. I did not see this surprise coming. I had no idea that Leon and Camille were the same person.*
Naturally, I blended right in. (p. 21)	*The author wants me to see exactly why Leon disappeared. He wants to be special and show his talent, so he starts singing.*
Leon was the singing sensation of the swamp. (p. 23)	*I love how the author repeats the s sounds there—it's fun to read "singing sensation of the swamp."*

Teaching Understanding the Author's Purpose in Grades K–2: Persuade *I Wanna Iguana* by Karen Orloff

Overview and Rationale

Written as a series of letters between a mother and her son Alex, this book presents Alex's attempt to persuade his mother to get him a pet iguana. He promises that he will be completely responsible for it, but Mom fears life with a six-foot iguana. Alex tries to assuage her fears as their negotiations continue. Because it is written in child-friendly language, kids will relate to Alex's efforts to convince his mother of what he wants.

Lexile Framework: 460
Grade-Level Equivalent: 2.3
Guided Reading Level: J

What the Text Says	What I Say
Signed, Your sensitive son, Alex (p. 1)	*I wonder why the author has started off with a letter. I'll have to keep reading to find out more. But I like—right from the start—how the author is showing me that Alex is trying to convince his mother of what he wants. He wants an iguana, and she does not.*
Love, Mom (p. 2)	*I like how we get a response from Alex's mom. I think the author is using these letters to let the characters give their side of the argument.*
Love, Your adorable son, Alex (p. 4)	*I like how the author signs the letters "adorable" and "sensitive" son. It makes me think that Alex is really trying to turn up the charm to get what he wants.*
Just thought I'd mention it. Love, Mom (p. 5)	*The author is showing me here that Mom won't give in without a fight. She's not convinced by Alex's efforts.*
. . . much less on your dresser (with or without your trophies) . . . (p. 7)	*Here I can see that Alex is trying a new route to persuading his mom—trying to make her think that she would never even know the iguana is there because it would be so small. But Mom comes back with a fact to show him he's wrong!*
Love, Your smart and mature kid, Alex (p. 9).	*I'm wondering why the author has Alex writing only to his mom, not to "Mom and Dad." Maybe he doesn't live with his dad. Or maybe his mom is the decision maker of the house, so he doesn't include his dad on the letters.*
. . . when you own a six-foot-long reptile? (p. 11)	*I'm noticing how clever his mom is. Not once has she said no. Instead she's just poking holes in his argument.*
This iguana can be the brother I've always wanted. (pp. 12–13)	*It looks like Alex is trying another route to persuading his mom. By saying he is "lonely" and has always wanted a brother, he's trying to make her feel guilty. If she feels guilty, maybe she will say yes.*
You have a brother. (p. 14)	*Ha! Looks like Mom wins again—he already has a brother, and she doesn't feel guilty!*
I could teach it tricks and things. (p. 16)	*The author is showing me here that Alex really won't quit. He must really want that iguana!*
Remember what happened when you took home the class fish? (p. 17)	*I like here how the author has Mom ask questions. Rather than lecturing Alex about responsibility, she's making Alex remember something bad that happened with the fish.*
I never would have taken the cover off of the jar! (p. 18)	*How did a fish jump into spaghetti sauce? The author is showing me that Alex has accepted his mistake, but maybe he's only saying this to get his iguana.*

continued . . .

. . . from previous

What the Text Says	What I Say
Let's say I let you have the iguana on a trial basis. (p. 19)	*A golden line here is "Let's say." The author is showing me that Alex's mom is considering the iguana!*
And I would clean his cage when it got messy. (p. 20)	*I like how the author uses all of these arguments to make me as the reader root for Alex. Here he's trying to show how responsible he is so he can persuade his mom.*
P.S. If you clean his cage as well as you clean your room, you're in trouble. (p. 22)	*I'm really liking the author's decision now to write this book in the form of letters. They are much funnier and more appealing than if Alex and his mom were just having a conversation about the iguana.*
I'll pay for the lettuce with my allowance. (p. 23)	*I'm seeing that the author is giving us another persuasion tactic—Alex will spend his allowance on the iguana's food.*
"Yes, Mom! I wanna iguana . . . Please!" (p. 24)	*The author has changed to speech. I wonder why? My guess is that this conversation is so important it can't just happen through letters.*
"YESSSS! Thank you! Thank you!" (p. 26)	*The author doesn't come right out and say it, but the picture and Alex's reaction let me know he was successful in persuading his mom to let him get the iguana. He used lots of different arguments to convince her, but I think the most important thing was his persistence! He did not give up.*

Teaching Understanding the Author's Purpose in Grades 3–5 *Balloons Over Broadway: The True Story of the Puppeteer of Macy's Parade* by Melissa Sweet

Overview and Rationale

Many of our students will be familiar with the iconic Macy's Thanksgiving Day Parade, but who really knows its behind-the-scenes story? This nonfiction book tells the story of puppeteer Tony Sarg, the creative genius of the parade's famous balloons. The winner of the 2012 Robert F. Sibert Informational Book Medal and the NCTE Orbis Pictus Award, this exemplary biography informs the reader about Tony's dedication, imagination, and perseverance.

Lexile Framework: 1,000

Grade-Level Equivalent: 4

Guided Reading Level: N

What the Text Says	What I Say
. . . when he was only six years old. (p. 1)	*I predict that the author is going to tell me how Tony became a marionette man. I don't really know what a marionette man is, so I also think the author is going to explain that to me.*
. . . and his dad, so impressed, never made Tony do another chore. (p. 2)	*I like how the author used this example of feeding the chickens to show how creative Tony was, and how he used these pulleys to avoid getting out of bed.*
Word soon spread about Tony's amazing marionettes. (p. 3)	*The author here wants me to understand exactly what a marionette is. She doesn't give me an exact definition but gives me hints so that I can figure it out myself—with the hints "wood, cloth, strings, and puppets," I can tell that marionettes are a kind of puppet made out of cloth and wood that have string to make them move.*
. . . then attached them to gears and pulleys to make them move. (pp. 3–4)	*The author is trying to show me how Tony started his career in New York City—first on Broadway, where there are plays and musicals, and next at Macy's store where he started a puppet parade.*
Macy's even arranged to bring in bears, elephants, and camels from the Central Park Zoo. (pp. 5–6)	*At first I thought the author wrote this story to tell me about Tony's life. Now I see that the author wrote the story more to tell about how he helped create the Macy's parade to help people celebrate Thanksgiving.*
. . . one every year on Thanksgiving Day—to celebrate America's own holiday. (pp. 7–8)	*The author really wants me to understand why this parade is so important—that it is a part of America's own holiday.*
Macy's asked Tony to replace the animals. (pp. 9–10)	*The author is showing me that Macy's was always trying to make the parade bigger and better, and that Tony is a part of that.*
. . . to hold up in bad weather yet light enough to move up and down the streets? (p. 11)	*I can see here how the author is trying to show me exactly the dilemma that Tony encountered in designing marionettes for the parade. Rather than just telling me the solution, the author is making it suspenseful so that I really want to keep reading and figure out what Tony did.*
. . . from an Indonesian rod puppet in his toy collection. (p. 12)	*The author is really entertaining me here—asking questions that Tony had to find answers for, showing me how creative and clever Tony had to be. I'm seeing that the author spent two pages telling me about the problem, rather than just telling me what Tony did.*
. . . the air-filled rubber bags wobbled down the avenues, propped up by wooden sticks. (pp. 13–14)	*Finally the author gives me Tony's solution and lets me see how much the crowds loved these marionettes. They were made out of rubber, filled with air, and high in the sky controlled by sticks.*

continued . . .

What the Text Says	What I Say
But how? (p. 15)	*The author is showing me how Tony likes to tackle problems and think through solutions. I'm getting the sense that Tony is never satisfied with his work and he is creative about making it better all the time.*
. . . but what if the controls were below and the puppet could rise up? (pp. 16–17)	*Note the typography in the illustrations on this page. *I'm seeing that the author wrote this part of the story so that the words look like a part of the picture. I wonder why she did that. I'm thinking that this shows me how creative Tony is in thinking through the problem of making the puppet rise up so that people could see it in the sky.*
Since helium is lighter than air, it would make the balloons rise. (p. 19)	*The author here is persuading me how smart, creative, and hardworking Tony is. I'm getting all of this evidence about how hard Tony works to make these puppets rise into the sky. The author is also informing me about helium and how it is lighter than air. This is an important detail about the puppets.*
Then, one by one, Tony cut the lines to the sandbags. (p. 20)	*Here, the author is building suspense to entertain me. The author doesn't just tell me if the balloons will work, but makes me want to keep reading to find out.*
. . . and the magnificent upside-down marionettes rose up to the skies! (p. 22)	*Note: This page turns to a vertical orientation. *Wow. Look how the author made it so I had to turn the whole book to read this page. I think she did this on purpose so that I can see how high in the sky Tony's puppets went. His idea worked!*
They shimmied and swayed through the canyons of New York City. (pp. 23–24)	*I'm seeing here that the author used so many different verbs, or action words—sailed, sallied, shimmied, swayed. I remember that it was really important to Tony that the puppets had movement in them—and I think the author chose these strong verbs to show that the puppets were moving and dancing through New York City.*
It was a parade New Yorkers would never forget! (pp. 25–26)	*The author really wants me to see how much people loved Tony's creations.*
. . . for a puppet to be anything anyone could imagine it to be. (pp. 27–28)	*At first, I thought this was going to be a boring biography of Tony Sarg. But now, I'm getting the sense that the author's purpose in writing this story was to inform me about how the Thanksgiving Day parade came to be, to persuade me how creative Tony was, and to entertain me with a fun story about how creative puppets can be.*

THINKING ALOUD WITH MONITORING AND CLARIFYING

Good readers are actively involved in knowing when they stop understanding a part of a text. They recognize when their comprehension breaks down. They take steps to clarify what they don't understand.

Teaching Monitoring and Clarifying in Grades K–2 *My Name Is Sangoel* by Karen Lynn Williams and Khadra Mohammed

Overview and Rationale

Sangoel is a young Sudanese refugee who leaves his native land during his country's civil war. When he arrives in the United States, everything is unfamiliar and intimidating. His struggles to fit in are complicated by the struggles of his teachers and classmates to correctly pronounce his name, one of his last reminders of his home and heritage. Upon its publication, this book was awarded multiple honors including the International Literacy Association's Children's Choices Reading List 2010, the Notable Social Studies Trade Books for Young People 2010, and the 2009 Notable Books for Children from *Smithsonian* Magazine. Young readers typically have more confusion with nonfiction text, so I have purposefully included a narrative text to model monitoring and clarifying using narrative text. With immigration and refugees being a hot topic in the news, I have included this book to help students understand the struggles of refugees to acclimate to American culture and schools.

Lexile Framework: 440

Grade-Level Equivalent: 2.1

Guided Reading Level: 2

What the Text Says	What I Say
"... It is the name of your father and of your ancestors before him." (p. 1)	*Wow. There's a lot in this first sentence I don't understand. Who is the Wise One, and is that someone's real name? What is a refugee camp? When I hear about a camp, I think of summer camps. What is Dinka? Is that a name? A religion? A place? I have to keep reading to have all of my questions answered.*

continued...

What the Text Says	What I Say
". . . You will be Sangoel. Even in America." (p. 1)	*I still don't understand what a Dinka is, and I'm not really sure why this old man is so thin and he's telling Sangoel about America. Does this have to do with the refugee camp?*
He did not have a country. (p. 3)	*I'm not sure why his father was killed. Was he a soldier? I know Sudan is a country in Africa, but I'm not sure why there was a war there. But this part also answered my question about what a refugee is—the text tells me that a refugee is a person who does not have a home or a country. So a refugee camp must be a place where lots of people without homes or countries come together to live.*
Sangoel knew he would never see his friends again. (p. 3)	*I need to know more about what it means to be "resettled." Do only young people who can work get resettled? Is America the only place refugees get resettled? I had to slow down when I read that Lili and Mama were crying. I can't tell yet if they are crying because they aren't going with Sangoel to America, or because they are sad to say goodbye to everyone in the refugee camp. Maybe I'll find out more in the next pages.*
The "sky boat" took them to America. (p. 5)	*I'm not sure what the sky boat is. I see the words are in quotation marks, so maybe that's a nickname for something. The only way to get to America from Sudan is either a boat or an airplane, so maybe sky boat is Sangoel's word for an airplane.*
He shivered and his head ached. (p. 6)	*I had to reread this whole part because I didn't understand why Mama was afraid of stairs and what magic doors were. But then I realized that Sangoel came from Sudan, where maybe he had never seen some of the things we are used to in America. It must be scary to be in a new place with unfamiliar things, like escalators and fluorescent lights.*
. . . and pointed across the room. (p. 8)	*Aha! The text clarified my confusion about what Dinka is. It's an old language from Sudan.*
Sangoel was only eight, but he was the man of the family. (p. 8)	*I'm wondering what the author means by "man of the family." I already know his father was killed, and he has a sister. Does this mean that he feels like he's trying be an adult like his father was? Is this a way for the author to tell me that Sangoel feels responsible for taking care of his family?*
. . . and pulled her and Lili through the crowd. (p. 8)	*Again—the text answered my question. Mama and Lili came to America. They must have been crying because they were sad to say goodbye to their friends in Sudan.*

What the Text Says	What I Say
Sangoel blinked back tears. (p. 8)	*I'm unclear on why this stranger would hug Sangoel and his family right after meeting them. I'm thinking that maybe she's trying to make them feel welcome or to show them that she cares and is there to help.*
There was no barbed wire to keep them in. (p. 10)	*I wonder why the author said there was no barbed wire in America. Does that mean that there was barbed wire in the refugee camp in Sudan?*
She cried again when he turned it off. (p. 11)	*I don't understand—does this mean Mama has never used a stove or a telephone? If they didn't eat with forks, did they use their hands? Do they not know there are not real people in a TV? This goes along with the idea that there are so many new things in America!*
"Education is your mother and your father." (p. 13)	*I'm lost with this last sentence—that education is his mother and father. What did the Wise One mean by that? I know school is not really his mother and father, so there's another message there. Maybe what the Wise One meant is that school is as important as his mother and father.*
"My name is Sangoel," he whispered, but no one heard. (p. 15)	*At first, I was unclear what was going on. I didn't know whom he was whispering to—I thought he was whispering to himself. But when I reread, I saw that the teacher couldn't pronounce his name correctly and the kids laughed at a mean nickname. Now I understand that he was trying to tell them his correct name, but the class couldn't hear him over their laughter.* *At this point, several people have mispronounced his name—which makes me wonder if I'm saying it wrong too! How do we really say his name?*
. . . but in America they called it soccer. (p. 16)	*When I first read this, I didn't understand what the author meant, but when I reread it, I got an important signal—the word but helped me to understand that soccer is the American term for the sport that Sangoel used to call football.*
"My name is Sangoel," he said before the coach could say it wrong. (p. 16)	*I'm not sure if the author is trying to hint that Sangoel is used to people saying his name wrong or if the message here is that Sangoel is getting braver, and not whispering anymore.*
"My name is Sangoel," he called softly as the boy ran off. (p. 17)	*I'm not certain if this boy is trying to be kind and just cannot pronounce his name, or if the boy is purposefully saying his name wrong to taunt Sangoel.*
. . . and he wished he were back at camp. (p. 18)	*There are some things that I wish the book would clarify for me—where does their food come from? Who is paying for their apartment? Does Mama have a job, or did they bring any money from Sudan?*

continued . . .

. . . from previous

What the Text Says	What I Say
You will always be Sangoel. (p. 18)	*I can't tell yet if Mama is trying to be helpful and make Sangoel fit in with an American name, or if Mama thinks a new name would help him forget some of the bad things about Sudan.*
He had bad dreams about war and running and hiding. (p. 19)	*I'm not sure why he'd choose the floor over a bed. Maybe the author is hinting that he used to sleep on the floor in the refugee camp, so he's returning to something that felt safe and comfortable.*
He put on his almost-white shirt and went to school. (p. 21)	*I need to know what he made with the markers and this shirt. The author has done a great job building suspense, so I want to keep reading to see what this shirt says.*
Sangoel nodded and smiled! (p. 22)	*Yes! I got the answer—I wanted! I kept reading to find out how his name was correctly pronounced. I was saying it "San-go-el" too, just like everyone else, but here I learned its correct pronunciation.*
"My name is Sangoel. Even in America." (p. 26)	*The author is making a really important point here—that his name is more than just a word. Sangoel's name is a link to his family and his past. Maybe that is why the Wise One was so insistent that he always be Sangoel, even in America.*
Author's Note (p. 28)	*I'm going to read the Author's Note because I'm hoping that it will give me some answers to some of the questions that the text did not answer for me.*
. . . and may not be able to bring along family members, money, clothing, or food. (p. 28)	*I was confused earlier about who was paying for Sangoel's apartment and food, and this part clarified for me that most refugees can't bring food and money and clothing with them.*
Often there are no schools, no electricity, and no clean drinking water. (p. 28)	*Wow—at first I had thought a refugee camp was like a summer camp, but I was really wrong. Refugee camps sound like terrible places to have to live.*
Years of war and persecution have forced many people to leave Sudan. (p. 28)	*This clarifies more about that unfamiliar word—Dinka—for me. It's not just a language, but a group of people in Sudan.*
Today more people choose to keep the name that connects them to their heritage. (p. 28)	*I'm understanding a lot more about why Sangoel and the Wise One are so insistent on keeping his name, and why Mama's idea of an American name just doesn't feel right to him.*

Teaching Monitoring and Clarifying in Grades 3–5
Simple Machines: Wheels, Levers, and Pulleys by David Adler

Overview and Rationale

This informational text provides readers with an engaging introduction to basic physics. Young readers will be surprised to know that they use simple machines every day—wedges such as knives and forks, inclined planes such as playground slides, and levers such as seesaws. Told by two young children and their comical cat, *Simple Machines* explains how these basic machines work.

Informational text—with its myriad of technical vocabulary, nonlinear text structure, and assumption of background knowledge—is a logical source of confusion and comprehension breakdowns. To model how I monitor my comprehension and clarify when it falters, I've selected this book because of its highly technical content. *Simple Machines* also does not have many of the features inherent in informational text—headings, glossary, and table of contents. Without the road map that these text features provide, young readers may struggle to navigate through this content-heavy book.

Lexile Framework: 690

Grade-Level Equivalent: 4.3

What the Text Says	What I Say
It's a simple machine that helps break things apart. (p. 2)	*I don't understand here why the author is comparing my smiling in the mirror to a machine called a wedge. When I look in the mirror at my smile, I see my teeth. It sounds like the author is trying to tell me that my teeth are a wedge, but I don't really understand that. I need to keep reading to see if I get more information about wedges.*
. . . that splits the apple into pieces small enough to swallow. (p. 2)	*I was correct—reading on gave me more information to see how my teeth are like wedges. If a wedge is a machine that breaks things apart, my teeth break apart the food I'm eating. So that's what the author meant by telling me my teeth are a machine—one called a wedge.*
The force of the lumberjacks' swing drives the wedge into the log. (p. 3)	*I'm unclear what force is. Does that mean how strong something is?*
. . . into a sideways force that breaks the log into smaller pieces. (p. 3)	*The author doesn't come right out and tell me what force is, but if I try to put the book into my own words, I see that force might be related to power. I'm learning here that the force of the ax helps to break the log.*

continued . . .

. . . from previous

What the Text Says	What I Say
The front is narrow so it can push easily through the water. (p. 4)	*Wow. I have to slow down here to think about how all of these things—stuff I use all the time—are wedges. It might help me to reread the part where the text tells me that a wedge "helps breaks things apart." That helps me understand that a thumbtack breaks apart paper, and knives break apart food.*
If you have, you played on a simple machine. (p. 5)	*Now I'm confused! Is a slide another example of a wedge? It doesn't seem like a slide breaks things apart. Let me keep reading.*
It makes it easier to carry things up or down. (p. 6)	*At first, I thought the author was saying that a slide is a wedge. But when I kept reading, I could see that the author wanted to introduce a new kind of machine—one called an inclined plane. I need to remember that this kind of machine makes it easier to move things up and down.*
The more gradual the slope of the ramp, the easier the work. (p. 7)	*That word slope at first was tricky. I'm not familiar with a slope of a ramp. But then I remembered I have heard slope used in the winter about ski slopes. It think it has to do with how steep something is. So this sentence means that if a slope were smaller—"more gradual"—then it would be easier to push something up a ramp.*
An inclined plane gets the same work done with less force over a greater distance. (p. 8)	*There's that word force again! It must be a really important word in talking about machines. Here I'm unclear if ramps and inclined planes are the exact same thing, so let me read on to see if this question gets answered.*
Mountain roads are inclined planes. (p. 9)	*Let me think about this with something more familiar to me—not driving a car, but riding my bike. The text is telling me it's too steep to drive a car right up a mountain—just like it's too steep to ride my bike. The road is an inclined plane to help move me and my bike up it.*
. . . the greater the distance you have to drive to reach the top. (p. 10)	*There's that word slope again—I'm glad I slowed down to think through that one. Let me break down these two long sentences into smaller parts to think through them more clearly. The road—an inclined plane—makes it easier to ride my bike up a steep mountain. But if the slope isn't very big, I will have to drive farther to get up. That makes sense.*
. . . to make it easier for people in wheelchairs to get around. (p. 11)	*I see wheelchair ramps outside most buildings, so now I see how that is an inclined plane to move wheelchairs up and down.*
. . . you are moving it in along a circular inclined plane. (p. 12)	*I don't do a lot of building, so this example of a screw as an inclined plane was not as helpful to me. But I think what it's saying here is that the twisting helps move something up and down, just like the road up a mountain twists around.*

What the Text Says	What I Say
Have you ever played on a seesaw? (p. 13)	*I recognize this kind of question! The last time I got confused and didn't realize it was the author's way of signaling that I'm about to read about a new kind of machine.*
It's a simple machine that makes lifting easier. (pp. 13–14)	*This is a lot of new vocabulary for me—so I need to slow down and repeat the words so I'm really clear on them. The most important thing is that a lever has a bar and a pivot. The pivot stays still. And a lever helps to lift things.*
The load feels lighter. (pp. 15–16)	*To really understand this, I need more information on why moving my hand makes it feel lighter. I'm thinking the author will explain this next.*
. . . it's making it easier to lift the sand. (p. 16)	*Wait a second. I thought a pivot stays still. My hand can move. I'm confused if pivots never move or if that was the pivot in the seesaw that doesn't move.*
. . . the rubbing of the bottom of the box against the ground—that makes moving the box so difficult. (pp. 17–18)	*I'm a bit confused if the box is hard to move because it's heavy or because of the friction—this rubbing against the ground. Why don't we just use a ramp to move the box? Is there a better machine for this?*
It's the wheels and axles on the wagon that makes your work easier. (p. 18)	*I certainly know the job of wheels, but I'm not familiar with this word axle. Let me read on to see if the author tells me more.*
Wheels reduce friction. (p. 19)	*So there's my answer to what an axle is. But this last sentence "Wheels reduce friction" is unclear to me. How do the wheels make less rubbing on the ground? Don't wheels touch the ground too?*
A wheel and axle also multiplies the distance something turns. (pp. 19–20)	*Let me see if I can clarify this confusing statement by rewriting it into my words. I know that the friction makes things hard to drag, but a wheel touches less of the ground and so it has less friction.*
On a Ferris wheel, the distance the axle turns is multiplied. (pp. 21–22)	*This is confusing. I'm having a hard time understanding what moves and what turns. I had to reread it a couple of times, but what I see now is that there are two circles on a Ferris wheel—one for the axle and one for the wheel with all the people in their seats. The axle does lots and lots of little turns to move the big wheel with the people in their seats.*
. . . you are turning a wheel and axle. (p. 23)	*I don't understand yet how my bathroom faucet is an axle. But I know that this author has a pattern where he explains in more detail, so I'm going to keep reading.*

continued . . .

. . . from previous

What the Text Says	What I Say
The larger the knob, the easier it is to turn the thin shaft. (p. 24)	*I had to reread this part twice, and I'm now beginning to understand that the part I turn is connected to an axle that moves to turn the water on and off.*
They spin around it. (p. 25)	*So what I think this is telling me is that when I peddle a bike, I'm not really peddling the wheels, but rather I'm peddling the axle.*
Gears can change the speed, power, and direction of a machine's work. (p. 26)	*The author is giving me another important vocabulary word—gears, which means wheels with teeth. It would have been useful if the author had given me a glossary to help me keep track of all these new words.*
It's fixed—attached—to the top of the pole. (p. 27)	*I was sort of confused at first because there is no real definition of a pulley. But when I reread the example of the flagpole, I could see that a pulley helps me to pull things.*
The more pulleys you add, the less force you need. (p. 28)	*That word force keeps popping up again and again. If I use the word power in its place, this paragraph tells me that two pulleys add more power.*
With the pulleys the motor in the crane needs less lifting power. (p. 29)	*This book doesn't really have much of a conclusion or a part where the author summarizes everything that I've read. But I'm getting the sense that these simple machines—pulleys, levers, ramps, axles, gears—all work together to lift and move heavy things and to make jobs easier.*

Appendix J

Putting It Together: Think Aloud Scripts

As proficient readers approach text, they apply multiple comprehension strategies simultaneously. Though we teach young readers strategies in isolation, it is somewhat inauthentic to think, "With this book, I'm only going to ask questions." Our end goal is to interweave comprehension strategies as the opportunity naturally arises in text. To showcase the application of multiple strategies at the same time, I've written transcripts where these strategies are interwoven. Again, I've selected culturally relevant high-quality children's literature across text genres. The chart below will help you track my text selections

Grade Level	Format	Title	Author
K–2	Nonfiction	*Apples*	Gail Gibbons
K–2	Poetry	"The Dentist and the Crocodile"	Roald Dahl
K–2	Narrative Picture Book	*Last Stop on Market Street*	Matt de la Peña
K–2	Historical Fiction	*The Watcher: Jane Goodall's Life With the Chimps*	Jeanette Winter
3–5	Narrative Picture Book	*Doctor De Soto*	William Steig
3–5	Chapter Book	*The Year of Billy Miller*	Kevin Henkes
3–5	Poetry	"Casey at the Bat"	Ernest Thayer
3–5	Narrative Picture Book	*An Angel for Solomon Singer*	Cynthia Rylant

Thinking Aloud With Nonfiction in Grades K–2
Apples by Gail Gibbons

Overview

This nonfiction book teaches young learners a plethora of factual information about different kinds of apples, how they grow, and their parts. In addition, it provides a brief history of apple trees in America. This book also beautifully illustrates the change of the seasons and fruit tree agriculture. Gail Gibbons is a renowned writer and illustrator of over one hundred children's books.

Lexile Framework: 650L
Guided Reading Level: N

What the Text Says	What I Say	The Comprehension Strategy I Model
It grows on an apple tree. (p. 1)	*Right away, I can tell that the author here is giving me facts about how apples grow. I think the author is trying to inform me.*	A **Understanding the author's purpose**
They have been in existence for about two million years. (p. 1)	*I wonder why apple trees grow more than other fruit trees. Does this mean that more people in the world eat apples than any other fruit?*	? **Asking questions**
. . . they brought apple seeds and seedlings with them from England. (p. 2)	*At first, I wasn't sure what the difference is between seeds and seedlings. When I kept reading, I got the sense that seedlings are seeds that have begun to sprout—sort of like tiny little apple trees.*	⇄ **Monitoring and clarifying**
. . . and had apple trees growing near their villages. (p. 3)	*When I began reading, I thought that the first apple trees in America were planted by English colonists. But as I read more, I found out that apples were already in America thanks to the Native Americans.*	**Synthesizing**
He became known as Johnny Appleseed. (p. 4)	*Why did Johnny Appleseed choose to give apples out? How were they useful to the people in the early 1800s?*	? **Asking questions**
. . . but most are grown commercially. (p. 5)	*The author is using this signal word but to show me that there is a difference between growing apples at home and growing them commercially. I wonder what those differences are.*	A **Understanding the author's purpose** ? **Asking questions**

What the Text Says	What I Say	The Comprehension Strategy I Model
. . . and about 28 million bushels are grown in Canada. (p. 6)	*Why does the United States grow so many more apples than Canada? I've already discovered that apples are grown everywhere around the world, so how many are grown elsewhere? And how many apples are in a bushel? How much does a bushel weigh?*	? **Asking questions**
The core has five seed chambers. (p. 7)	*The author wants me to know key parts of an apple, like the core. She introduces the new word, and then restates it to tell me that a core holds seeds.*	A **Understanding the author's purpose**
Each blossom has to be pollinated in order for an apple to grow. (p. 9)	*I'm not sure what is meant by* pollinated, *so let me keep reading to find out. Before, the author introduced the words and then defined them later, so maybe she does that here.*	**Monitoring and clarifying**
The blossoms are usually pollinated by insects or by the wind. (p. 9)	*Note: The text box on the illustration reads as follows: "POLLINATION happens when a grain of pollen from a stamen lands on the stigma of another blossom." *I did find out what* pollinated *means. It is a word to explain how the plants make seeds to reproduce, or make more plants.*	**Monitoring and clarifying**
During the late summer or early fall the apples ripen. (p. 12)	*Here the author is explaining the life cycle of apples to me—how they grow and change over the seasons.*	A **Understanding the author's purpose**
Workers pick the apples by hand. (p. 13)	*Are there any machines that can help pick apples? It seems like there are so many to pick, and it would be very slow to do it by hand.*	? **Asking questions**
. . . it is fun to go apple picking. (p. 16)	*Here I have learned that apples are picked mostly in the fall, but I see them in my grocery store in the winter and spring. How is that possible?*	? **Asking questions**
There is apple cider, too. (p. 17)	*What is the difference between apple juice and apple cider? How are the recipes different?*	? **Asking questions**
Some people bob for apples. (p. 19)	*Before I learned the different purposes for apples—mostly for eating and making things. Here I'm getting new information to tell me that apples also have a fun purpose—like in candy and different games.*	**Synthesizing**

continued . . .

. . . from previous

What the Text Says	What I Say	The Comprehension Strategy I Model
. . . when the trees will produce a new crop of apples! (p. 21)	*Uh oh. Let me slow down and scan the text features to figure out what dormant means. I see here that dormant means alive but not actively growing [point to text feature in illustration]. So that sounds like the apple trees are sort of sleeping.*	⇄ **Monitoring and clarifying**
Apples are different shades of yellow, green, and red, or a mix of all those colors. (p. 23)	*The author wants me to understand that apples come in a variety of colors and flavors.*	A **Understanding the author's purpose**
This is called pruning. (p. 24)	*Why do we prune trees? Is it to get the dead branches off?*	? **Asking questions**
The pruning and fertilizing help produce lots of good apples. (p. 25)	*I'm getting the sense that apples take a lot more care than just dropping a seed in the dirt. The author is giving me details about pruning and fertilizing.*	III **Making inferences**
They are nutritious and delicious. (p. 29)	*These last two sentences are golden lines for me because they help me remember that even though there are many kinds of apples, they are all healthy and good to eat. I think the author ended the book on them so we'd remember how important apples are in many countries around the world.*	A **Understanding the author's purpose**

Thinking Aloud With Poetry in Grades K–2
"The Dentist and the Crocodile" by Roald Dahl

Overview

This poem's plot centers on a crocodile's visit to the dentist due to a toothache. With humor and delight, the text portrays the dentist's fear of the crocodile while humanizing dentists in the eyes of children. The crocodile sits in the dentist's chair and tries to trick the dentist into putting his head into his mouth by asking him to check his back teeth. Young learners will enjoy the rhymes and humoristic language used in this poem. Roald Dahl is a world-renowned poet and novelist who has sold over 250 million copies of his books.

Lexile Framework: 410L

Guided Reading Level: N

What the Text Says	What I Say	The Comprehension Strategy I Model
He said, "Right here and everywhere my teeth require repair." (line 2)	*Hmm, I'm getting some clues, like the* word cunning, *that make me think this crocodile is up to no good. And if his teeth need so much repair, or fixing, why is he smiling so much?*	**Making inferences**
He muttered, "I suppose I'm going to have to take a look." (line 5)	*Now I understand how nervous this dentist feels! His face is pale, he's shaking, and he's trying to convince himself that he has to look at this crocodile's teeth! I know I'd be scared!*	**Synthesizing**
At least three hundred pointed teeth, all sharp and shining white. (line 9)	*I like how the author is painting a scary picture here—the words* massive, fearsome, *and* three hundred pointed teeth *really show me exactly why the dentist might feel afraid.*	**Understanding the author's purpose**
"You're much too far away, dear sir, to see what you're about." (line 14)	*This makes me wonder what the crocodile is planning. Does he want the dentist to start with the molars so he can bite down and eat him?*	**Asking questions**
He cried, "No no! I see them all extremely well from here!" (line 16)	*Why isn't the dentist running away? The author is really showing me how tense this situation is—the crocodile is trying to convince the dentist to put his head way inside of his mouth, and the dentist is crying because he's so afraid!*	**Asking questions** **Understanding the author's purpose**
"Oh Croc, you naughty boy, you're playing tricks again!" (line 18)	*Aha! The dentist might be rescued—the words in* burst a lady *make me think that she's there to save the dentist—she even scolds the crocodile for playing tricks!*	**Making inferences** **Understanding the author's purpose**
"He's after me! He's after you! He's going to eat us all!" (line 20)	*I wonder who this lady is. Where did she come from?*	**Asking questions**
". . . He's my little pet, my lovely crocodile." (line 24)	*What? When I first read this, I thought that the lady was going to rescue the dentist. But when I reread it, I thought that the lady was not a part of the solution—but a part of the problem! Did she send the crocodile in to trick the dentist? Who keeps a crocodile for a pet? In a nutshell, maybe this dentist should be afraid of the lady and the crocodile!*	**Monitoring and clarifying** **Synthesizing** **Asking questions**

Thinking Aloud With a Narrative Picture Book in Grades K–2 *Last Stop on Market Street* by Matt de la Peña

Overview

Every Sunday after church, CJ takes a crosstown bus with his grandmother. At the start of the book, he questions this routine, but the tender moments with his Nana help him to understand the beauty in his community and in everyday life. This book has racked up multiple awards, including a 2016 Newbery Medal, a 2016 Caldecott Honor, a 2016 Coretta Scott King Illustrator Honor, a 2015 *New York Times* Book Review Notable Children's Book, and a 2015 *Wall Street Journal* Best Children's Book.

Lexile Framework: 610L

Guided Reading Level: M

What the Text Says	What I Say	The Comprehension Strategy I Model
. . . which freckled CJ's shirt and dripped down his nose. (p. 2)	*The author doesn't tell me CJ's exact age, but this information makes me think he is a child. He is skipping down the steps—kids are more likely to skip than adults. And being outside smells like freedom, which makes me think he didn't go to church on his own—maybe an adult forced him to go there.*	**Making inferences**
"How come we gotta wait for the bus in all this wet?" (p. 3)	*I'm getting more evidence that CJ is young. He is with his nana, which is nickname for a grandmother. I also wonder why they are not leaving church in their car. Do they live in a city, where people take buses more often to avoid traffic? Do they not have money for a car?*	**Making inferences** ? **Asking questions**
"Nana, how come we don't got a car?" (p. 5)	*I'm noticing that the author really tries to make CJ sound like a child—he's using slang words, like gotta and don't got. I'm also guessing that CJ is a little embarrassed. He is waiting in the rain for a bus, while his friend gets into a car and waves. This is making me think CJ's family doesn't have enough money for their own car.*	A **Understanding the author's purpose** **Making inferences**
". . . old Mr. Dennis, who always has a trick for you." (p. 7)	*I'm not sure what she means by a bus that breathes fire or who Mr. Dennis is. If I keep reading, maybe I will find out more.*	**Monitoring and clarifying**

What the Text Says	What I Say	The Comprehension Strategy I Model
It sighed and sagged and the doors swung open. (p. 7)	*Now I'm thinking that this book takes place in a neighborhood without a lot of money. The bus CJ is riding sounds old and used.*	**Synthesizing**
Nana laughed her deep laugh and pushed CJ along. (p. 9)	*I'm thinking that Mr. Dennis is the bus driver, and that he's very used to seeing CJ. They seem to have a routine of these tricks, which hints to me that CJ is on the bus a lot.*	**Making inferences**
She made sure CJ did the same. (p. 10)	*In a nutshell, Nana and CJ are used to riding this bus and interacting with the people on it. They greet all of the passengers and don't seem to be embarrassed to be riding the bus.*	**Synthesizing**
Nana hummed as she knit. (p. 11)	*I'm getting the sense that Nana is quite comfortable on this bus—even though it's stopping and lurching, she's humming and knitting. She's not ashamed to be riding this bus.*	**Synthesizing**
"Miguel and Colby never have to go nowhere." (p. 11)	*Where are they going after church? It sounds like they have a habit of going to the same place every week after church, and the hint gotta go makes me think CJ isn't that excited about where they are going.*	**Asking questions** **Making inferences**
". . . And I hear Trixie got herself a brand-new hat." (p. 12)	*Now I can really see that CJ and his nana always go to this place—they have nicknames for the people they see there! And Nana is so excited to go there, so much so she feels sorry for kids who don't meet these people. Why doesn't CJ feel as excited as Nana does?*	**Synthesizing** **Asking questions**
CJ gave up his seat. (p. 13)	*Why does CJ give up his seat? I know that it's polite to give up your seat to someone older than you or someone who can't stand as well as you can. If I keep reading, maybe I'll find out why.*	**Asking questions** **Monitoring and clarifying**
"How come that man can't see?" (p. 13)	*The author answered my question! I reread to find out that CJ gave up his seat to a blind man. The picture shows me a man holding a cane, which confirms that he's blind.*	**Monitoring and clarifying**

continued . . .

. . . from previous

What the Text Says	What I Say	The Comprehension Strategy I Model
"Some people watch the world with their ears." (p. 13)	*I like how the author shows Nana as firm and wise. She doesn't tolerate CJ's whining, and she makes him treat strangers politely.*	A **Understanding the author's purpose**
Nana squeezed the man's hand and laughed her deep laugh. (p. 14)	*I'm getting more information that makes me see how likable Nana is to everyone. Right after meeting a stranger, she is laughing with him and squeezing his hand.*	**Synthesizing**
". . . Why don't you ask the man if he'll play us a song?" (p. 15)	*Note: The picture shows one of the boys holding an iPod. Be sure to point this out to students. *Here's more important evidence of how comfortable Nana feels—she would ask a stranger on the bus to play his guitar for her! She also doesn't allow CJ to feel sorry for himself that he doesn't have an iPod, like the older boys. She's comfortable with where she is and how she is.*	**Synthesizing**
So did CJ and the spotted dog. (p. 16)	*Now I think the passengers on this bus are enjoying a happy moment together, listening to music and appreciating each other's company. Even CJ—who was complaining about having to ride the bus before—joins in.*	**Synthesizing**
. . . and the sound gave him the feeling of magic. (p. 18)	*At first, I was confused because the bus becomes dark. CJ is lifted out of the city, and he sees crashing waves and butterflies in the moon. Then I reread, and I thought that maybe the music is making him see all these beautiful sights in his mind's eye. So he's not really seeing these things—he's just imagining them as he listens to the guitar.*	**Monitoring and clarifying**
CJ dropped it in the man's hat. (p. 19)	*I'm getting more confirmation that Nana is firm and CJ respects her. Without a word, she can tell him what she wants him to do—to give money to the guitar player.*	**Synthesizing**
"Last stop on Market Street," Mr. Dennis called. (p. 20)	*I want to know what's so important about Market Street. Why is Market Street so important that they've ridden this crowded bus all the way there?*	? **Asking questions**

What the Text Says	What I Say	The Comprehension Strategy I Model
"How come it's always so dirty over here?" (p. 21)	*The author is suggesting that Market Street is a poor area in the city. There are so many clues—the broken doors and the graffiti and the stores that are not open anymore—to make me think that people here are poor.*	**Making inferences**
"Sometimes when you're surrounded by dirt, CJ, you're a better witness for what's beautiful." (p. 22)	*I wonder what Nana means here. Why doesn't she just tell CJ that this area is dirty because people are poor? I think it's a really important line, so I want to spend some time with it. Let me reread again her line about the dirt. "You're a better witness for what's beautiful." Maybe Nana is telling CJ to look for what is beautiful—even in places that might not look beautiful to the outside. Nana is teaching CJ to look for the positive things in life.*	? **Asking questions** **Synthesizing** **Monitoring and clarifying**
... the perfect rainbow arcing over their soup kitchen. (p. 23)	*Aha! Throughout this book, I've been wondering where CJ and Nana are going. Finally, I get an answer. They are going to a soup kitchen, a place where people who need help can get free food. Are they taking food from the soup kitchen, or are they volunteering to help at the soup kitchen?*	? **Asking questions**
... where he never even thought to look. (p. 23)	*This is a golden line for me because it describes exactly what is so likable about Nana—how she easily makes friends with strangers and how she is so positive. It seems like CJ admires this quality in his nana.*	A **Understanding the author's purpose**
... he said, "I'm glad we came." (p. 25)	*This is another golden line for me! The author shows me that there's been a change in CJ—at first, he didn't want to come here, but now he's thankful he did.*	A **Understanding the author's purpose**
... told him, "Me too, CJ. Now, come on." (p. 27)	*Note: The picture shows CJ and his Nana serving food to people who have come to the soup kitchen. *I had wondered if CJ and Nana came to the soup kitchen to get food for themselves, since I got the sense they didn't have much money. But this illustration makes me realize that they are there to help. This information confirms that Nana is helping CJ realize the positive things in life, like helping out people in need.*	**Synthesizing**

Thinking Aloud With Historical Fiction in Grades K–2
The Watcher: Jane Goodall's Life With the Chimps
by Jeanette Winter

Overview

This picture book depicts Jane Goodall's life and scientific accomplishments. The plot begins in Jane's childhood and illustrates her love of animals. After graduating high school, Jane immigrates to Africa where she meets a professor who sends her to observe chimps in their natural habitat. The plot continues and details the struggles Jane encountered on this unique journey. This book was named Best Book of the Year by the *Boston Globe*, *Kirkus Reviews*, *Booklist*, and the Bank Street College of Education.

Lexile Framework: 820

Guided Reading Level: O

What the Text Says	What I Say	The Comprehension Strategy I Model
. . . looking for little Valerie Jane Goodall. (p. 1)	*Who is everyone? Who is searching for Jane? Where have they searched? The author is giving me clues that she's gone off somewhere alone, so I want to know how that happened. And I get the clue that she's little, but exactly how old is she?*	**Asking questions**
"I know how an egg comes out!" (p. 2)	*I have a question about the setting. I get a clue about the henhouse, so maybe this takes place on a farm. And Jane tells her mother that she knows how an egg came out, so I'm thinking that her hiding spot was in the henhouse where she watched chickens lay eggs.*	**Making inferences**
At five years old, Jane was already a watcher. (p. 2)	*This is an important sentence that answers my question about how old Jane is. And the author is describing her as a "watcher." I know she watched what happened in the henhouse, so I wonder what else she likes to watch.*	**Synthesizing**
When spring came, the robin even built a nest in Jane's bookcase! (p. 4)	*The author is using all of these examples to show me that Jane is curious about nature. The author is showing me that Jane is patient and observant, because she watched this bird for weeks. The author is also hinting that animals trust Jane, because this bird lives in Jane's room.*	**Making inferences** **Synthesizing**

What the Text Says	What I Say	The Comprehension Strategy I Model
. . . talk to the animals and live with the apes. (p. 5)	*I think the author's purpose here is to show how important apes and Africa are to Jane. There are lots of places in the world that have animals, but apes in Africa seem especially important.*	**A** **Understanding the author's purpose**
. . . She hid her earnings under the parlor rug for safekeeping. (p. 6)	*I wonder what her school days were like. The author doesn't give me any information about Jane as a student, but tells me that she saved her money for a plane trip to Kenya—which is in Africa. This confirms my earlier thought that the author wants me to know the importance of Jane's dream of Africa.*	**?** **Asking questions**
. . . and fish that glowed through the dark water. (p. 7)	*The author's purpose here is to confirm what I already thought about Jane—that she's observant and patient. She watches nature even in the cold wind.*	**A** **Understanding the author's purpose**
Yes, she would! (p. 9)	*The part about chimpanzees being most like humans makes me ask questions. How are humans and chimpanzees alike? How are they different? Why is it important that we are so alike? Why is it important to study them? I think the author here wants me to ask questions, so I can understand the job Jane is going to take.*	**?** **Asking questions**
"I wanted to learn things that no one else knew, uncover secrets . . . ," she wrote. (p. 10)	*Here the author seems to be quoting directly from what Jane wrote—maybe in a journal or in a letter. I like how the author used Jane's words to show how curious and observant Jane was.*	**A** **Understanding the author's purpose**
She knew she was Home. (p. 11)	*The author doesn't come right out and say it, but I'm making an inference that the message here is about how brave Jane is. She's all alone in the woods in the dark, with strange sounds, yet she feels safe there. I also think the author was deliberate in capitalizing Home. The capital H makes me think how important this place was to Jane.*	**A** **Understanding the author's purpose** **III** **Making inferences**
. . . she didn't see them. (p. 14)	*The author is hinting that the chimps are hiding from Jane. I know from a previous description about the robin that Jane is a patient watcher, so I'm thinking that the author is telling me that Jane's patience will be important.*	**A** **Understanding the author's purpose** **III** **Making inferences**

continued . . .

What the Text Says	What I Say	The Comprehension Strategy I Model
When will I see a chimp? She wondered. (p. 16)	*I like how the author writes "when will I" rather than "will I." This makes me think that Jane is confident that with enough patience, eventually she will see a chimp.*	A **Understanding the author's purpose**
. . . she almost lost hope. (p. 17)	*The word* almost *stands out for me here. It seems like the author is showing me all of Jane's challenges—being alone, being sick, not seeing the chimps. The word* almost *confirms that Jane will continue to be brave and patient until she sees the chimps.*	A **Understanding the author's purpose** **Synthesizing**
She stayed in the background, never hid, acted uninterested, and quietly watched. (p. 18)	*I think the author is deliberately making this part sound just like what happened with the robin. Eventually, it was comfortable enough with Jane to build a nest in her room. I wonder then if the chimps will be just as comfortable.*	? **Asking questions** A **Understanding the author's purpose**
"You have to be patient if you want to learn about animals," she wrote. (p. 20)	*Again the author incorporated Jane's writing to show her patience. I'm getting more evidence of her perseverance, bravery, and desire to learn about the chimps.*	A **Understanding the author's purpose**
To her, each one was different—just like us. (p. 23)	*It seems to me that Jane is growing very close to the chimps, sleeping with them and naming them. Maybe they are more than just animals to her.*	**Synthesizing**
". . . So gently. No snatching," she wrote. (p. 23)	*I like how the author chose this passage of Jane writing in capital letters. Those capital letters show how important this was to Jane. Maybe she was surprised or excited that this chimp has gotten so close to her.*	A **Understanding the author's purpose**
Before this, everybody thought chimps ate only plants. (p. 24)	*Here the author is informing me of things that we know about chimps all because of Jane. This makes me understand how important Jane's work was.*	**Synthesizing**
". . . What a day—chimps near, chimps far, old men, young men, ladies, children, babies, teenagers—the lot," she wrote. (p. 26)	*Here Jane thinks of chimps just like human beings—she calls them ladies and children, not female chimps and baby chimps. This makes me understand how much love she feels for them.*	**Synthesizing** **Making inferences**

What the Text Says	What I Say	The Comprehension Strategy I Model
She saw them swagger and throw tantrums, and kept out of the way. (p. 28)	*At the beginning of the book, I asked about the ways that chimps are similar to humans. The purpose of this part is to answer that question—I see here that chimps have emotions—love, anger, sadness. The author is telling me how alike chimps and humans are.*	**A** **Understanding the author's purpose** **Synthesizing**
And so assistants came to watch and write. (p. 31)	*The author is giving me just enough information here to make me ask more questions. I wonder how long Jane was alone—I know there are "years of notes," but how many years did she spend with the chimps? How did she survive on her own for so long? Who were these assistants? How many came? What did Jane do with her notes?*	**?** **Asking questions**
One day Jane sadly left Gombe. (p. 32)	*The author has included a powerful word in this short sentence—the word sadly. I can tell that over the years Jane has come to love the chimps. So it makes sense that she'd feel sad to leave. But why did she leave? What was her reason for leaving?*	**A** **Understanding the author's purpose** **?** **Asking questions**
They needed Jane to speak for them. (p. 34)	*That word extinct is so important—extinct means there would be no more left. I think by saying "They needed Jane to speak for them," the author is telling me that Jane has to tell people to protect chimps. Maybe the reason Jane left was to educate people about chimps so we could protect them and their habitats.*	**Synthesizing**
. . . year after year, asking for help to save the chimps and the forests. (p. 35)	*I notice here that this is the first time the author has referred to the chimps as Jane's friends. I was right that she loved them. I'm also confirming my idea that Jane left Africa to educate people to save the chimps.*	**A** **Understanding the author's purpose** **Synthesizing**
. . . David Greybeard at her side. (p. 36)	*As I read this, I wondered if the chimps would remember her like she remembered them. But the author gave me a clue—David Greybeard at her side—that makes me think they remember her as well.*	**III** **Making inferences**

continued . . .

. . . from previous

What the Text Says	What I Say	The Comprehension Strategy I Model
. . . and opened a window for us to the world of the chimpanzees. (p. 39)	*I like how the author reminds me of the things Jane did as a little girl—Dr. Dolittle and Tarzan. It makes me think that the author's purpose is to inform us about Jane, a woman who worked hard to achieve her childhood dreams. The last sentence also makes me think that the author's message is how important Jane is to chimpanzees.*	A **Understanding the author's purpose**

Thinking Aloud With a Narrative Picture Book in Grades 3–5 *Doctor De Soto* by William Steig

Overview and Rationale

Doctor De Soto is a talented and sought-after dentist who is assisted by his wife. Animals—large and small—seek him out for his ability to stop their pain. Since he is a mouse, he refuses to treat animals who have a taste for mice. One day, he takes mercy on a fox suffering from a toothache. In a race to see who outfoxes whom, this picture book has readers rooting for the De Sotos.

Lexile Framework: 560L

Guided Reading Level: M

What the Text Says	What I Say	The Comprehension Strategy I Model
Larger animals sat on the floor, while Doctor De Soto stood on a ladder. (p. 1)	*The author is telling me that small animals are close to Doctor De Soto's size and that he needs a ladder to reach bigger animals, so I can guess that Doctor De Soto is small too—maybe a squirrel, or a mouse, or a hamster.*	**Making inferences**
There Doctor De Soto was hoisted up to the patient's mouth by his assistant, who happened to be his wife. (p. 2)	*I'm getting the sense that Doctor De Soto has lots of patients—animals of all sizes. He seems to be a talented and popular dentist.*	**Synthesizing**
Doctor De Soto was especially popular with the big animals. (p. 4)	*When I hear big animals, I think of things like elephants and horses. I wonder why they like him so much.*	? **Asking questions**

What the Text Says	What I Say	The Comprehension Strategy I Model
. . . they could hardly feel any pain. (p. 4)	*Before I asked why the big animals liked him, and I get information here that tells me he is a delicate dentist who barely hurts his patients.*	**Monitoring and clarifying**
Being a mouse . . . (p. 5)	*Aha! I was right that Doctor De Soto is small.*	**Monitoring and clarifying**
They wouldn't even admit the most timid looking cat. (p. 5)	*The big idea here is that there are no cats allowed. Are there any other animals that are dangerous to mice?*	**Synthesizing** **Asking questions**
. . . they saw a well-dressed fox with a flannel bandage around his jaw. (p. 6)	*I wonder how Doctor De Soto and his wife will handle this. I'm guessing foxes are dangerous to mice, so he will be forbidden.*	**Making inferences**
And he wept so bitterly it was pitiful to see. (pp. 7–8)	*At first I thought that Doctor De Soto wouldn't help the fox, but now I'm thinking that because the fox is so miserable, he will allow him in.*	**Synthesizing**
She pressed the buzzer and let the fox in. (p. 9)	*Why do they change their mind? I'm seeing these characters now as very sympathetic toward the fox.*	**Asking questions** **Monitoring and clarifying**
" . . . and remove the bandage, please." (pp. 10–11)	*I like how the author shows the fox begging and in terrible pain to show me why the De Sotos changed their minds.*	**Understanding the author's purpose**
. . . and his jaw began to quiver. (pp. 12–13)	*When I first met the fox, I thought he was in such pain that he'd never hurt the mice. But now I'm thinking that the fox will not be able to resist temptation and will try to eat the De Sotos!*	**Synthesizing**
"Wide open!" yelled his wife. (p. 13)	*At first, I wasn't sure about the word* quiver. *I know* quiver *means to shake, and at first I thought his mouth was quivering because he was in so much pain. But when I reread it and noticed the phrase* despite his misery, *I thought his mouth was shaking because he wanted to close it with Doctor De Soto and his wife inside!*	**Monitoring and clarifying**

continued . . .

. . . from previous

What the Text Says	What I Say	The Comprehension Strategy I Model
"You won't feel a feel when I yank that tooth." (p. 14)	*I was confused at first with gas. I was thinking the doctor was giving him gas like we give our cars gas! But when I kept reading, I realized he was using gas to numb the fox and make him not feel pain.*	⇄ **Monitoring and clarifying**
"How I love them raw . . . with just a pinch of salt, and a . . . dry . . . white wine." (p. 14)	*Hmm, I know here he's talking in his sleep because the author gives the clue of dreamland. But I wonder what he is talking about. What does he love raw, with salt and white wine?*	? **Asking questions**
Mrs. De Soto handed her husband a pole to keep the fox's mouth open. (p. 15)	*I'm getting the sense here that Doctor De Soto and his wife think the fox is talking about how he loves mice and calls them yummy! Maybe they are using the pole so he can't snap his jaws shut and eat them.*	III **Making inferences**
. . . if it would be shabby of him to eat the De Sotos when the job was done. (pp. 16–17)	*I like how the author makes it so the fox has to wait and come back for his new tooth. It makes the story go on longer and builds suspense for me.*	A **Understanding the author's purpose**
"They're wicked, wicked creatures." (p. 18)	*I'm really getting the sense here that Doctor De Soto and his wife are plotting something. They call themselves foolish to trust a fox, but they are still planning to give him a new tooth. I like how the author introduced conflict between Doctor De Soto and his wife—she thinks the fox is trustworthy, but he is suspicious of the fox. This conflict makes me want to keep reading to see if either of them is right!*	III **Making inferences** A **Understanding the author's purpose**
A minute later he was snoring. (p. 19)	*Now I'm really curious to see what this plan is! I wonder what they are plotting.*	? **Asking questions**
. . . and laughed. "Just a joke!" he chortled. (pp. 20–21)	*I like how the author has the fox snap his mouth shut here as a joke. The mood was so tense up until this point, and the author used a bit of humor to break through some of the tension.*	A **Understanding the author's purpose**
. . . and hooked it up to the teeth on both sides. (pp. 21–22)	*I'm getting these clues that the fox is really appreciative—he loves the gold tooth, he's cheerful because he's not in pain, and he's making jokes. That makes me think that the fox will not try to eat the De Sotos.*	III **Making inferences**

What the Text Says	What I Say	The Comprehension Strategy I Model
"On the other hand, how can I resist?" (p. 22)	*This word* shouldn't *is important to me—and so is the phrase* on the other hand. *The author is telling me that the fox is really in a dilemma. He doesn't want to eat the De Sotos, but he's not sure he can say no to the temptation!*	A **Understanding the author's purpose**
". . . How would you like to be the first one to receive this unique treatment?" (p. 23)	*Now I think that something is going on with this preparation. I know the De Sotos were up late at night making a plan, and all of a sudden, they are introducing this brand-new application. I think it's a trick, and I want to read on to see if the fox will fall for it.*	**Synthesizing**
. . . with the help of his brand-new tooth. (p. 24)	*I was a bit confused when I saw that the words* no one *were in italics. I know the author uses that to show something important. When I wasn't sure why he said no one would see them again, I read more to find out that the fox is going to eat them. So when he says no one will see them again, the fox means that they will be gone forever in his belly!*	**Monitoring and clarifying** A **Understanding the author's purpose**
The fox looked very happy. (p. 25)	*I like how the author shows here that everyone is relaxed—Doctor De Soto is humming, his wife is helping out her husband, and the fox is happy. It makes me think that the De Sotos have no idea what the fox is planning to do—and the fox has no idea that the De Sotos are plotting something!*	A **Understanding the author's purpose**
. . . but his teeth were stuck together! (p. 26)	*Stuck together! I wonder if there was something—like super glue—in that gold tooth to make it so that he couldn't open his mouth again!*	? **Asking questions**
". . . No pain ever again!" (p. 26)	*"Permeate the dentine"? What does that mean? I see a part of* dentist *in* dentine, *so I think it has to do with teeth. And maybe* permeate *has something to do with sitting there. Doctor De Soto is saying the formula won't work unless it permeates the teeth.*	**Monitoring and clarifying**
. . . He tried to do so with dignity. (p. 27)	*The gist here is that the fox knows he got tricked! He can't talk well with his mouth glued shut, and he's trying to leave without being totally embarrassed. I now see that the fox is embarrassed that he was outsmarted.*	**Synthesizing**

continued . . .

... from previous

What the Text Says	What I Say	The Comprehension Strategy I Model
They kissed each other and took the rest of the day off. (p. 28)	*I'm ending the book with questions. Will the fox never be able to open his mouth again? Will the De Sotos ever treat any animals who are dangerous to mice again? What does the fox think about mice now? What do the De Sotos think about foxes now? I know these questions aren't answered in the book, but I sure am curious!*	? **Asking questions**

Thinking Aloud With a Chapter Book in Grades 3–5 *The Year of Billy Miller* by Kevin Henkes

Overview and Rationale

Most children and teachers know and love Kevin Henkes for his popular picture books, but his works for the middle-grade reader are equally as appealing. A Newbery Honor book, *The Year of Billy Miller* is a story about friendship, sibling rivalry, and elementary school.

Lexile Framework: 620L
Guided Reading Level: P

What the Text Says	What I Say	The Comprehension Strategy I Model
Part One: Teacher	*Hmm, I can tell this book is going to be written in several parts. I wonder why there are so many parts. Will each part be written from a different person, like this one is from the teacher?*	A **Understanding the author's purpose**
It was the first day of second grade, and Billy Miller was worried.	*Who is Billy Miller? Is he a second-grade student? A second-grade teacher? What is he worried about?*	? **Asking questions**

What the Text Says	What I Say	The Comprehension Strategy I Model
He was worried that he wouldn't be smart enough for school this year.	*Before I wasn't sure who Billy was and why he was worried. Now I'm getting the hint that he's worried about not being smart enough, so that makes me think Billy is a kid.*	**Synthesizing**
There was a reason he was worried. Two weeks earlier on their drive home from visiting Mount Rushmore and the Black Hills of South Dakota, Billy Miller and his family stopped in Blue Earth, Minnesota to see the statue of the Jolly Green Giant. Billy instantly recognized the Giant from the labels of canned and frozen vegetables. The statue was spectacular—so tall, and the greenest green Billy had ever seen.	*I got lost here because I thought I was going to hear about the reason Billy was worried about not being smart enough, and instead the author is telling me about his trip to see a statue. Maybe if I keep reading I will find out why the author is telling me the part about the statue.*	**Monitoring and clarifying**
Billy was wearing his new baseball cap that said BLACK HILLS in glossy silver embroidery. It was a blustery day. The flag on the nearby pole snapped in the wind. Billy raced ahead of his family—up the steps to the lookout platform. As he stood between the Giant's enormous feet, a sudden gust lifted his cap from his head. His cap sailed away. Without thinking, Billy stepped onto the middle rung of the guardrail, leaned over, and reached as far as he could. He fell to the pavement below. The next thing Billy remembered was waking up in a hospital.	*The author doesn't come right out and say it, but I'm getting the sense that he fell a long way down to the pavement below. I'm inferring that when he fell, he got hurt badly. It could be that he hurt his head when he fell. Maybe that is why he's worried about not being smart enough for second grade.*	**Making inferences**
His parents, whom he called Mama and Papa, were with him, as was his three-year-old sister, Sally, whom everyone called Sal. After tests were done, the doctor proclaimed Billy miraculously unharmed, except for a lump on his head. "You fell exactly the right way to protect yourself," the doctor told him. "You're a lucky young man." "And Papa got your hat back!" said Sal.	*I've got lots of questions here. Why does Billy call his parents Mama and Papa? That sounds sort of old-fashioned, when kids today mostly call their parents Mom and Dad. That makes me wonder when this story takes place. What kind of tests did they run?*	**Asking questions**

continued...

. . . from previous

What the Text Says	What I Say	The Comprehension Strategy I Model
When they returned home, Billy proudly showed his lump—and his cap—to his best friend, Ned. He called his grandmother on the phone and told her about the incident, too. Everything seemed all right until a few nights later when Billy overheard his parents taking in the kitchen. "I'm worried about him," said Mama. "He's fine," said Papa. "Everyone said he's fine. And he seems fine. He *is* fine." "You're probably right," said Mama. "But I worry that down the line something will show up. He'll start forgetting things." "He already forgets things," said Papa. "He's a seven-year old boy." "You know what I mean," said Mama. She paused. "Or he'll be confused at school. Or . . ." That's all Billy heard. He snuck up to his room and closed the door. And that's when he started to worry.	*Now I understand why Billy is so worried about not being smart enough for second grade. He had a bad fall, went to the hospital, and has a lump on his head. He overhears his parents worrying that he is forgetful.*	**Synthesizing**
Billy didn't tell anyone that he was worried. Sometimes, he didn't know how to say what he was thinking. He had words in his head, but they didn't always make it to his mouth. This happened often, even before the fall.	*I'm getting the sense that Billy has a lot on his mind. He worries a lot, and sometimes he has a hard time telling people things. I think this will be an important part of Billy's character, since the author is telling it to me right at the start of the book.*	**Synthesizing**
"Happy first day of school," said Mama. "Happy first day of school," said Papa. Billy had noticed long ago that one of his parents often repeated what the other said. Without taking the time to sit at the table, Mama rushed about the kitchen, stealing a few bites of Papa's toast and a gulp of his coffee. She hoisted her big canvas bag onto the counter and reorganized its contents. It was Mama's first day of school, too. She taught English at the high school down the street.	*I wonder how Billy feels about his mom being a teacher. Will she eventually be his teacher? And do we know yet what kind of job Billy's father has?*	? **Asking questions**

What the Text Says	What I Say	The Comprehension Strategy I Model
While Billy was eating his pancakes, Papa reread aloud the letter that Ms. Silver, the second grade teacher, had sent during the summer. In the letter Ms. Silver greeted the students and said she was looking forward to the new school year. She said that she and her husband had a baby boy at home. And two dogs. She said that second grade would be a "safe, happy year of growth" and "a wonderful, joyful, exciting challenge." Billy stopped chewing when he heard the word *challenge*. He put down his fork and touched the lump on his head. He didn't want a challenge.	*The author is giving me more clues that Billy is really nervous about second grade. He stops eating, and touches the lump on his head. I get the sense that Billy is anxious.*	**Synthesizing**
Papa continued. "Ms. Silver says you'll be studying colors and habitats and the world of names." "That sounds like fun," said Mama. "My students will be studying *Beowulf* and *Paradise Lost*." "I'd rather be in second grade," said Papa, smiling.	*The author doesn't come right out and say it, but I get the sense Papa thinks those books are boring. He smiles and says that second grade sounds more fun than the work Mama's students will be doing.*	**Making inferences**
Unlike the other fathers Billy knew, Papa stayed home and took care of Sal and the house. Papa was an artist.	*Aha! Earlier, I had asked if Papa had a job—and here I got my answer.*	**Asking questions**
He was waiting for a breakthrough.	*What does that mean—"waiting for a breakthrough"? Maybe if I keep rereading the author will explain it to me.*	**Monitoring and clarifying**
That's what he always said. He was currently working on big sculptures made of found objects. Pieces of old machines, tree limbs, and broken furniture filled the garage and spilled out onto the driveway. They were scattered across the yard too. Billy loved watching Papa work. There was always something lying around that was fun to play with.	*The author doesn't really explain to me what a breakthrough is, but I know that artists sometimes have a hard time selling their work and making money. I wonder if that is the case for Papa.*	**Asking questions**
"Gotta go," said Mama. She kissed Papa on his bushy orange beard. She kissed Billy on his lump. "Have a fantastic day," she said. "And kiss Sal for me when she wakes up." Just like that, Mama was gone, the smell of her lemony shampoo hanging in the air for a moment.	*I get the sense here that Billy is a bit sad about his mother leaving. She kisses him on his lump—a spot that she knows he is worried about. When she leaves, he still smells her scent. Perhaps he wants his mother to make him feel better on the first day of school.*	**Making inferences**

continued . . .

. . . from previous

What the Text Says	What I Say	The Comprehension Strategy I Model
Papa cleared his throat and shook Ms. Silver's letter with a flourish.	*What does it mean that he shook the letter "with a flourish"? Why is he shaking it like that? Let me keep reading for more clues.*	**Monitoring and clarifying**
Billy could tell he was trying to be funny. In a deep, rumbly voice he said, "This utterly fascinating letter concludes by stating that currently this is, in fact, according to the Chinese, the Year of the Rabbit." Papa used his regular voice again. "That's pretty great, don't you think? The Year of the Rabbit." Billy shrugged. Normally this would have interested him, but he was preoccupied.	*I'm getting the sense that Papa knows Billy is nervous and maybe a bit sad about Mama leaving. Maybe Papa is trying to distract him, or to be funny to make Billy feel better on the first day of school.*	**Making inferences**
"Maybe you'll have carrots for a snack every day," said Papa. Silence. "Papa?" said Billy. "Hmm?" "But, Papa, will I be smart enough for second grade?"	*The key point here is that Billy is nervous about how smart he is. The author started out by saying that at the very beginning of the story, but I had sort of forgotten why he was so worried.*	**Synthesizing**
"Of course you will," said Papa. He was looking right down at Billy, directly into his eyes. Billy glanced down at was what left of his pancakes. With his thick, work-gnarled finger, Papa lifted Billy's chin. Their eyes met and held.	*I like how the author uses a gesture from Papa to show how kind he is and how much he loves Billy. He looks him right in the eyes and lifts his chin, which makes me think Papa really wants Billy to understand that he's smart enough.*	A **Understanding the author's purpose**
"Ms. Silver and the great nation of China might think that this is the Year of the Rabbit," said Papa. "But I know—and I know everything—that this is the Year of Billy Miller." Billy smiled. He couldn't not. He repeated Papa's words in his head. This is the Year of Billy Miller.	*I want to keep reading so that I know exactly why this is the Year of Billy Miller—just like the title and this last line say. What happens to make second grade the Year of Billy Miller? Is that a good thing or a bad thing?*	? **Asking questions**

Thinking Aloud With Poetry in Grades 3–5
"Casey at the Bat" by Ernest Thayer

Overview and Rationale

This legendary poem depicts the last half-inning of a baseball game. The plot follows Casey and his team who are at a disadvantage with a score of four to two. The poem illustrates the thrill, fun, and disappointments experienced at such ballgames.

Lexile Framework: 810L

Guided Reading Level: Z

What the Text Says	What I Say	The Comprehension Strategy I Model
The outlook wasn't brilliant for the Mudville nine that day: (stanza 1)	*Who are the Mudville nine? Where is Mudville?*	? **Asking questions**
The score stood four to two; with but one inning more to play, (stanza 1)	*I'm getting the sense that this is a poem about baseball—I've got the hint that there are nine players, and that there is an inning left—which lets me know this is a baseball game.*	**Making inferences**
A pall-like silence fell upon the patrons of the game. (stanza 1)	*At first I thought that these two players really died, but when I reread, I realized they were out at first base and the two outs made the crowd grow quiet.*	**Monitoring and clarifying**
The rest Clung to the hope which springs eternal in the human breast. (stanza 2)	*I'm getting the sense that some of the fans think their team—the Mudville one—is about to lose. Some fans are leaving early, but a couple of die-hard fans are still watching.*	**Synthesizing**
". . . We'd put up even money now, with Casey at the bat." (stanza 2)	*I like how the author uses* if only. *That shows me that the crowd sees Casey as their last hope to get a hit and win this game.*	A **Understanding the author's purpose**
For there seemed but little chance of Casey getting to the bat. (stanza 3)	*I don't really understand what the author means by these two players being a* hoodoo *and a* cake. *When I reread this whole stanza, I can guess that these are negative terms to describe a player. The author is hinting that the crowd is melancholy because of these two players—if they get out, there will be no chance for Casey to come up to bat.*	**Monitoring and clarifying** **Making inferences**
There was Jimmy safe at second and Flynn a-hugging third. (stanza 4)	*At first, I thought that Flynn and Jimmy were going to strike out or get out so that Casey wouldn't get the chance to hit. But both Flynn and Jimmy got on base! Jimmy is on second base, and Flynn is on third, with Casey about to bat.*	**Synthesizing**
For Casey, mighty Casey, was advancing to the bat. (stanza 5)	*I like how the author uses the yells from the throats of the fans to show that they are cheering on Casey. The golden phrase is* mighty Casey. *This makes me think the crowd is expecting him to get a hit and to win the game for Mudville!*	A **Understanding the author's purpose**

continued . . .

. . . from previous

What the Text Says	What I Say	The Comprehension Strategy I Model
No stranger in the crowd could doubt 'twas Casey at the bat. (stanza 6)	*What does* doffed his hat *mean? When I reread it and when I read on, I don't get much of a sense of the word, but I do get this image that Casey is cool and collected—the words* ease, pride, *and* smile *show he's confident! This mood makes me think a hit is a sure thing for Casey!*	**Monitoring and clarifying**
Defiance flashed in Casey's eye, a sneer curled Casey's lip. (stanza 7)	*I wonder why Casey's face changes from a smile to a sneer. Maybe he's trying to intimidate the pitcher?*	? **Asking questions**
"That ain't my style," said Casey. "Strike one!" the umpire said. (stanza 8)	*I don't understand why the author uses* leather-covered sphere. *Is that just an overly descriptive way to say* ball? *I know that sometimes poets like to use vivid imagery as they write, so maybe that's why he didn't simply say* ball. *Also, at first I thought Casey was going to hit the ball, but I know that it might be more interesting to have some strikes against Casey—to increase the suspense and to make me read more!*	**Monitoring and clarifying** A **Understanding the author's purpose**
And it's likely they'd have killed him had not Casey raised his hand. (stanza 9)	*Okay, now I'm not sure why the fans are yelling to kill the umpire. Do they think he made a bad call? Maybe I should go back and reread the previous stanza carefully. This line* "close by the sturdy batsman" *makes me think that maybe the pitch was really close and almost hit Casey. That might make the fans angry! I missed that the first time I read.*	**Monitoring and clarifying**
But Casey still ignored it and the umpire said, "Strike two!" (stanza 10)	*Why did Casey ignore this pitch? What was wrong with it that he didn't want to swing?*	? **Asking questions**
And they knew that Casey wouldn't let that ball go by again. (stanza 11)	*The author wants me to see how outraged the fans are, and how determined Casey is. It's really clear how much these fans need Casey to get a hit.*	A **Understanding the author's purpose**
He pounds with cruel violence his bat upon the plate; (stanza 12)	*Okay, the smiling, confident Casey is gone! The words* hate, clenched, *and* cruel violence *show me how tense this scene is.*	A **Understanding the author's purpose**

What the Text Says	What I Say	The Comprehension Strategy I Model
And now the air is shattered by the force of Casey's blow. (stanza 12)	*I need to know more about what is meant by Casey's blow. Did he blow through the air, like he missed the ball? Or did he blow it out of the park, like a home run? I need to keep reading to understand the action here.*	**Monitoring and clarifying**
But there is no joy in Mudville—mighty Casey has struck out. (stanza 13)	*What? I'm so surprised here—I've got these clues like bright sunshine, a band, light hearts, laughing men, and shouting children that make me think this was a good outcome—that Casey got a hit and Mudville won the game. And then I see the signal word but, and I have to revise what I was thinking—mighty Casey has struck out!*	**Synthesizing**

Thinking Aloud With a Narrative Picture Book in Grades 3–5
An Angel for Solomon Singer by Cynthia Rylant

Overview and Rationale

This poignant picture book tells the story of Solomon Singer, a lonely middle-aged New Yorker. As he walks the city streets, he dreams of his boyhood in Indiana. His dreams are realized at the magical Westway Café, where he befriends a waiter named Angel. Because of this blossoming friendship, Solomon begins to see the beauty of the world around him and leaves behind his loneliness.

Lexile Framework: 1120

Guided Reading Level: P

What the Text Says	What I Say	The Comprehension Strategy I Model
The hotel had none of the things he loved. (p. 1)	*At first I wasn't sure what the "it" was. Did Solomon not like the hotel, or did he not like New York City? As I kept reading, I realized he did not like the hotel, as the author tells me it had none of the things he loved.* *Also, why would someone live in a hotel, especially one he didn't like? What are the things he loved?*	**Monitoring and clarifying** **Asking questions**

continued . . .

. . . from previous

What the Text Says	What I Say	The Comprehension Strategy I Model
. . . and no picture window for watching the birds. (p. 3)	*The author tells me exactly what Solomon likes—watching birds, windows, porch swings. This evidence suggests that Solomon likes the outdoors and nature.*	**Making inferences**
. . . oh, what a difference a yellow wall or a purple wall would have made! (p. 4)	*No animals and no color in his hotel room. From all of what Solomon doesn't have in his room, it sounds to me like this hotel is drab and lonely.*	**Making inferences**
It was dreams of balconies and purple walls that took him to the street. (p. 6)	*Now I understand that Solomon leaves the place that he does not love so he can wander to places that he might like better.*	**Synthesizing**
. . . and listened to the voices of all who passed, wishing for the conversations of crickets. (p. 8)	*Why did he leave Indiana? What brought him to New York City?*	? **Asking questions**
He didn't feel happy as he wandered. (p. 10)	*I'm really getting the sense that Solomon is lonely and unhappy—no family to love. He doesn't like where he lives, and even wandering does not bring him happiness. I got the clue that he's at least fifty years old, but does he have a job?*	**Synthesizing** ? **Asking questions**
. . . and so the name meant something to him. (p. 12)	*If he loves the Midwest so much, why does he not move back? Does he not have enough money to move halfway across the country?*	? **Asking questions**
But it didn't put a price on dreams. (p. 12)	*I'm not sure what that final line means—"It didn't put a price on dreams." When I reread it, I can tell the "it" is the menu, so literally this sentence tells me that there is no price for dreams on the menu. Maybe the author is telling me that dreams are priceless?*	**Monitoring and clarifying** A **Understanding the author's purpose**
. . . a pair of brown eyes that were lined at the corners from a life of smiling. (p. 14)	*I like how the author uses a sweet, familiar voice and smiling eyes to show the kindness of whomever is talking to Solomon. I'm guessing he feels comfortable right away.*	A **Understanding the author's purpose** **Making inferences**

What the Text Says	What I Say	The Comprehension Strategy I Model
. . . (but he didn't say the balcony out loud). (p. 14)	*I'm wondering what the author meant when he wrote that Solomon ordered a balcony, but didn't say it out loud. Why did he write that? First of all, you can't order a balcony at a café! I already know that a balcony is one of the things that Solomon wants at home. So maybe this shows that he feels so comfortable at the café that it feels like home.*	A **Understanding the author's purpose**
Solomon Singer did, the very next night. (p. 14)	*Does he come back because the soup is so good? Or because it's a comfortable place for a lonely man? Or because the waiter is so friendly? Or maybe because of all of those reasons?*	? **Asking questions**
. . . and a fireplace (but he didn't say the fireplace out loud). (p. 16)	*There it is again! A thing that he wanted to order but didn't really. The author saying it twice shows me that it's a really important symbol, so I think it represents the idea that this café gives Solomon a feeling of home and a feeling of belonging.*	A **Understanding the author's purpose** **Synthesizing**
. . . and Solomon Singer did, the very next night. (p. 16)	*So far Solomon and the waiter haven't really talked. Will they ever have a conversation?*	? **Asking questions**
. . . and ordered up a balcony (but he didn't say the balcony out loud). (p. 17)	*I was confused by this part—I am not sure if "he made his way west" means that he went to Indiana or if it means he went to the café. I've also just noticed that the café's name is Westway—like the Midwest where Solomon is from. I wonder if the author did that on purpose! When I reread this whole part, I'm getting the sense that Solomon keeps going back to this café because it reminds him of home and the things he loves.*	**Monitoring and clarifying** A **Understanding the author's purpose** ? **Asking questions**
. . . and he thought them beautiful. (p. 19)	*What a beautiful sentence—the streets moved before him like fields of wheat. I'm getting the sense that because of this new place, New York City is starting to feel more beautiful and more like home.*	**Making inferences**

continued . . .

. . . from previous

What the Text Says	What I Say	The Comprehension Strategy I Model
. . . and he felt friendly toward them. (p. 20)	*Here the author repeated some of those images from Solomon's Indiana home—the shining stars, the wheat fields, and the crickets. I saw those exact same things at the beginning of the book—now I'm really sure that New York City is feeling like home.*	A **Understanding the author's purpose**
. . . when he would come in from wandering the roads he loved. (p. 24)	*The important idea here is that Solomon is reliving the happiness he felt in his Indiana childhood. The Westway Café makes him feel like he's home and no longer lonely.*	**Synthesizing**
The waiter's name, it turned out, was Angel. (p. 25)	*Angel! I know angels are symbols of love and good things. I don't think that it's a coincidence that the author named the waiter Angel.*	A **Understanding the author's purpose**
. . . and one of his dreams has even come true (he has sneaked a cat into his hotel room). (p. 26)	*I'm noticing that the book changes verb tense here. It was all written in the past tense—but then the author writes, "he dines there still." That makes me feel like this story is still going on—that Solomon is still eating at the Westway Café.*	A **Understanding the author's purpose**
. . . and Solomon Singer will smile and make you feel you are home. (p. 28)	*I wonder if this is a true story. Is there really a Westway Café and a man named Solomon Singer? I think the message here is that everyone—even people who are lonely—can find a place that feels like home to them.*	? **Asking questions**

online resources

Available for download at **resources.corwin.com/ness-thinkalouds**

References

Afflerbach, P., & Johnston, P. (1986). What do expert readers do when the main idea is not explicit? In J. Baumann (Ed.), *Teaching main idea comprehension* (pp. 49–72). Newark, DE: International Reading Association.

Anderson, V., & Roit, M. (1993). Planning and implementing collaborative strategy instruction for delayed readers in grades 6–10. *The Elementary School Journal, 94*(2), 121–137.

Baker, L. (1979). Comprehension monitoring: Identifying and coping with text confusions. *Journal of Reading Behavior, 11*(4), 366–374.

Baker, L., & Brown, A. L. (1984). Metacognitive skills and reading. In P. D. Pearson (Ed.), *Handbook of reading research* (pp. 353–394). New York, NY: Longman.

Bandura, A. (1977). Self-efficacy: Toward a unifying theory of behavioral change. *Psychological Review*, *84*(2), 191.

Barrentine, S. J. (1996). Engaging with reading through interactive read-alouds. *The Reading Teacher*, *50*(1), 36–43.

Baumann, J. F., Jones, L. A., & Seifert-Kessell, N. (1993). Using think alouds to enhance children's comprehension monitoring abilities. *The Reading Teacher, 47*(3), 184–193.

Baumann, J. F., Seifert-Kessell, N., & Jones, L. A. (1992). Effect of think-aloud instruction on elementary students' comprehension monitoring abilities. *Journal of Literacy Research*, *24*(2), 143–172.

Beers, K. (2003). *When kids can't read, what teachers can do: A guide for teachers, 6–12*. Portsmouth, NH: Heinemann.

Beers, K., & Probst, R. E. (2013). *Notice & note: Strategies for close reading*. Portsmouth, NH: Heinemann.

Bereiter, C., & Bird, M. (1985). Use of thinking aloud in identification and teaching of reading comprehension strategies. *Cognition and Instruction, 2*(2), 131–156.

Block, C. C. (2004). *Teaching comprehension: The comprehension process approach*. Boston, MA: Allyn & Bacon.

Block, C. C., & Duffy, G. G. (2008). Research on teaching comprehension: Where we've been and where we're going. *Comprehension Instruction: Research-Based Best Practices* (2nd ed., pp. 19–37). New York, NY: Guilford Press.

Block, C. C., & Israel, S. E. (2004). The ABCs of performing highly effective think alouds. *The Reading Teacher, 58*(2), 154–167.

Chin, C., Brown, D. E., & Bruce, B. C. (2002). Student-generated questions: A meaningful aspect of learning in science. *International Journal of Science Education, 24*(5), 521–549.

Chouinard, M. M., Harris, P. L., & Maratsos, M. P. (2007). Children's questions: A mechanism for cognitive development. *Monographs of the Society for Research in Child Development*, 72(1), i–129.

Coiro, J. (2008). *A beginning understanding of the interplay between offline and online reading comprehension when adolescents read for information on the Internet.* Unpublished dissertation monograph, University of Connecticut.

Coiro, J. (2011). Talking about reading as thinking: Modeling the hidden complexities of online reading comprehension. *Theory Into Practice, 50*(2), 107–115.

Common Core State Standards (CCSS) Initiative. (2010). *English language arts standards.* Retrieved from http://www.corestandards.org/ELA-Literacy

Cummins, S., & Stallmeyer-Gerard, C. (2011). Teaching for synthesis of informational texts with read-alouds. *The Reading Teacher, 64*(6), 394–405.

Davey, B. (1983). Think aloud: Modeling the cognitive processes of reading comprehension. *Journal of Reading, 27*(1), 44–47.

Davey, B., & McBride, S. (1986). Effects of question-generation training on reading comprehension. *Journal of Educational Psychology, 78*(4), 256.

Donovan, C. A., & Smolkin, L. B. (2002). Children's genre knowledge: An examination of K–5 students' performance on multiple tasks providing differing levels of scaffolding. *Reading Research Quarterly, 37*(4), 428–465.

Dorl, J. (2007). Think aloud! Increase your teaching power. *Young Children, 62*(4), 101–105.

Dowhower, S. L. (1999). Supporting a strategic stance in the classroom: A comprehension framework for helping teachers help students to be strategic. *The Reading Teacher, 52*(7), 672–688.

Duffy G. G. (2003). Explaining reading: A resource for teaching concepts, skills, and strategies. Newark, DE: International Reading Association.

Duffy, G. G., & Roehler, L. R. (1989). Why strategy instruction is so difficult and what we need to do about it. In C. B. McCormick, G. E. Miller, & M. Pressley (Eds.), *Cognitive strategy research* (pp. 133–154). New York, NY: Springer.

Duke, N. K. (2000). 3.6 minutes per day: The scarcity of informational texts in first grade. *Reading Research Quarterly, 35*(2), 202–224.

Duke, N. K., & Kays, J. (1998). "Can I say 'Once upon a time'?" Kindergarten children developing knowledge of information book language. *Early Childhood Research Quarterly, 13*(2), 295–318.

Duke, N. K., & Pearson, P. (2002). Effective practices for developing reading comprehension. In A. E. Farstrup & S. J. Samuels (Eds.), *What research has to say about reading Instruction* (3rd ed., pp. 205–242). Newark, DE: International Reading Association.

Duke, N. K., & Purcell-Gates, V. (2003). Genres at home and at school: Bridging the known to the new. *The Reading Teacher, 57*(1), 30–37.

Durkin, D. (1978). What classroom observations reveal about reading comprehension instruction. *Reading Research Quarterly, 14*(4), 481–533.

Durkin, D. (1981). *Reading comprehension instruction in five basal reader series* (Reading Education Report No. 26). Retrieved from http://files.eric.ed.gov/fulltext/ED205914.pdf

Dymock, S. (2007). Comprehension strategy instruction: Teaching narrative text structure awareness. *The Reading Teacher, 61*(2), 161–167.

El-Dinary, P. B., Pressley, M., & Schuder, T. (1992). Teachers learning transactional strategies instruction. In C. K. Kinzer & D. J. Leu (Eds.), *Literacy research, theory, and practice: Views from many perspectives. 41st yearbook of the National Reading Conference* (pp. 453–462). Chicago, IL: National Reading Conference.

Farest, C., Miller, C., & Fewin, S. (1995). Lewis & Clark: An incredible journey into the world of information books. *New Advocate, 8*(4), 271–288.

Fisher, D., Flood, J., Lapp, D., & Frey, N. (2004). Interactive read-alouds: Is there a common set of implementation practices? *The Reading Teacher, 58*(1).

Fisher, D. & Frey, N. (2012). Close reading in elementary schools. *The Reading Teacher, 66*(3), 179–188.

Fisher, D., Frey, N., & Hattie, J. (2016). Visible learning for literacy, grades K–12: Implementing the practices that work best to accelerate student learning. Thousand Oaks, CA: Corwin.

Fisher, D., Frey, N., & Hattie, J. (2017). *Teaching literacy in the visible learning classroom.* Thousand Oaks, CA: Corwin.

Fisher, D., Frey, N., & Lapp, D. (2011). Coaching middle-level teachers to think aloud improves comprehension instruction and student reading achievement. *The Teacher Educator, 46*(3), 231–243.

Flavell, J. H. (1976). Metacognitive aspects of problem solving. In L. B. Resnick (Ed.), *The nature of intelligence* (pp. 231–235). Hillsdale, NJ: Erlbaum.

Frazier, B. N., Gelman, S. A., & Wellman, H. M. (2009). Preschoolers' search for explanatory information within adult–child conversation. *Child Development, 80*(6), 1592–1611.

Frey, N., & Fisher, D. (2013). *Rigorous reading: 5 access points for comprehending complex texts.* Thousand Oaks, CA: Corwin.

Garcia, G. E. (2002, December). *Issues surrounding cross-linguistic transfer in bilingual students' reading: A study of Mexican-American fourth graders*. Paper presented at the National Reading Conference, Miami, FL.

Ghaith, G., & Obeid, H. (2004). Effect of think alouds on literal and higher-order reading comprehension. *Educational Research Quarterly, 27*(3), 49.

Hall, K. M., & Sabey, B. L. (2007). Focus on the facts: Using informational texts effectively in early elementary classrooms. *Early Childhood Education Journal, 35*(3), 261–268.

Harvey, S., & Goudvis, A. (2000). *Strategies that work: Teaching comprehension to enhance understanding*. Portland, ME: Stenhouse.

Heller, M. (2006). Telling stories and talking facts: First graders' engagements in a nonfiction book club. *The Reading Teacher, 60*(4), 358–369.

Israel, S. E., & Massey, D. (2005). Metacognitive think-alouds: Using a gradual release model with middle school students. In S. E. Israel, C. C. Block, K. L. Bauserman, & K. Kinnucan-Welsch (Eds.), *Metacognition in literacy learning: Theory, assessment, instruction, and professional development* (pp. 183–198). Mahwah, NJ: Erlbaum.

Ivey, G., & Broaddus, K. (2001). "Just plain reading": A survey of what makes students want to read in middle school classrooms. *Reading Research Quarterly, 36*(4), 350–377.

Jongsma, K. (2000). Vocabulary and comprehension strategy development. *Reading Teacher, 53*(4), 310–312.

Kelley, M. J., & Clausen-Grace, N. (2010). Guiding students through expository text with text feature walks. *The Reading Teacher, 64*(3), 191–195.

King, A., & Rosenshine, B. (1993). Effects of guided cooperative questioning on children's knowledge construction. *The Journal of Experimental Education, 61*(2), 127–148.

Kucan, L. (2007). Insights from teachers who analyzed transcripts of their own classroom discussions. *The Reading Teacher, 61*(3), 228–236.

Kymes, A. (2005). Teaching online comprehension strategies using think-alouds. *Journal of Adolescent and Adult Literacy, 48*(6), 492–500.

Lapp, D., Fisher, D., & Grant, G. (2008). "You can read this text—I'll show you how": Interactive comprehension instruction. *Journal of Adolescent and Adult Literacy, 51*(5), 372–383.

Leal, D. J. (1994). A comparison of third grade children's listening comprehension and retention of scientific information using an informational book and an informational storybook. In C. K. Kinzer & D. J. Leu (Eds.), *Multidimensional aspects of literacy research, theory, and practice* (Vol. 43, pp. 135–147). Chicago, IL: National Reading Conference.

Leven, T., & Long, R. (1981). *Effective instruction*. Washington, DC: Association for Supervision and Curriculum Development.

Loxterman, J. A., Beck, I. L., & McKeown, M. G. (1994). The effects of thinking aloud during reading on students' comprehension of more or less coherent text. *Reading Research Quarterly, 29*(4), 353–368.

Maloch, B. (2008). Beyond exposure: The uses of informational texts in a second grade classroom. *Research in the Teaching of English, 42*(3), 315–362.

Maria, K., & Hathaway, K. (1993). Using think alouds with teachers to develop awareness of reading strategies. *Journal of Reading, 37*(1), 12–18.

Marzano, R. J. (2010). Teaching inference. *Educational Leadership, 67*(7), 80–81.

McKeown, R. G., & Gentilucci, J. L. (2007). Think-aloud strategy: Metacognitive development and monitoring comprehension in the middle school second-language classroom. *Journal of Adolescent & Adult Literacy, 51*(2), 136–147.

Migyanka, J. M., Policastro, C., & Lui, G. (2005). Using a think-aloud with diverse students: Three primary grade students experience *Chrysanthemum*. *Early Childhood Education Journal, 33*(3), 171–177.

Mokhtari, K., & Reichard, C. A. (2002). Assessing students' metacognitive awareness of reading strategies. *Journal of Educational Psychology, 94*(2), 249.

Moss, B. (1997). A quantitative assessment of first graders' retelling of expository text. *Reading Research and Instruction*, 37, 1–13.

Moss, B., & Leal, D. J. (1994, December). *A comparison of children's written responses to science-related information books and informational storybooks*. Paper presented at the annual meeting of the National Reading Conference, San Diego, CA.

Ness, M. (2015). *The question is the answer: Supporting student-generated queries in elementary classrooms*. Landover, MD: Rowman & Littlefield.

Nolte, R. Y., & Singer, H. (1985). Active comprehension: Teaching a process of reading comprehension and its effects on reading achievement. *The Reading Teacher, 39*(1), 24–31.

Oczkus, L. D. (2004). Super six comprehension strategies: 35 lessons and more for reading success. Norwood, MA: Christopher-Gordon.

Oczkus, L. D. (2009). Interactive think-aloud lessons: 25 surefire ways to engage students and improve comprehension. New York, NY: Scholastic.

Ortlieb, E., & Norris, M. R. (2012). Preventing the development of struggling readers: Comprehension instruction in the science classroom. *Current Issues in Education, 15*(1).

Oster, L. (2001). Using the think-aloud for reading instruction. *The Reading Teacher, 55*(1), 64–69.

Oyler, C., & Barry, A. (1996). Intertextual connections in read-alouds of information books. *Language Arts, 73*(5), 324–329.

Pappas, C. C. (1993). Is narrative "primary"? Some insights from kindergartners' pretend readings of stories and informational books. *Journal of Reading Behavior, 25*(1), 97–129.

Paris, S. G., Lipson, M. Y., & Wixson, K. (1994). Becoming a strategic reader. In R. B. Rudell, M. R. Rudell, & H. Singer (Eds.), *Theoretical models and processes of reading* (4th ed., pp. 788–810). Newark, DE: International Reading Association.

Pearson, P. D., & Gallagher, M. (1983a). The gradual release of responsibility model of instruction. *Contemporary Educational Psychology, 8*(3), 112–123.

Pearson, P. D., & Gallagher, M. (1983b). The instruction of reading comprehension. *Contemporary Educational Psychology, 8*(3), 317–344.

Peitzman, L. (2013, May 31). 25 most challenging books you will ever read. *BuzzFeed.* Retrieved from https://www.buzzfeed.com/louispeitzman/the-25-most-challenging-books-you-will-ever-read?utm_term=.aakglGEbr#.npRG37V81

Piaget, J. (1952). *The origins of intelligence in children* (Vol. 8, No. 5). New York, NY: International Universities Press.

Pressley, M. (2002). Metacognition and self-regulated comprehension. In A. E. Farstrup & S. J. Samuels (Eds.), *What research has to say about reading instruction* (pp. 291–309). Newark, DE: International Reading Association.

Richgels, D. (2002). Informational texts in kindergarten. *The Reading Teacher, 55*(6), 586–595.

Rosenblatt, L. M. (1994). *The reader, the text, the poem: The transactional theory of the literary work* (Paperback ed.). Carbondale: Southern Illinois University Press.

Rosenshine, B., Meister, C., & Chapman, S. (1996). Teaching students to generate questions: A review of the intervention studies. *Review of Educational Research, 66*(2), 181–221.

Saenz, L. M., & Fuchs, L. S. (2002). Examining the reading difficulty of secondary students with learning disabilities expository versus narrative text. *Remedial and Special Education, 23*(1), 31–41.

Schunk, D. H., & Rice, J. M. (1985). Verbalization of comprehension strategies: Effects on children's achievement outcomes. *Human Learning: Journal of Practical Research & Applications, 4*(1), 1–10.

Silvén, M., & Vauras, M. (1992). Improving reading through thinking aloud. *Learning and Instruction, 2*(2), 69–88.

Singh, M. (2014, October 27). What's going on inside the brain of a curious child? *National Public Radio*. Retrieved from https://ww2.kqed.org/mindshift/2014/10/27/whats-going-on-inside-the-brain-of-a-curious-child

Smith, L. A. (2006). Think-aloud mysteries: Using structured, sentence-by-sentence text passages to teach comprehension strategies. *The Reading Teacher, 59*(8), 764–773.

Snow, C. (2002). *Reading for understanding: Towards an R&D program in reading comprehension* (No. MR-1465-DERI). Santa Monica, CA: RAND.

Snow, C. E., Griffin, P., & Burns, M. S. (2005). Knowledge to support the teaching of reading: Preparing teachers for a changing world. San Francisco, CA: Jossey-Bass.

Spider-hunting nudist ends with ring of fire. (2006, April 5). *Zee News*. Retrieved from http://zeenews.india.com/home/spiderhunting-nudist-ends-with-ring-of-fire_286368.html

Taboada, A., & Guthrie, J. T. (2006). Contributions of student questioning and prior knowledge to construction of knowledge from reading information text. *Journal of Literacy Research, 38*(1), 1–35.

Taylor, L. K., Alber, S. R., & Walker, D. W. (2002). The comparative effects of a modified self-questioning strategy and story mapping on the reading comprehension of elementary students with learning disabilities. *Journal of Behavioral Education, 11*(2), 69–87.

Therrien, W. J., & Hughes, C. (2008). Comparison of repeated reading and question generation on students' reading fluency and comprehension. *Learning Disabilities: A Contemporary Journal, 6*(1), 1–16.

Thomas, K., & Barksdale-Ladd, M. (2000). Metacognitive processes: Teaching strategies in literacy education classes. *Reading Psychology, 21*(1), 67–84.

Tovani, C. (2000). *I read it, but I don't get it: Comprehension strategies for adolescent readers.* Portland, ME: Stenhouse.

Vygotsky, L. S. (1962). *Thought and language* (E. Hanfmann & G. Vakar, trans.). Cambridge, MA: MIT Press. (Original work published in 1934)

Vygotsky, L. S. (1978). *Mind in society: The development of higher psychological processes.* Cambridge, MA: Harvard University Press.

Walker, B. J. (2005). Thinking aloud: Struggling readers often require more than a model. *The Reading Teacher, 58*(7), 688–692.

Ward, L., & Traweek, D. (1993). Application of a metacognitive strategy to assessment, intervention, and consultation: A think-aloud technique. *Journal of School Psychology, 31*(4), 469–485.

A "whopper" of a burger bill. (2006, March 28). *USA Today*. Retrieved from http://usatoday30.usatoday.com/news/offbeat/2006-03-28-burger_x.htm

Wilhelm, J. D. (2001). Improving comprehension with think-aloud strategies. New York, NY: Scholastic.

Wilhelm, J. D. (2013). *Improving comprehension with think-aloud strategies* (2nd ed.). New York, NY: Scholastic Inc.

Williams, J. A. (2010). Taking on the role of questioner: Revisiting reciprocal teaching. *The Reading Teacher, 64*(4), 278–281.

Wong, B. Y., & Jones, W. (1982). Increasing meta-comprehension in learning disabled and normally achieving students through self-questioning training. *Learning Disability Quarterly, 5*(3), 228–240.

Wood, D., Bruner, J. S., & Ross, G. (1976). The role of tutoring in problem solving. *Journal of Child Psychology and Psychiatry, 17*(2), 89–100.

Yoğurtçu, K. (2012, January). The impact of self-efficacy perception on reading comprehension on academic achievement. *Procedia-Social and Behavioral Sciences, 70*, 375–386.

Yopp, R. H., & Yopp, H. K. (2006). Informational texts as read-alouds at school and home. *Journal of Literacy Research, 38*(1), 37–51.

Children's Literature Reference List

Al-Abdullah, Queen R., & DiPucchio, K. (2010). *The sandwich swap*. New York, NY: Disney-Hyperion.

Arnosky, J. (2000). *A manatee morning*. New York, NY: Simon & Schuster.

Babbitt, N. (1975). *Tuck everlasting*. New York, NY: Farrar, Straus & Giroux.

Burnett, F. H. (1911). *The secret garden*. New York, NY: Frederick A. Stokes.

Churnin, N. (2016). The William Hoy story: How a deaf baseball player changed the game. Park Ridge, IL: Albert Whitman & Co.

Cisneros, S. (1984). *The house on Mango Street.* Houston, TX: Arte Público Press.

Clements, A. (1996). *Frindle*. New York, NY: Simon & Schuster Books for Children.

Creech, S. (1994). *Walk two moons*. New York, NY: HarperCollins.

Dahl, R. (1964). *Charlie and the chocolate factory*. New York, NY: Knopf.

dePaola, T. (1975). *Strega nona*. New York, NY: Simon & Schuster Books for Children.

DiCamillo, K. (2005). *Mercy Watson to the rescue*. Cambridge, MA: Candlewick Press.

Franzen, J. (2001). *The corrections*. New York, NY: Farrar, Straus & Giroux.

Frazee, M. (2003). *Roller coaster*. Boston, MA: Houghton Mifflin Harcourt.

Freedman, R. (1987). The mysterious Mr. Lincoln. In R. Freedman (Ed.), *Lincoln: A photobiography* (pp. 1–6). New York, NY: Clarion Books.

Gibbons, G. (2005). *Owls*. New York, NY: Holiday House.

Hurd, E. T. (2000). *Starfish*. New York, NY: HarperCollins.

Lear, E. (1871). The owl and the pussy-cat. In E. Lear (Ed.), *Nonsense Songs, Stories, Botany, and Alphabets*. London, UK: Robert John Bush.

Levine, E. (2007). Henry's freedom box: A true story from the Underground Railroad. New York, NY: Scholastic.

Lobel, A. (1975). *Owl at home*. New York, NY: HarperCollins.

Lowry, L. (1989). *Number the stars*. New York, NY: Houghton Mifflin Books for Children.

Lowry, L. (1993). *The giver*. New York, NY: Houghton Mifflin Books for Children.

MacLachlan, P. (1985). *Sarah, plain and tall*. New York, NY: HarperCollins.

Melville, H. (1851). *Moby-Dick*. New York, NY: Harper & Bros.

Moss, M. (2004). *Mighty Jackie: The strike-out queen*. New York, NY: Simon & Schuster Books for Young Readers.

Munson, D. (2000). *Enemy pie*. San Francisco, CA: Chronicle Books.

Neuman, R. (1999). Organic molecules and chemical bonding. In *Organic chemistry* (pp. 1–55). Retrieved from http://people.chem.ucsb.edu/neuman/robert/orgchembyneuman.book/01%20OrganicMolecules/01Separates/01Text.pdf

O'Dell, S. (1960). *Island of the blue dolphins*. New York, NY: Houghton Mifflin Harcourt.

Penn, A. (1993). *The kissing hand*. Washington, DC: Child Welfare League of America.

Peterson, I., & Henderson, N. (2000). Trek 7: The fractal pond race. In I. Peterson & N. Henderson (Eds.), *Math trek: Adventures in the math zone* (pp. 39–52). New York, NY: Wiley.

Polacco, P. (1998). *Thank you, Mr. Falker*. New York, NY: Philomel Books.

Pynchon, T. (1973). *Gravity's rainbow*. New York, NY: Penguin Books.

Recorvits, H. (2003). *My name is Yoon*. New York, NY: Frances Foster Books.

Sarcone-Roach, J. (2015). *The bear ate your sandwich*. New York, NY: Knopf Books for Young Readers.

Shannon, D. (1998). *A bad case of stripes*. New York, NY: Blue Sky Press.

Silverstein, S. (1964). *The giving tree*. New York, NY: Evil Eye Music.

Silverstein, S. (1974). Sick. In S. Silverstein (Ed.), *Where the sidewalk ends* (pp. 58–59). New York, NY: HarperCollins.

Simon, S. (2003). *Eyes and ears*. New York, NY: HarperCollins.

Slate, J. (2000). *Miss Bindergarten stays home from kindergarten*. New York, NY: Puffin Books.

Steig, W. (1986). *Brave Irene*. New York, NY: Farrar, Straus & Giroux.

Upadhyay, R. (2003, January 24). Hard at work. *Time for Kids*.

Van Dusen, C. (2009). *The circus ship*. Somerville, MA: Candlewick Press.

White, E. B. (1952). *Charlotte's web*. New York, NY: HarperCollins.

Index

Abramson, A., 191–195
Achievement, impact of think alouds on, 24
Adler, D., 217–220
Afflerbach, P., 107
Al-Abdullah, R. (Queen), 56–57, 157–159, 163–165
Allard, H., 195–198
An Angel for Solomon Singer (Rylant), 245–248
Apples (Gibbons), 222–224
Asking questions, 7, 28–31
  benefits of, 28–29
  defining, 31
  sentence starters for, 31, 84, 168
  skill building for, 29–31, 30
  think aloud scripts for, 187–195
  think aloud scripts for Grades K–2, 187–191
  think aloud scripts for Grades 3–5, 191–195

Babbitt, N., 9
A Bad Case of Stripes (Shannon), 9, 131–138
  think aloud script for, 181–184
  "We Do" phase for, 131–137
Balloons Over Broadway: The True Story of the Puppeteer of Macy's Parade (Sweet), 210–212
Bandura, A., 25
Barrentine, S. J., 25
Baumann, J. F., 6, 8
The Bear Ate Your Sandwich (Sarcone-Roach), 108–113
Beers, K., 31, 56
Block, C. C., 24, 34
Brainstorming, 42, 56, 104
Brave Irene (Steig), 12–13
Broaddus, K., 25
Bunting, E., 187–191

"Casey at the Bat" (Thayer), 242–245
Charlie and the Chocolate Factory (Dahl), 9
Charlotte's Web (White), 13–14
Chouinard, M. M., 29
Churin, Nancy, 56–57, 159–161, 166–167
The Circus Ship (Van Dusen), 120
  think aloud script for, 172–180
Cisneros, S., 7
Clarifying. *See* Monitoring and clarifying
Clement, A., 143–144
Closed-ended questions, 29
Coles, Robert, 202–204
Common Core State Standards (CCSS Initiative)
  on question generation, 29
  on weight of informational text, 144

Dahl, Roald, 9, 224–225
de la Peña, Matt, 226–229
"The Dentist and the Crocodile" (Dahl), 224–225
DePaola, T., 30
Die template for sentence starters, 82, 149
DiPucchio, K., 56–57, 157–159, 163–165
Doctor De Soto (Steig), 234–238
Duffy, G. G., 34, 40
Duke, N. K., 45, 126, 129
Durkin, D., 12

Enemy Pie (Munson), 18
  chart for thinking aloud in third grade, 89–93
  stopping points in first reading, 43, 45, 46–49
  stopping points in second reading, 62–67
Eyes and Ears (Simon), 18, 50
  chart for thinking aloud in fifth grade, 94–99
  stopping points in, 51–56

Fisher, D., 1, 4, 10, 11, 16, 18–19, 24
Flavell, J. H., 25, 39
Flood, J., 11

Frazee, M., 30
Freedman, R., 152
Frey, N., 1, 10, 11, 14, 16, 18–19
Frindle (Clement), 143–144

Gallagher, M., 14–15
Game spinner, 81, 83, 149
Gibbons, G., 7, 9, 222–224
The Giver (Lowry), 114–115
Goudvis, A., 28
Gradual release of responsibility model, 125–152
  "I Do" phase of, 126–129
  self-evaluation for readers, 144, 145
  steps in, 14–15
  "We Do" phase of, 129–142
  "You Do" phase of, 142–144, 149–150
Grant, M., 4, 24
Guthrie, J. T., 28

"Hard at Work" (Upadhyay), 146
Harris, P. L., 29
Harvey, S., 28
Hathaway, K., 40
Hattie, J., 16, 18–19
Henderson, N., 152
Henkes, K., 238–242
Henry's Freedom Box: A True Story From the Underground Railroad (Levine), 8
The House on Mango Street (Cisneros), 7
Hughes, C., 28
Hurd, E. T., 151

"I Do" phase, in gradual release of responsibility, 126–129
  checklist for, 128
  encouraging noticing and noting, 127–129
Improving Comprehension With Think-Aloud Strategies (Wilhelm), 26
Inferences. *See* Making inferences
Informational text, 217–220
  Common Core Standards on, 144
  in fifth grade, 43, 49–50, 51–56, 67–75
Interactive Think-Aloud Lessons (Oczkus), 26
International Literacy Association, 26
"I" statements, 16
Ivey, G., 25
I Wanna Iguana (Orloff), 208–210

Johnston, P., 107
Jones, L. A., 6, 8
Journalistic-type questions, 29

Kasza, K., 200–202
The Kissing Hand (Penn), 115–116
Kucan, L., 123

Laden, N., 206–208
Lapp, D., 4, 10, 11, 17, 24
Last Stop on Market Street (de la Peña), 226–229
Lear, E., 13, 56–57, 156–157, 162–163
Levine, E., 8
Lizards (Marsh), 205–206
Lobel, A., 13
Lowry, L., 114–115

MacLachlan, P., 7
Making inferences, 7, 31–34
  classroom application of, 32
  defining inference, 31, 33, 195
  sentence starters for, 33–34, 84, 168
  skill building for, 33–34
  think aloud scripts for, 195–200
  think aloud scripts for Grades K–2, 195–198
  think aloud scripts for Grades 3–5, 198–200
Maratsos, M. P., 29
Maria, K., 40
Marsh, L., 205–206
MARSI (Metacognitive Awareness of Reading Strategies Inventory), 40
Marzano, R. J., 33
Math, thinking aloud in, 146, 152
Metacognition, 25, 39–40
Metacognitive Awareness of Reading Strategies Inventory (MARSI), 40
Mighty Jackie: The Strike-Out Queen (Moss), 138–142
Miss Bindergarten Stays Home from Kindergarten (Slate), 117–119
Miss Nelson is Missing! (Allard), 195–198
Mohammed, K., 213–216
Monitoring and clarifying, 7, 37–39, 108
  defining, 38
  sentence starters for, 38–39, 85, 170
  skill building for, 38–39
  think aloud scripts for, 213–220

think aloud scripts for Grades K–2, 213–216
think aloud scripts for Grades 3–5, 217–220
Moss, M., 138–142
Munson, D., 18, 43, 45, 46–49, 62–67, 89–93
My Lucky Day (Kasza), 200–202
My Name is Sangoel (Williams & Mohammed), 213–216
My Name is Yoon (Recorvits), 7
"The Mysterious Mr. Lincoln" (Freedman), 152

National Council of Teachers of English, 26
Norris, M. R., 24
Noticing and noting, 57, 127–138
checklist for, 128
stopping points/comprehension strategies for, 129–138
NowComment.com, 122

Oczkus, L., 26, 28
Open-ended questions, 29
Orloff, K., 208–210
Ortlieb, E., 24
"The Owl and the Pussycat" (Lear), 13, 56–57
overview and rationale, 156–157
think aloud for, 162–163
Owl at Home (Lobel), 13
Owls (Gibbons), 7

Pearson, P., 14–15, 126, 129
Penn, A., 115–116
Peterson, I., 152
PIE (persuade, inform, entertain), 36
Poetry
kindergarten students and, 43–44, 60–62
think aloud scripts for interwoven strategies, 224–225, 242–245
Prediction, difference from inference, 33
Private I. Guana: The Case of the Missing Chameleon (Laden), 206–208
Probst, R., 57
Purpose. *See* Understanding author's purpose

Questions. *See* Asking questions

Reading comprehension strategies, 24–25
previous research on, 26
strategy symbols and, 27
See also Asking questions; Gradual release of responsibility model; Making inferences; Monitoring and clarifying; Research study, yearlong investigation; Sentence starters; Synthesizing; Think aloud scripts; Think aloud scripts for interwoven strategies; Understanding author's purpose
Recorvits, H., 7
Research study, yearlong investigation, 2
author's evaluation of teacher think alouds, 108–113, 109–112, 114–116
example of successful think aloud, 117–119
feedback form for think aloud reflections, 121
findings of, 103–107
reading comprehension strategies and, 105–106
summary of, 3, 102–103
teacher self-evaluation of think alouds, 108–113, 109–112
tips for honing skills, 107–108
See also Reading comprehension strategies
Roller Coaster (Frazee), 30
Rosenblatt, L. M., 42
Rylant, C., 245–248

Sage and Scribe, 150
The Sandwich Swap (Al-Abdullah & DiPucchio), 56–57
overview and rationale, 157–159
think aloud for, 163–165
Sarah, Plain and Tall (MacLachlan), 7
Sarcone-Roach, J., 108–113
Science, thinking aloud in, 147, 151
Scripts. *See* Think aloud scripts
The Secret Garden (Burnett), 14
Seifert-Kessel, N., 6, 8
Self-efficacy, 25
Self-evaluation for think aloud, sample template, 185

Sentence starters, 28
asking questions and, 31, 84, 168
die template for, 82, 149
making inferences and, 33–34, 84, 168
monitoring and clarifying and, 38–39, 85, 170
spinner template for, 81, 83, 149
synthesizing and, 35, 84–85, 169
three-step process and, 81–85
understanding author's purpose and, 37, 85, 169
Shannon, D., 9, 131–138, 181–184
"Sick" (Silverstein), 18
stopping points in first reading, 43–44
stopping points in second reading, 60–62
thinking aloud in kindergarten, 88–89
Silverstein, S., 18, 43–44, 60–62
Simon, S., 9, 18, 50, 51–56, 94–99
Simple Machines: Wheels, Levers, and Pulleys (Adler), 217–220
Skill building
for asking questions, 29–31, 30
for making inferences, 33–34
for monitoring and clarifying, 38–39
for synthesizing, 34–35
for understanding author's purpose, 36–37
Slate, J., 117–119
Smoky Night (Bunting), 187–191
Social studies, thinking aloud in, 146, 152
"Spider-Hunting Nudist Ends With Ring of Fire," 153–155
Spinner template, 81, 83, 149
Starfish (Hurd), 151
Steig, W., 12–13, 234–238
Stopping points
in gradual release of responsibility model, 129–138
in three-step process, 16, 41–57
See also *individual texts*
The Story of Ruby Bridges (Coles), 202–204
The Stranger (Van Allsburg), 198–200
Strategy symbols, 27
Strega Nona (dePaola), 30
Student engagement, 25
Stump the Chump, 107–108
Super Six comprehension strategies (Oczkua), 26
Sweet, M., 210–212
Synthesizing, 7, 34–35, 67
defining, 34
sentence starters for, 35, 84–85, 169
skill building for, 34–35
think aloud scripts for, 200–204
think aloud scripts for Grades K–2, 200–202
think aloud scripts for Grades 3–5, 202–204

Taboada, A., 28
Teaching Literacy in the Visible Learning Classroom (Fisher et al.), 18–19
Technology, incorporating into think alouds, 122
Text feature walk, 50
Thank you, Mr. Falker (Polacco), 32
Thayer, E., 242–245
Therrien, W. J., 28
Think Aloud Chart, 17, 86
example of, 87, 171
for *Enemy Pie* in third grade, 89–93
for *Eyes and Ears* in fifth grade, 94–99
for "Sick" in kindergarten, 88–89
Think alouds
achievement, impact on, 24
application to *USA Today* article, 4–6
applying across content areas, 144, 146–147
benefits of, 24–25
characteristics of, 8–10
defining, 6, 8
educational theories behind, 14–15
examples applied to texts, 7–8
mathematics and, 146, 152
newspaper article sample, 153–155
relevance of, 13–14
science and, 147, 151
signals, using for, 79–80
social studies and, 146, 152
technology, incorporating into, 122
visuals and, 147–149
what think alouds are not, 10–13
See also Think Aloud Chart; Think aloud scripts; Think aloud

scripts for interwoven strategies; Three-step process
Think aloud scripts
for asking questions, 187–195
for making inferences, 195–200
for monitoring and clarifying, 213–220
for synthesizing, 200–204
for understanding author's purpose, 204–212
See also Think Aloud Chart; Think aloud scripts for interwoven strategies; Three-step process
Think aloud scripts for interwoven strategies, 221–248
for chapter book, Grades 3–5, 238–242
for historical fiction, Grades K–2, 230–234
for narrative picture book, Grades K–2, 226–229
for narrative picture book, Grades 3–5, 234–238, 245–248
for nonfiction, Grades K–2, 222–224
for poetry, Grades K–2, 224–225
for poetry, Grades 3–5, 242–245
Three-step process, 15–17. *See also* Think Aloud Chart; Think alouds; Three-step process, determining where and when to think aloud; Three-step process, identifying juicy stopping points; Three-step process, writing scripts on sticky notes
Three-step process, determining where and when to think aloud, 16, 59–76
in informational text in fifth grade, 67–75
in narrative text in third grade, 62–67
in poetry in kindergarten, 60–62
Three-step process, identifying juicy stopping points, 16, 41–57
defining stopping points, 42
in informational text in fifth grade, 43, 49–50, 51–56
in narrative text in third grade, 45, 46–49
in poetry in kindergarten, 43–44
sticky-noting during, 42–43
Three-step process, writing scripts on sticky notes, 16, 77–100
sentence starters for, 81–85
sentence starters, die template for, 82
sentence starters, spinner template for, 83
signals, using for think alouds, 79–80
time commitment for, 79
Tovani, C., 37
Transactional theory of reading, 42
"Trek 7: The Fractal Pond Race" (Peterson & Henderson), 152
Tuck Everlasting (Babbit), 9

Understanding author's purpose, 8, 35–37
defining purpose, 36
sentence starters for, 37, 85, 169
skill building for, 36–37
think aloud scripts for, 204–212
think aloud scripts for Grades K–2, 205–210
think aloud scripts for Grades 3–5, 210–212
to entertain, 206–208
to inform, 205–206
to persuade, 208–210
Upadhyay, R., 146
USA Today, 4, 5–6

Van Allsburg, C., 198–200
Van Dusen, C., 120, 172–180
Visuals, thinking aloud with, 147–149

Walker, B. J., 144
The Watcher: Jane Goodall's Life With the Chimps (Winter), 230–234
"We Do" phase, of gradual release of responsibility, 129–142
chart for, 130
for *A Bad Case of Stripes,* 131–137
for *Mighty Jackie: The Strike-Out Queen,* 138–142
White, E. B., 13–14
Who Was Anne Frank? (Abramson), 191–195
Wilhelm, J., 10, 15–17, 26, 104, 125, 129, 144
The William Hoy Story: How a Deaf Baseball Player Changed the Game (Churin), 56–57
overview and rationale, 159–161
think aloud for, 166–167

Williams, K. L., 213–216
Winter, J., 230–234

The Year of Billy Miller (Henkes), 238–242
Yoğurtçu, K., 25
Yopp, H. K., 45
Yopp, R. H., 45
"You Do" phase, of gradual release of responsibility, 142–144
monitoring of student progress, 143–144
tips for encouraging thinking aloud, 149–150

Notes

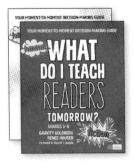

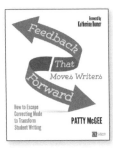

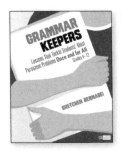

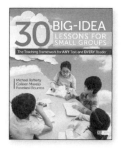

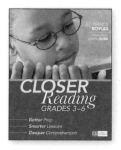